The Norton Anthology of World Masterpieces

Sixth Edition

Volume One

Instructor's Guide

Maynard Mack, <u>General Editor</u>

Bernard M. W. Knox

John C. McGalliard

P. M. Pasinetti

Jerome Clinton

The Norton Anthology of World Masterpieces

SIXTH EDITION

Volume One

Instructor's Guide

W·W·Norton & Company
New York · London

ISBN 0 393 96192 3

W. W. Norton & Company, Inc.
500 Fifth Avenue, New York, New York 10110

W. W. Norton & Company Ltd.
10 Coptic Street, London WC1A 1PU

3 4 5 6 7 8 9 0

Contents

Masterpieces of the Ancient World

Masterpieces of the Middle Ages

Masterpieces of the Renaissance

Preface

In this guide for instructors, we offer the many loyal friends of *The Norton Anthology of World Masterpieces* a systematic overview of useful class procedures. Most derive from our own experience, some from yours, which many of you through the years have been kind enough to share with us. We hope that you will continue to contribute whenever the spirit moves, for a collection of this kind is only valuable if it is alive, always hospitable to ideas that have proved their viability, always ready to jettison those that fail.

It goes without saying that not all the suggestions put forward here will work equally for all teachers, classes, or occasions. No teacher needs reminding how different various classes can be, or how different the same class on different days. Yet we like to think that there will be something in these pages to assist even the most seasoned voyagers among masterpieces, particularly when they are outside their familiar waters (certainly this has been the case with the seven of us!); and we firmly believe that there is much here to give confidence to the newcomer.

We include, for instance, summaries pointing up what seem to us the main characteristics of each work, not forgetting those qualities that constitute its claim to our attention, as well as background material, additional to that in the anthology introductions and headnotes, on the several factors that may have helped shape the work (*Backgrounds*). These are followed by generously full discussions of ways in which the work may profitably be approached under classroom conditions, and, likewise, of the difficulties we have found that students sometimes have with it, owing to social, political, cultural, or linguistic change (*Classroom Strategies*). Following this, we propose a number of points for class discussion or for writing that, at least in our own experience, can be counted on to engage student interest while at that same time lighting up the work in hand (*Topics for Discussion and Writing*). There is at the close a special annotated bibliography of writings likely to prove particularly helpful in preparing either a class lecture or a class discussion (*Further Reading*).

It is our conviction that this guide supplies an important addendum to our anthology, if used with imagination and good sense. It is not, and is not intended to be, a teachers' "answer-book." In the first place, because your own inspirations are what finally matter: ours will work best if they serve primarily as a warm-up for yours. And in the second place, because in the profound world of human feelings and failings, agonies and joys of which world literature treats, there are no "answers"—only understandings that are better or worse according as they do justice to the full reality of that impassioned image of ourselves which great works of art bring before us.

THE EDITORS

Masterpieces of the Ancient World

The Epic of Gilgamesh

Backgrounds

In an ancient and legendary time, the gods of Mesopotamia create a king for the great city of Uruk whose name is Gilgamesh. He is perfect in beauty and strength and is, in fact, more god than man. His superiority makes him arrogant and he serves his people badly. He fights wars that devour the young men of the city and he takes women from their husbands and lovers for his own pleasure and amusement. The people of Uruk complain of his oppression, and the gods hear them. On humankind's behalf they implore Aruru, the goddess of creation, to create a second being equal in strength and ferocity to Gilgamesh to serve as a kind of counterbalance to him. This she does by first conceiving the image of the being who will satisfy their need and then making him of clay and water. The result is Enkidu, a creature who is half human and half wild animal. He falls to the ground in the wilderness, and at first he lives with wild beasts, hunting with them and eating only uncooked food. He knows nothing of the city and its people.

He becomes a kind of protector god for wild game, breaking the hunter's traps and filling in his pits. The first hunter to encounter him is terrified of him and asks his father what to do. His suggestion is to go to Uruk, to Gilgamesh, to request a prostitute from him. This he does, although it is not clear that he actually speaks with Gilgamesh. The prostitute seduces Enkidu across the line separating wild from human, and educates him in the elements of human social behavior. The shepherds then teach him to eat prepared food and wear clothing and anoint himself as humans do. At this point he has become so human that the animals who were his companions shy away from him, and, indeed, he now protects the shepherds' flocks rather than the wild animals.

The prostitute sees that he is ready and leads him to Uruk and the confrontation with Gilgamesh for which Aruru has created him. Gilgamesh has already learned of his coming through a dream which his mother interprets as portending that he will find a true companion. When they meet, they fight but are so evenly matched that only with great difficulty does Gilgamesh throw Enkidu to the ground. Once he has established his superiority, his anger vanishes, and they embrace as friends. The consequence of their union is that their prodigious energies, particularly those of Gilgamesh, are directed outward toward heroic achievements and not against the people of Uruk.

The first adventure that Gilgamesh proposes is a journey to the great Cedar Forest in the Country of the Living to slay the terrible giant Humbaba. His only reason for undertaking this adventure is to gain the immortality of fame. Enkidu, who knows how ferocious Humbaba is, is reluctant, but allows himself to be persuaded. After lengthy preparations and with the blessing of the sun god, Shamash, they proceed. They defeat Humbaba after a terrible battle, but the monster first begs for mercy, then curses them before he dies. Enlil, the god of wind and storm, is enraged by the slaying of his creature, curses the heroes as well, and gives to others the seven splendors that had been Humbaba's.

Their second adventure is provoked by Ishtar. She desires Gilgamesh as her lover, but he rejects her insultingly. This provokes her to send the bull of Heaven against the people of Uruk. The terrible destruction the Bull causes obliges Gilgamesh and Enkidu to destroy it. Ishtar demands vengeance for its death, and the gods grant that one of the two heroes, Enkidu, must die. At first, Enkidu is enraged by his fate and curses all those who transformed him from a wild creature into a man; later, he softens when Shamash, the sun god, reminds him of the glory he has enjoyed as a man.

Gilgamesh is devastated by the death of his companion and sobered by the discovery of the limits of mortality. He learns that one human, Utnapishtim, has been given the gift of immortality, and he decides to undertake a journey in search of him. His journey takes him out of the human realm into a world that seems to exist between this world and that of the gods. He begins it by first abandoning the city and becoming somewhat wild himself. Then he must pass the fierce lions who guard the entrance to the dark tunnel that brings him to a prototypical garden of paradise. He later makes a puzzling and perilous voyage to Dilmun—an island that lies beyond the reach of human voyaging. Although he is discouraged at every step, Gilgamesh perseveres and, at last, finds his way to Utnapishtim, who tells him the story of how he won the gratitude of the gods. When he learns that Gilgamesh, too, desires immortality, he tests him by asking him to stay awake for six days and seven nights. He is unable to do so, but Utnapishtim offers him, by way of consolation, the secret of a plant that assures eternal renewal, if not immortality. Gilgamesh undertakes to find the plant, which grows at the bottom of the sea where fresh and salt waters come together. He succeeds, but, in a moment of carelessness, loses the plant to the serpent. Discouraged and defeated, Gilgamesh returns at last to Uruk empty-handed. His consolation is the assurance that his worldly accomplishments will endure beyond his own lifetime.

Classroom Strategies

Suggested Assignments:
Prologue and Parts 1, 2, and 3
Parts 4, 5, 6, and 7

Topics for Discussion

The Sandars translation smoothes out a lot of rough spots in the original, but the text is still full of puzzles. There are so many gods, and all of them new. The names have a puzzling and comic sound (i.e., Humbaba). It is not always clear what is happening in narrative, as is the case with the expedition to the forest to kill Humbaba. It may be helpful to point out that the gods are not organized in a clear hierarchy as is true with the gods of the Greeks and Romans. They are more like a large and noisy family with no generally acknowledged patriarch or matriarch to pull them together, an alliance of semi-independent chiefs. Despite the occasional obscurities in the text, however, certain themes stand out quite clearly and are linked with individual sections of the work.

In the first, the arrogance of power offers itself for discussion, as does the thin line that divides enmity from deep friendship. There are also suggestive parallels between the account of the creation of Gilgamesh and Enkidu and Genesis 1–3. The process of civilizing Enkidu, of bringing him out of the wild and into civilization, opens up a discussion of the relation of civilization to nature. After all, Enkidu both gains and loses by his transformation. And it is surely worth noting that, even at this very early stage of human history, the settled live in conflict with the wild. The roles of hunters and shepherds as liminal figures standing between the two spheres is worth exploring as is the special function of the prostitute who is principally responsible for Enkidu's transformation. (She may be a temple prostitute here, a figure with a more complicated role in society than that of the Mesopotamian equivalent of a "hooker.")

The campaign against Humbaba opens up a discussion of the importance of fame as conferring immortality, and also the mixed results that come about when the goal of an adventure is a selfish one. Humbaba poses no threat to Uruk and his death brings no benefits, at least as the story is told here. Gilgamesh's encounter with Ishtar shows how risky the relations of humans to gods can be, at least for humans. He has the right to reject her advances, and good reason for doing so, but he oversteps himself in rejecting her so insultingly. He pays a heavy price for his bad manners.

The remainder of the poem focuses on the tragedy of mortality. The tragedy is made more poignant because it takes place in an era before the development of a belief in the afterlife.

Topics for Writing

1. Any of the questions raised above under *Topics for Discussion.*

2. Dreams are so recurrent in *Gilgamesh*, and so important. They serve as a vehicle of communication between gods and mortals, anticipating events symbolically, but accurately. What narrative function do they serve? That is, why is it useful to know what is going to happen before it does?

The poem of Gilgamesh offers several opportunities for comparison with other works:

3. *Gilgamesh* has the earliest version of the Flood Story, a narrative which appears later in both Genesis 6–9 and the Koran, Sura 71. Each version has very different emphases and draws a different moral.

4. As the earliest epic, *Gilgamesh* also invites comparisons with later epics like the *Odyssey* and the *Aeneid*. Each, for instance, provides a different goal as an organizing principal—the return home, the

founding of a state, the search for immortality. The involvement of the gods in human affairs also differs among them. Finally, the *Aeneid* is consciously and explicitly derived from Homer, yet Homer shows no awareness of *Gilgamesh*. How is this apparent?

Further Reading

See also the reading suggestions in the anthology, p. 13.

Delaney, Stephanie, *Myths from Mesopotamia: Creation, the Flood, Gilgamesh, and Others*. Oxford, 1989.
Translations with commentary of a number of myths that illuminate the context of *Gilgamesh*. The translations are more scholarly and less literary than Sandars's.

Kirk, G. S. *Myth: Its Meaning and Functions in Ancient and Other Cultures*. Cambridge and Berkeley, 1970.
Kirk's work contains an extended discussion of both Mesopotamian and Greek mythology, and of similarities between *Gilgamesh* and some Greek myths. There is also a useful discussion of structuralism and myth.

Kovacs, Maureen Gallery, *The Epic of Gilgamesh*. Stanford, California, 1989.
Another recent translation that also includes excellent notes and commentary.

Tigay, Jeffrey A., *The Evolution of the Gilgamesh Epic*. Philadelphia, 1982.
Very detailed and informative discussion of the various stages in the evolution of the epic.

THE OLD TESTAMENT
Genesis
[The Creation—The Fall; The First Murder;
The Flood; The Origin of Languages]

Backgrounds

The creation of the world in seven days: light and darkness on the first day; the sky (firmament) on the second; on the third, land and sea and also vegetation on the land; on the fourth, sun, moon, and stars; on the fifth, fish and birds; on the sixth, animals and man (Adam). On the seventh day God rested. Adam, in the garden of Eden, is given permission to eat the fruit of any tree except the tree of knowledge of good and evil. He is also given a mate, Eve, who, tempted by the serpent, persuades Adam to eat the forbidden fruit. They are punished by expulsion from the garden and must now work in order to live; they must also face the inevitability of death: "Dust thou art and to dust shalt thou return..."

In the next generation, violent death comes into the world: Cain murders his brother Abel. Their descendants become so wicked that God is sorry he ever created the human race and decides to destroy it. But one just man, Noah, is allowed to survive the flood, with his family and specimens of all the animals, fish, and birds. So the earth is repopulated but men, in their pride, begin to build a tower as high as heaven. God prevents this by confusing their speech; before, there was one universal language but now the builders of the tower speak different languages and cannot understand one another.

Though Genesis is traditionally assigned to the prophet Moses, it bears the marks of a document that has a long history of revision, addition, and reinterpretation over a period of time. (There are, for example, two different accounts of the creation which do not agree in detail.) The book probably preserves ancient oral tradition but shows signs also of priestly revision at a later stage. Its original language is Hebrew, and Genesis, together with the next four books of the Old Testament, forms the Torah (the Law) of the Jewish faith.

Classroom Strategies

The selections are short but have matter enough in them to form one assignment. Refer students to the headnote (p. 45–49) for some of the problems raised by these texts.

The main difficulties for the modern student are:

—The concept of God that underlies the stories of Adam, Noah, and Babel. You should explain that the punishments inflicted by God are in each case just: Adam disobeys the one prohibition imposed on him, the Flood is sent to punish almost universal wickedness, and the builders of the tower are encroaching on God's space. But in every case justice is tempered with mercy: Adam and Eve are not destroyed, only expelled from the garden; Cain is not killed but condemned to be a wanderer on the face of the earth; Noah and his family are saved, to repopulate the earth, and God makes a covenant with him never to destroy the human race again; the builders of the tower are not destroyed or even hurt, they are simply divided by language. You can point out that these stories, like myths in many societies, have an explanatory function: they answer questions. Why do we have to work in order to live and eventually die? Why don't we all speak the same language? Why does the serpent crawl? And why do we feel revulsion when we see it?

—The subordinate role of Eve and her responsibility for the Fall. A difficult subject, but you can point out that this story is the creation of a firmly patriarchal society in which sons were more highly regarded than daughters and authority was the prerogative of the male. (We are told the names of Noah's sons, for example, but not the name of his wife.) It can be pointed out too, that the Hebrews were not alone in this attitude; the Greek myth of Pandora has exactly the same moral: it's all the woman's fault.

Topics for Discussion

1. The significance of the fact that God forbids eating the fruit of the tree of knowledge. Why should the knowledge of "good and evil" be forbidden? *Are* there kinds of knowledge that it is risky for human beings to have?

2. The role of the serpent (refer ahead to Milton where the serpent has become Satan). Is the serpent a way of passing the buck—of saying it's not *our* fault?

3. Cain and Abel, symbolic of two different ways of life, farmers and pastoral nomads.

Genesis
[The Story of Joseph]

Backgrounds

Noah has three sons—one of them, Shem, the ancestor of the Semitic peoples, including the Hebrews. One of the descendants of Shem, Abraham, settles in Palestine, which is to be the home of the Jewish people. His grandson Jacob has thirteen sons; his favorite is one of the youngest, Joseph, to whom he gives a coat of many colors. (Modern scholars translate the phrase "a long robe with sleeves" but the coat of many colors is now proverbial in the English language.) Joseph has dreams which he interprets to mean that he will be the greatest of the brothers. They are enraged and leave him to die in a dry cistern in the outland pastures. They smear his coat with goat's blood and convince Jacob he has been killed by a wild beast.

But Joseph is rescued by passing merchants who sell him as a slave to Potiphar, the captain of the guard of Pharaoh, the ruler of Egypt. Joseph rises rapidly in his master's esteem and soon is entrusted with great responsibilities. Potiphar's wife tries to seduce him; rejected, she accuses him of an attempt at rape and Joseph is sent to prison. There he interprets the dreams of fellow prisoners, and one of them, released and restored to his post as Pharaoh's butler, remembers Joseph when the Pharaoh has some disturbing dreams. Joseph interprets them as a prophecy of seven years of plenty followed by seven years of famine; he suggests storing food as a reserve. Pharaoh puts him in charge of the program; he becomes Pharaoh's chief minister.

The seven lean years begin as predicted; the Egyptians are provided for but in Israel there is famine. Jacob sends his sons to Egypt to buy grain; they come to Joseph, whom they do not recognize. He denounces them as spies and tells them to come back, this time with the youngest of the brothers, Benjamin. Jacob is unwilling to let Benjamin go but in the end he has to yield. Once in Egypt the brothers are entertained royally, their sacks filled with grain. But in Benjamin's sack Joseph has his servants, in secret, put his own silver cup. When it is found there after a search he tells the others to go home; he will keep Benjamin with him in Egypt. They beg him to let Benjamin go, saying that Jacob will die of grief. Joseph can conceal his feelings no longer and reveals his identity. He sends for Jacob and so the Israelites settle in Egypt. After many years when a later Pharaoh begins to oppress them they escape from Egypt (the Exodus) led by the prophet Moses.

The story has some historical plausibility; for two centuries (1720–1550 B.C.) Egypt was under the domination of the Hyksos, a non-Egyptian people, and Semitic settlers were favored. Joseph's rise to power and influence could in such circumstances have happened. The sophisticated literary form of the story may owe something to a model: an Egyptian tale of a man who rejected the advances of his brother's wife, who then falsely accused him and almost caused his death at his brother's hands (see Thomas in *Further Reading*). The belief that dreams foretold the future, taken for granted in the Joseph story, is common to most of the civilizations of the ancient world; the teacher can refer forward, for example, to Penelope's dream in the *Odyssey* (XIX. 462ff.). The basic mechanism of the plot, the hero in disguise (compare the scene between Joseph and his brothers), is also found on a larger scale in the *Odyssey*.

Classroom Strategies

One assignment. No special difficulties.

Topics for Discussion

1. Discuss Joseph's statement to his brothers: "So now it was not you that sent me hither but God" (45:8).

2. "This dreamer cometh . . .": Joseph as visionary and a man of action.

Topics for Writing

1. Discuss the function in the story of one of the following recurrent motifs: Joseph's clothes; dreams and their interpretation.

2. Recast the story as a play in five acts.

3. Why do you think Joseph put the silver cup in Benjamin's sack?

4. Does the "success story" of Joseph differ in any way from its

modern counterparts in which an awkward, clumsy, ugly, or despised person makes good?

Job

Backgrounds

Satan—the Hebrew word means "the adversary"—challenges God to test the piety of Job, a rich and fortunate man famous for his devotion to the Almighty. How will his piety stand up in the face of calamity? God gives Satan permission to inflict any suffering short of physical harm on Job to see if, as Satan claims, he will curse God.

In the course of one day Job learns that all his servants, his flocks, and his sons and daughters have been killed but he does not blame God. Satan demands and receives permission to inflict bodily harm; he covers Job's body with sores. Job's wife tells him: "Curse God and die," but he rebukes her.

Now three friends (Job's comforters) come to sympathize with him. From this point on the story is cast in dramatic and poetic form until the short narrative conclusion.

Job wishes he had not been born and the first of his friends replies: since Job has been punished, he must have sinned. His attitude is arrogant; he should show humility before God. The second friend suggests he may be paying for the sins of his children. The third returns to the theme of the first but more harshly: Job *must* be guilty or he would not be suffering. Job refuses to accept these arguments; the disasters inflicted on him are out of proportion to any sin he may unknowingly have committed. He appeals to God, and wishes he could speak to him directly and learn what the reason for his suffering is: "My desire is, that the Almighty would answer me...." (31:35) His desire is fulfilled as God speaks from the whirlwind. His speech contains no justification for the suffering he inflicted on Job; it is a magnificent celebration of the power and greatness of God. Job accepts God's answer; he feels overwhelmed by God's personal intervention—now he has faith in him: "I have heard of thee...but now mine eye seeth thee" (42:5). God does not answer Job's question but he does dismiss the beliefs of his friends: "Ye have not spoken of me the thing that is right, as my servant Job has" (42:7). And "the Lord gave Job twice as much as he had before" (42:10).

The basis of the work is an oral folktale, the story of the patient sufferer. Onto a Hebrew version of the tale has been grafted a poetic dialogue between Job and three friends and also the voice of God speaking from the whirlwind. The text probably was set in its present form some time in the sixth century B.C.

Classroom Strategies

Ideally this should be one assignment, but if necessary it can be divided: 1–14 and 15 to the end.

Satan is a problem for most people new to this text. He is not the Devil of later literature but one of the "sons of God" (1:6). His name means "the adversary"; perhaps he is a sort of loyal opposition. Students can be told to watch for the transformation of this figure in later texts (especially Milton), his identification with the serpent of Genesis and the Evil One of the New Testament.

Topics for Discussion

Job (in Chapter 31) makes the claim that his life has been virtuous and devoted to the worship of God and so does not deserve the calamities that have fallen on him. He asks God for an answer, but the voice from the whirlwind does not deal with his question at all. Why does Job accept God's assertion of divine power (42) and not press for an answer to his question? Why is he satisfied with what he is given? Do you find the end of the dialogue satisfactory?

[The answer should be along the lines that Job is content with the fact that the Almighty has condescended to speak to him in person. Even if his question is not answered, he has the assurance that God cares for him enough to speak to him directly. Before this he has only known of God by hearsay, but now he has direct experience (42:5). The question of justice in the world, of apparently undeserved suffering (and its opposite, the prosperity of the wicked) is not resolved; it is a question, too, that will be debated by the Greeks (*Odyssey* I. 39ff., for example).]

Topics for Writing

1. Recast in your own (plain) language the core of the arguments offered by the three comforters. How do they differ from one another?

2. Discuss the statement that although God does not answer Job's complaint he "reveals himself personally to him and shares with him the vision of his cosmic responsibilities."

Psalms

Our selection offers five texts from what might be called the Hebrew hymnal, a collection of no less than 150 songs (*psalm* is a Greek word that describes the sound made by a plucked string, and many of these psalms have come down to us with musical directions attached—"for flutes," for example, or "with stringed instruments"). They are of various types; our selection offers specimens of hymns celebrating the majesty of God (Psalms 8, 19, and 104 in our selection), songs of trust in the Lord (Psalm 23), and laments (Psalm 137).

Hebrew poetry is not based on strict metrical pattern alone (as in Greek or Latin) or on metrical pattern and rhyme (as in English and many other modern languages); it works by what is known as "parallelism." A first statement is repeated or amplified in a different form—"The statutes of the Lord are right, rejoicing the heart; the commandment of the Lord is pure, enlightening the eyes" (19:8)—and this second form may echo the original thought, as in this example, build on it toward a climax, or contrast with it.

Isaiah
[The Song of the Suffering Servant]

This is the third of four so-called Servant Songs which are incorporated in a section of the Book of the prophet Isaiah that was probably written around the time of the fall of Babylon to the Persian armies of Cyrus, an event that was followed by the return of the Jewish people from the exile lamented in Psalm 137. Though in every case the text speaks of the Servant as an individual and has so been understood, it is also possible to take the Servant as a symbol of Israel itself, the nation that "will be a light to the gentiles" (46:6, not included in this anthology). Christian interpreters, however, very soon saw this passage as a prophecy of Jesus Christ; in the Acts of the Apostles (Chapter 8) one of the apostles finds a man from Ethiopia reading the words "He was led like a sheep to the slaughter," convinces him that they refer to Christ, and baptizes him.

See also the reading suggestions in the anthology, p. 49.

Eissfeldt, O. *The Old Testament: An Introduction.* Oxford, 1965.
Very full, authoritative discussion of every aspect of the problems posed by the Old Testament by one of the greatest modern scholars in the field.

The New Oxford Annotated Bible (with the Apocrypha). New York, 1977.
The Revised Standard Version, which corrects misunderstandings in the Authorized and frequently translates a better text. It is equipped with helpful introductions to the different books and very useful footnotes. See pp. 1523–29, "Characteristics of Hebrew Poetry," for help with the Psalms.

Thomas, D. Winton, ed. *Documents from Old Testament Times.* London, 1958; New York, 1961.
Contains documents, translated by experts in the different fields from Babylonian, Egyptian, and other ancient Near Eastern texts, that parallel or throw light on the biblical accounts. See especially the Babylonian Creation Myth, the Flood Story in the Gilgamesh Epic, the Babylonian Theodicy (a dialogue on divine justice and human suffering, comparable in theme to Job), and the Egyptian Tale of Two Brothers (for comparison with the story of Joseph and Potiphar's wife).

HOMER
The Iliad

Backgrounds

In the tenth year of the Achaean siege of Troy, a rich city in Asia Minor, Agamemnon, the most powerful king among the Achaean allies, quarrels with the bravest of them, Achilles. Agamemnon had taken as his concubine the captive daughter of a Trojan priest of Apollo; at the priest's request, the god had sent a plague to devastate the army. Agamemnon agrees to give back the girl but demands compensation from the army for the loss of his share of the spoils of war. Achilles opposes this demand as unreasonable and Agamemnon, at the end of a furious argument announces he will take away Achilles' girl Briseis, whom Achilles had captured in a raid. Achilles draws his sword to kill Agamemnon but is dissuaded from violence by the goddess Athena, who promises that he will be amply recompensed for Agamemnon's insults at some future date. He goes back to his tent and pulls his men out of the fighting. But he also asks his mother, the goddess Thetis, to intervene. She is to use her influence with Zeus, the king of the gods, and ask him to inflict defeat and suffering on the Achaeans, so that they will turn against Agamemnon. She goes to Olympus and, in spite of the opposition of Zeus' wife Hera (who favors the Achaean side), Zeus grants her prayer.

[In books II–V (not included in our selection) Agamemnon calls an assembly of the troops. In an attempt to test morale he suggests abandoning the war; the ensuing stampede for the ships is stopped only by Odysseus with the aid of the goddess Athena. The Achaeans then muster for battle and the poet describes each contingent in what is known as the Catalogue of Ships; he then proceeds to list the Trojan forces. The two sides join battle but Hector, the Trojan leader, proposes that the war be settled by a duel between Menelaus, the Achaean king, and Paris, the Trojan prince who had run off with Menelaus' wife, Helen. Both sides agree; Menelaus wins the fight and is about to kill Paris when the goddess Aphrodite, who protects Paris because he gave her the prize for beauty, rescues him and sends him to join Helen in Troy. Agamemnon tells the Trojans to give back Helen and all her possessions and also to pay an indemnity; it looks as if the two sides will make peace on those terms but the gods, at the urging of Hera and Athena, prevent it. Athena persuades Pandarus to shoot an arrow at Menelaus during the truce. Menelaus receives only a light wound, but the truce is broken; the battle resumes. Zeus' promise is not fulfilled immediately; the Achaean hero Diomedes dominates the battle and the Trojans are hard pressed.]

In Book VI Hector goes to Troy to organize prayers to Athena; the poet gives us a glimpse of the rich, civilized city which the Achaeans will in the end destroy. Hector meets his mother Hecuba, his brother, Paris, and Helen, the cause of the war; he then sees, for the last time as it turns out, his wife Andromache and his infant son.

[In books VII and VIII the promise of Zeus is fulfilled. After an inconclusive duel between Hector and Ajax the Achaeans are driven back and the Trojans, who usually retire behind their city walls at night, camp out on the field, ready to deliver a decisive assault in the morning.]

In Book IX Agamemnon summons a council; they advise him to make amends to Achilles. He agrees and proposes not only a magnificent list of gifts but also to restore Briseis (whom he swears he has not touched) and to offer one of his daughters in marriage to Achilles after the war. This offer is made to Achilles by Odysseus, Ajax, and Phoenix, an old retainer of Achilles; but Achilles refuses outright. The insult to his honor is too great to be wiped out by gifts. He will go home, with all his men. Phoenix tries to persuade him, reminding him of the story of Alcmaeon, who also withdrew from the fighting alliance in anger, was begged to return, and refused. When in the end he came back to the fighting, he had forfeited all of the gifts he would have been given if he had complied earlier. Achilles still refuses to fight but he has been moved; he will stay at Troy. And the final appeal from Ajax moves him still more; he will not join the battle, he says, until Hector fights his way to the Greek ships and sets them on fire. Phoenix stays with Achilles; Odysseus and Ajax return to report the failure of their mission.

[In Book X Odysseus and Diomedes make a successful night raid on the Trojan lines, but this is the last Achaean success for some time. In books XII to XVII the tide of battle turns against the Achaeans. Paris wounds Diomedes with an arrow; Odysseus is wounded and withdraws; Machaon, the Achaean physician, is also wounded. Achilles, who is watching the fighting and rejoicing in the Achaean losses sends his friend Patroclus to see if the wounded man he saw was indeed Machaon and this, the poet says, "is the beginning of his evil." For Patroclus, moved to pity by the wounded men he sees in the Achaean camp and by Hector's assault on the wall the Achaeans have built to protect their ships, will appeal to Achilles on the Achaeans' behalf (XIII–XIV). Achilles refuses to join the fighting himself but allows Patroclus, equipped with his own armor, to take the field. After driving the Trojans back, Patroclus is killed by Hector, who strips off the armor of Achilles and puts it on. After a desperate fight, the Achaeans recover the body of Patroclus and take it back to their camp (XV–XVII).]

When Achilles hears of the death of Patroclus, he resolves to avenge him by killing Hector, but he must wait until his goddess mother brings him new armor; it is forged by Hephaestus, the divine smith, and includes a marvelous picture shield. Achilles then calls an assembly of the Achaeans, accepts Agamemnon's apology and, after mourning over the corpse of Patroclus, puts on the armor and goes into battle.

[In the final battle even the gods take part, but Achilles drives all before him as he cuts the Trojan warriors down. He drives the Trojans inside the gates of the city but is distracted by the god Apollo, a protector of Troy who, taking the shape of a Trojan warrior, leads him on a futile chase. Hector, feeling responsible for the defeat of his people, stays outside the gate to face Achilles.]

In Book XXII the two great adversaries face each other at last. Hector is beaten but before he dies prophesies Achilles' imminent death. Achilles ties the corpse to his chariot and drags it out to his camp.

[Book XXIII deals with the burial of Patroclus and the funeral games in his honor. Achilles distributes rich prizes to the winners of athletic events: chariot race, boxing, wrestling, foot race, armed combat, weight casting, and archery.]

In the last book (p. 187), Priam, king of Troy and father of Hector, is led by a divine messenger, Hermes, to the tent of Achilles to offer a rich ransom for his son's body. Achilles has been told by Thetis that Zeus is angry with him for his desecration of Hector's corpse and Achilles agrees to give it up. But he is not prepared to see Hector's father, king of Troy, a suppliant at his feet, and his pity for the old man puts an end to the inhuman fury which has ruled him since the death of Patroclus. He lets Priam take the body, gives him eleven days for the burial of Hector; on the twelfth day the war will be renewed. Hector's people lament for him and give him a magnificent funeral; the last line of the poem—"And so the Trojans buried Hector, breaker of horses"—reminds us that the fighting will begin again at once and that Achilles, in his turn, will face the death he has inflicted on others.

Nothing is known about Homer's life or personality. It has even been thought that there was no one poet who composed the *Iliad*, that it was the creation of many generations of illiterate bards, the product of an epic tradition. That it comes out of some such background there can be no doubt; not only does it contain linguistic forms and refer to customs that predate the Greek adoption of literacy in the middle of the eighth century B.C., it also shows in its repetition of epithets ("Achilleus of the swift feet"), phrases, lines, and even whole passages (compare I. 13–16, 25–29 with I. 438–49) the characteristic features of oral composition. The products of such a tradition are, however, usually much shorter than the *Iliad* and *Odyssey*; further, they rarely display the masterly construction and internal cross-reference that distinguish the Homeric poems.

Critical opinion now tends to assume a poet who was a master of the oral techniques and repertory but who exploited the new resource of the alphabet (adapted from a Phoenician script) for the construction of large-scale epics. This does not mean that overnight the *Iliad* and *Odyssey* became poems for reading; they were still performed by professional reciters, but the poem was no longer the creation, from memory and improvisation, of an individual bard; it was the dramatic recitation of a known and admired text. By the late sixth century B.C. public recitation of the poems was a highlight of the great festival of Athena at Athens and the poems were also studied in schools. Scholars of the Library at Alexandria in Egypt worked on the text in the third century B.C. and from that time on written copies for readers were the almost exclusive medium for Homer's survival to our own day.

Classroom Strategies

Suggested assignments:

1. Book I
2. Book IX, the selection from Book VIII on p. 124
3. XVIII and XIX
4. XXII and XXIV

The longer assignments, 3 and 4, are possible because in the first two the student will have become familiar with the style and character of the work.

One thing that may puzzle the student is the organization (if it deserves that name) of the Achaean army. It should be explained first of all that the poem does not reflect any real historical situation; the oral tradition on which Homer draws is not concerned with historical fact but with stories of heroes who surpass ordinary human standards of courage and martial achievement. The Achaean army is simply an alliance of independent chieftains, each one in command of his own men, who have come together to help Menelaus recover his wife and punish the Trojans but also to share in the plunder which will result from the capture and destruction of Troy. They owe no loyalty to Agamemnon, as feudal nobles did to a king; Agamemnon has to command by a diplomatic exploitation of the fact that he is in control of the biggest contingent of armed men. On every important decision he consults his "council"—the chieftains of the separate bands; when he acts impulsively and without consultation, as in the quarrel with Achilles, he eventually comes to regret that action and comes as close to an apology as he can (XIX. 72–78ff.).

The political organization of the army is an imaginary, epic phenomenon and the fighting is just as unrealistic. There are large numbers of nameless infantry who presumably fight with spear and shield but we never hear about them; the poem deals exclusively with the duels of the chief heroes. These heroes have horse-drawn chariots, but they do not use them against the enemy infantry; they ride to the battlefield in them, then dismount to fight. This is not the way war chariots were in fact used, as we know from the art and historical literature of the ancient Egyptians and Babylonians; the epic poets had kept the memory of the chariots but forgotten how they were used. From the point of view of the epic bard, the chariots would in any case get in the way of his story, for time and time again he pits one hero against another not just in combat but in verbal exchanges of threats, insults, taunts, and boasts, which would not have been possible if they had been racing past each other in chariots.

This does not mean that Homer's picture of war is totally unrealistic; his descriptions of what happens when bronze weapons cut human flesh are all too accurate. But the realistic wounding and killing are set in a framework of single combat which allows the heroes to speak to each other before, during, and after the fighting and allows the poet to create dramatic tension out of these exchanges. (See especially the speeches of Hector and Achilles [XXII. 296–321, 390–432].)

Topics for Discussion

1. Freedom and responsibility. To what extent are the decisions made by the heroes independent, individual decisions? Discuss, along these lines, Agamemnon's decision to take Briseis from Achilles.

[Agamemnon's decision is presented in Book I as completely independent of divine persuasion or command (unlike Achilles' decision not to kill Agamemnon); his motives are anger (121), hatred for Achilles (208ff.), a wish to assert his superiority (219ff.). And when in Book IX he regrets his action and wishes to be reconciled with Achilles, he blames his action as "madness" (IX. 138) and speaks of being "lost in my own inhuman rage" (143). It is noticeable, however, that he uses these words in a council from which Achilles is absent; the ambassadors to Achilles carry no apology from Agamemnon, only the offer of gifts. When finally, after the death of Patroclus, the two men meet, Agamemnon denies responsibility, claiming that his decision was not free. "But I am not to blame," he says (XIX. 100); he blames his action on Zeus and Delusion, the daughter of Zeus, who took his wits away. In this case Homer shows us a man who evades responsibility for his free decision by blaming a god, but sometimes a god did in fact affect human decision as in the case of Achilles in Book I who had clearly, after thinking over the alternatives, decided to kill Agamemnon (194) but was dissuaded by the goddess Athena.]

2. Discuss the statement (from the Introduction, p. 4): "Morality is a human creation, and though the gods may approve of it, they are not bound by it."

[The fate of Troy depends on the will of the gods, and its final destruction is a product of a power struggle among them: Hera, Athena, and Poseidon are inexorably hostile to Troy, Apollo its champion, and Zeus is swayed now by one side, now by the other. The fact that Troy is a civilized city besieged by soldiers bent on its destruction, the massacre of its men and the enslavement of its women and children, plays no part in the gods' decision, nor does the fact that, as Zeus says, Hector, the Trojan champion, worshipped Zeus with gifts and sacrifice ("The immortals loved Prince Hector," Zeus says, "best of all the mortals born in Troy" [XXIV. 81–82]). Hera and Athena have no pity for Troy, even though the Trojans (in Book VI) make offerings to Athena and pray for her help. They and their children will pay with their lives and freedom for the injury done to Athena's (and Hera's) pride when the Trojan prince Paris chose Aphrodite over them for the prize of beauty (XXIV. 33ff.).

[However, in Book XXIV, the gods (with the exception of Athena, Hera, and Poseidon) are appalled by Achilles' treatment of Hector's body and finally agree to order Achilles to give it up to his father Priam.]

Topics for Writing

1. Aristotle said that the man who is incapable of working in common, or who in his self-sufficiency has no need of others, is no part of the community, like a beast or a god. Discuss the figure of Achilles in the light of this statement.

2. In spite of the constraints imposed by the formulaic language of the oral tradition, Homer, according to one critic, "sees his people as individually distinct and makes us aware of their individuality." Discuss the ways in which Homer succeeds in presenting as differentiated individuals Hector, Nestor, Ajax, Odysseus, Agamemnon, Priam, Phoenix.

3. Homer's preferred medium of poetic comparison is simile rather than metaphor and his similes are "extended": the simile does more than establish a likeness between A and B, it goes on to describe B in great detail, some of the details not like A at all. Yet these details, the apparent development of B for its own sake, often do suggest points of comparison that lie below the surface and often, too, they make significant comments on broader aspects of the situation in which they appear. Discuss the function of the extended simile in the following passages:

VI. 503–14	XIX. 373–80
XXIV. 476–84	XXII. 26–32
XVIII. 207–14	XXII. 194–251
XVIII. 316–23	

Further Reading

See also the suggestions in the anthology, p. 98.

Chadwick, John. *The Mycenean World.* New York, 1976.
An up-to-date and critical survey of Mycenean civilization (including full discussion of the Linear B tablets and the light they throw on the period). Chadwick concludes that the Homeric poems

preserve very little of the real facts of the Mycenean period.

Dodds, Eric R. *The Greeks and the Irrational.* Berkeley and Los Angeles, 1951.
Chapter 1, "Agamemnon's Apology," deals with the problem posed above in *Topics for Discussion*, #1.

Hogan, James C. *A Guide to the* Iliad. New York, 1979.
Based on the Fitzgerald translation. A volume similar to Willcock, but based on a different translation: reference is more difficult but not impossible. It often explains passages Willcock passes over and also contains a valuable introduction.

Kirk, Geoffrey. *Homer and the Epic.* Cambridge, 1965.
A masterly survey of the whole field of modern Homeric controversy distinguished by its firm grip on the historical background, the fairness of its critique of the various theories, and the reassuring moderation of its conclusions.

Lloyd-Jones, H. *The Justice of Zeus.* Berkeley and Los Angeles, 1971.
Chapter 1 makes a case for the Homeric gods as dealing justly with mankind. (Relevant to *Topics for Discussion*, #2.)

Lord, A. B. *The Singer of Tales.* Cambridge, Mass., 1960.
Lord explains the background and methods of composition of modern Yugoslav oral epic and compares the results of his researches to the Homeric text. This is the authoritative treatment of Homer as an oral poet.

Luce, J. V. *Homer and the Heroic Age.* New York, 1975.
A survey of all the archeological and historical evidence for the Mycenean and Dark Age periods which may have some bearing on Homer; Luce is much less skeptical than Chadwick.

Owen, E. T. *The Story of the* Iliad. London, 1947.]
For ordinary readers, probably the most exciting account of the *Iliad* ever written. Brief but stirring.

Schein, Seth L. *The Mortal Hero: An Introduction to Homer's* Iliad. Berkeley and Los Angeles, 1984.

A brilliant literary study of the *Iliad* as a tragic poem, which concentrates attention on the moral values of the Homeric world and which summons to its literary purpose the latest results of linguistic, archeological, and historical research.

Whitman, Cedric. *Homer and the Heroic Tradition.* Cambridge, Mass., 1958; New York (Norton Library), 1965.
Contains a brilliant literary analysis of the *Iliad* which, though its elaborate analysis of the poem's structure fails to convince, is rich in revealing insights.

Willcock, Malcolm M. *A Companion to the* Iliad. Chicago, 1976.
Based on the Lattimore translation. A detailed commentary which deals with difficulties in the text, explains mythological and historical details and provides internal cross-references. An extremely useful volume for the teacher. (It is keyed to Lattimore's line numbers, which are those of our text.)

The Odyssey

Backgrounds

At a council of the gods on Olympus (Book I), Athena pleads the case of Odysseus. It is now ten years since Troy was captured, but Odysseus, shipwrecked on his way home, is stranded on an island where the goddess Calypso keeps him as her mate. The sea-god Poseidon—angry with Odysseus because the hero had blinded Poseidon's son, the Cyclops, Polyphemus—is absent from the council; Athena has her way, and Hermes, the messenger god, is sent to Calypso with the order to release Odysseus. Athena goes to Odysseus' home on Ithaca to encourage his son, Telemachus, whose household is occupied by the young and violent suitors of his mother Penelope; they are convinced Odysseus is dead and demand that she marry one of them. Athena, taking the shape of Mentes, king of a neighboring city, advises Telemachus to visit old Nestor at Pylos and Menelaus at Sparta to see if they have any news of his father.

Encouraged by the goddess (II), Telemachus calls an assembly of the people of Ithaca and assails the suitors for their unlawful occupancy of his house; he announces that he is off to find news of his father. The suitors realize that this is no longer a timid boy but a resolute and dangerous man; when they find out that he has actually left, they decide to set an ambush for him at sea and kill him on his way back. At Pylos (III) Telemachus meets old Nestor and hears from him how Agamemnon was killed by his own wife when he came home from Troy and how Menelaus, blown by adverse winds as far as Egypt, came home in the seventh year after Troy's fall. Accompanied by Nestor's son Pisistratus, Telemachus goes to Sparta (IV) where he is welcomed by Menelaus and Helen and told by Menelaus that, when last heard of, Odysseus was on the island of Calypso, without ship or crew, longing to return home.

Meanwhile, the god Hermes arrives (V) to bring Calypso the command of Zeus. She accepts it with reluctance and when Hermes is gone makes one last attempt to keep Odysseus; she offers to make him immortal if he will stay with her. He refuses and she helps him build a boat and sail off. The god Poseidon wrecks his boat and Odysseus eventually crawls ashore naked and battered, on the island of Scheria, home of the Phaeacians. Here he meets the daughter of the king Alcinous, Nausicaa (VI), who had come down to the shore with her retinue of girls to wash clothes. She is charmed by him and sends him off to the palace where he is hospitably entertained (VII). The next day, at a banquet in the hall (VIII), Odysseus, moved to tears by a minstrel's tales of Troy, is challenged to reveal his identity. He does so (IX) as he tells the Phaeacians (and us) the whole story of his wanderings since he left Troy (IX–XII).

Rounding the southern cape of Greece on his way to Ithaca he was blown out to sea, southwest presumably, but from this point on his itinerary leaves real geography behind. His first landfall is the country of the Lotus Eaters from which he rescues those of his crew who have tasted the Lotus and lost their wish to return home. From the next trial, the land of the Cyclops, he does not escape without casualties; four of his men are eaten by the one-eyed giant in his cave and Odysseus would have been eaten, too, if he had not made the Cyclops drunk and then put out his one eye. After escaping from the cave, Odysseus, taunting the blind giant from shipboard as he prepares to leave, tells Polyphemus his name and the giant prays to his father Poseidon to make Odysseus' homecoming a hard one. On the next island (X) he reaches Aeolus, King of the Winds, who gives him a bag containing all the winds except the one that will take him home. But, in sight of Ithaca, his crew, thinking the bag contains treasure, open it and the winds, let loose, blow the ship back to where it came from.

At his next landfall he loses all his ships but one to the Laestrygonians, giants and cannibals. He goes on to the island of Circe, who turns his advance party into swine, but, dominated by Odysseus, she restores their human shape and entertains them all in royal style. They stay for a year but before they leave, Circe tells Odysseus that he must go to the land of the dead and consult the seer Tiresias. There (XI) he is warned by Tiresias not to eat the cattle of the Sun when he lands on the island of Thrinacia; speaks to the shade of his dead mother, who tells him what is going on in his house at home; sees a procession of famous women; and then meets the ghosts of his companions at Troy—Agamemnon, Achilles, and Ajax.

Back on Circe's island (XII), he bids farewell to her and passes the Sirens who lure men to their doom by their song, makes the passage between the monster Scylla and the whirlpool Charybdis, and lands on the island of Thrinacia where, in spite of his appeals, his men eat the sacred cattle of the Sun. Once again at sea, the ship is sunk in a storm, the crew lost; only Odysseus survives, to land at last on Calypso's island.

The Phaeacians take Odysseus home to Ithaca (XIII); Poseidon, with the consent of Zeus, punishes them for helping his enemy. Odysseus meets the goddess Athena and they plan a stealthy approach to his house in disguise: if he goes home in his own person the suitors may kill him. She transforms him into an aged, ragged beggar and he goes to his swineherd Eumaeus for hospitality (XIV). He tells his generous host a tall tale of wanderings in Egypt and the story of Odysseus at Troy. Meanwhile, Telemachus returns from Sparta (XV), avoiding the suitors' ambush. While Eumaeus tells Odysseus how he was kidnapped as a child and sold to Odysseus' father as a slave, Telemachus makes his way to the swineherd's hut. Without letting Eumaeus know the truth, Odysseus reveals his identity to his son (XVI); together they plot the overthrow of the suitors.

Odysseus and Telemachus make their separate ways to the palace (XVII). As Odysseus comes into the palace yard Argus, his dog, on the point of death from old age, recognizes his master. Odysseus goes begging bread from the suitors; Antinous, the most violent of them, throws a stool at him. Odysseus is challenged by a real beggar, Irus (XVIII), but beats him handily in a fight and wins the exclusive right to beg at the palace. Another prominent suitor Eurymachus, insults Odysseus and throws a stool at him. Later that night (XIX) Penelope sends for Odysseus to see if the beggar has any news; he tells her of meeting Odysseus on the nearby mainland and assures her he will soon return. The old nurse Euryclea, told to wash his feet before he goes to bed, recognizes him by a scar on his leg, but he silences her.

Penelope decides to announce for the next day an archery contest which will decide which of the suitors may claim her hand. The suitors feast and revel (XX); one more of them, Ctesippus, throws something at Odysseus, a cow's hoof this time. They all start to laugh hysterically; the tension is mounting. The archery contest is set up (XXI); the bow of Odysseus is brought out but none of the suitors can string it. Telemachus tells Eumaeus to give it to Odysseus who strings it and kills Antinous (XXII), Eurymachus, and then—with the help of Telemachus, Eumaeus, and some loyal servants—all the rest of the suitors. Only the poet-minstrel Phemius is spared. When Penelope is told the news she cannot believe it (XXIII); she tests Odysseus' knowledge of a detail in their bedroom (the fact that the bed could not be moved since it was carved out of a standing olive tree) and accepts him as her husband.

But trouble is brewing in Ithaca. As Odysseus goes off to the country to see his father, Laertes, and the ghosts of the suitors go to the land of the dead (XXIV) to be interrogated by Agamemnon and others, the relatives of the suitors gather to attack Odysseus and his family. But their attack is thwarted by the goddess Athena, and the two sides make peace.

There was a theory in the ancient world that the *Odyssey* was a work of Homer's old age and that this accounts for the more mellow tone and the happy ending. Modern scholars have claimed that it must be later than the *Iliad* on other grounds: they discern a closer connection between human morality and divine judgment (in, for example, the speech of Zeus in I. 45ff.) and assume that a higher morality must belong to a later age. Others have based the same later dating on the wanderings in books IX–XII, seeing in them a reflection of the early days of Greek colonization. Since, however, the geography of the wanderings suggests fairyland rather than the real western Mediterranean, this thesis, like the other, is controversial. There have been many attempts to identify the island of the Cyclopes and the land of the Lotus Eaters but none of them has won general acceptance. The ancient critics were skeptical on this point: the great Greek geographer Eratosthenes of Alexandria (Third-Second centuries B.C.) said that you would be able to place the site of Odysseus' wanderings when you had found the cobbler who sewed up the leather bag containing the winds.

It is true, however, that the *Odyssey* takes for granted a knowledge of the *Iliad* on the part of the audience; it is remarkable that in all the tales told about Troy and the heroes of the war, by Odysseus, Menelaus, Nestor, Demodokos, and the ghost of Agamemnon, not one single episode is duplicated in the *Iliad*. Such a complete avoidance of the material treated in the *Iliad* suggests knowledge of it in something like its present form.

Classroom Strategies

The obvious assignments are: I–IV (Telemachus); V–VIII (Odysseus and the Phaeacians); IX–XII (the wanderings); XIII–XVI (at the hut of Eumaeus); XVII–XX (the beggar in the palace); XXI–XXIV (revenge and reunion). If shorter assignments are desired, take two books at a time.

If there is not time to read the whole poem, an Odyssean core (the wanderings) can be used: V–VI, VIII, IX–XII (from Calypso's island back to starting point). In this case, you will have to supply the bridge between VI and VIII, e.g.: "Odysseus follows Nausicaa's instructions and is received as a guest in the palace by her mother Arete and her father, Alcinous, who promises to help him return home."

Perhaps the main possibility of misunderstanding for today's students lies in the nature of the heroic ideal presented in the *Odyssey*. Odysseus is not an Achillean character (see p. 97 in the anthology), but he is bound by a heroic ethic just the same. Lies and stratagems are his natural weapons, since most of the time he is pitted against superior force; he is a survivor, one who fights "to save his life" (I. 9), but there are limits to what he will do to save it. On Circe's island, for example, he will not abandon his advance party which has not returned, even though the rest of his crew urge him to leave. He fights not only "to save his life" but also "to bring his shipmates home" (I. 9). In this he fails, but at least in the case of those who killed the cattle of the Sun, this is no fault of his.

In the famous contrast between Odysseus and Achilles in the lower world, many critics have seen a repudiation of the heroic ideal of the *Iliad*; Achilles would rather be alive and a peasant than a king over all the dead. Yet when told of the heroic achievements of his son Neoptolemus, he goes off "glorying" (XI. 604) and in XXIV the shade of Agamemnon contrasts the glory of Achilles' funeral with the ignominy of his own death and burial. As for Odysseus, in the last books of the poem, he exemplifies one heroic ideal in spectacular fashion. The hero avenges insults to his honor, and Odysseus' slaughter of the entire younger generation of the nobility of Ithaca is a heroic revenge on a grand scale. It is also a revenge that the poet obviously approves of and expects his audience to admire.

Topics for Discussion

1. The heroic ideal in the *Iliad* and the *Odyssey*.
   [See *Backgrounds*, above.]

2. Hospitality as a criterion of civilization in the *Odyssey*.
   [Polyphemus and Calypso as opposite extremes—no hospitality at all and too much; the Phaeacians as ideal hosts; courtly hospitality at Pylos (Nestor) and Sparta (Menelaus and Helen); hospitality abused (the suitors), etc. Students should discuss the startling fact that the Phaeacians, the most civilized hosts in the epic, are punished for it by Poseidon and Zeus, who make sure they will not help travelers again. Does this conform to the picture of divine good intentions thwarted by human wickedness offered by Zeus in his speech in Book I?]

3. Telemachus' growth to manhood. Analyze the stages of his assumption of responsibility and the recognition of the fact by others.
   [His mother's reaction is fear and anxiety; Nestor and Menelaus recognize him as Odysseus' son (whereas Athena in Book I professes not to); the suitors recognize his attainment of maturity by planning to kill him—*now* he is dangerous.]

Topics for Writing

1. Two ancient Greek critics, Aristophanes of Byzantium and Aristarchus, thought that Homer ended his poem on the lines "So they came / into that bed so steadfast, loved of old, / opening glad arms to one another" (XXIII. 298–300). In other words, they thought Book XXIV unnecessary. What in fact does Book XXIV contribute to the epic?
   [The ending at XXIII would have been a romantic ending: husband and wife reunited, nothing else matters. In fact there are still a great many problems to be solved, especially the consequences of Odysseus' slaughter of the suitors. Homer sees that Odysseus, who has established himself as master in his own house by violence, still has to be accepted by the community—the succession of his line depends on the community's goodwill. The epic ends with a reconciliation, engineered by Athena, but before the threat of conflict is removed, we are shown three generations of Odysseus'

family—father Laertes, Odysseus, his son, Telemachus—standing side by side ready for battle. Odysseus has been reintegrated in his family as he shortly will be in the community of Ithaca.]

2. Woman's role in the *Odyssey*.
[Faithful consort (Penelope, Arete) or temptation (Circe, Calypso, the Sirens, even Nausicaa). Helen has been one and is now the other. How "female" is Athena?]

3. Odysseus and Athena. Compare their relationship with that of Job and God. What does this suggest about the religious attitudes of the Hebrews and the Greeks?
[For Odysseus-Athena analyze carefully the long interview between them in XIII. 218ff.]

4. From the moment he hears from Athena in XIII how things stand in his own home Odysseus, in his disguise as a beggar, puts everyone to the test, to see if they are loyal to him or even whether they are decent human beings. List the incidents in which he puts people to the test and the results in each case.
[Eumaeus with the story of the cloak at Troy in XIV; the suitors by begging—Antinous in XVII, Eurymachus in XVIII, etc.]

5. List and differentiate the different recognitions of Odysseus, intended and unintended.
[Intended: Telemachus in XVI; the suitors in XXII; Eumaeus and Philoetius in XXI; Penelope in XXIII; Laertes in XXIV. Unintended: Argus in XVII; Eurycleia in XIX.]

6. Penelope and Telemachus: a complicated relationship between mother and son. Analyze the process of Telemachus' assertion of independent manhood and Penelope's reluctant acceptance of it.
[Telemachus' first action after Athena encourages him, is to contradict his mother (I. 386–96); she "gazed in wonder and withdrew" (397). Telemachus forbids Eurycleia to tell his mother he is going to Sparta (II. 391–95). Penelope is distressed when she hears he has gone: "Why has my child left me?" (IV. 739–42, 851–57). Athena inspires Telemachus with suspicions about Penelope's intentions (or does he have them anyway?) (XV. 14ff.). Telemachus is afraid she has already married one of the suitors

(XVI. 38–40). Their meeting after his return (XVII.40ff.). She reproaches him (XVIII. 243ff.). Penelope on Telemachus (XIX. 578–82); Telemachus on Penelope (XX. 138–41). Telemachus sends her out of the hall (XXI. 359–70). Telemachus berates her for not recognizing Odysseus at once (XXIII. 97–104).]

Further Reading

See also the reading suggestions in the anthology, p. 98.

Finley, M. I. *The World of* Odysseus. Revised edition, New York, 1978.
A historical-anthropological approach to Homeric "society" (in fact, to the "society" of the *Odyssey*) based on a study of the function of the gift in primitive societies. Stimulating, like everything Finley writes, and extremely good background for a discussion of the "economic" aspect of Homeric hospitality.

Griffin, Jasper. *Homer on Life and Death*. Oxford, 1980.
A limpid and informed discussion of both the *Iliad* and the *Odyssey* as poems that embody a consistent and civilized code of heroic, moral, and religious values.

Stanford, W. B. *The Ulysses Theme*. Oxford, 1963; Ann Arbor, 1968.
A rich and suggestive examination of the figure of Odysseus from Homer to James Joyce. Chapters II–V deal with Homer's hero. (Chapter V, "The Untypical Hero," is reprinted in Steiner and Fagles.)

Steiner, George, and Robert Fagles. *Homer: A Collection of Critical Essays*. Englewood Cliffs, N. J., 1962.
George E. Dimock's "The Name of Odysseus" is a brilliant discussion of the hero's identity, contained in a name he is proud to proclaim but must time after time conceal, a name that announces his nature and destiny. This volume also contains Erich Auerbach's famous but controversial essay on the scar of Odysseus (XIX), that explores fundamental contrasts between Homeric and Old Testament narrative, and W. B. Stanford's essay "The Untypical Hero" on the character of Odysseus.

Whitman, Cedric. *Homer and the Heroic Tradition*. Cambridge, Mass., 1958; New York (Norton Library), 1965.
Contains a chapter "The *Odyssey* and Change" that deals sensitively with differences of tone and feeling between the two epic poems.

Kirk, Lord, and Luce (see *Further Reading* for the *Iliad*, above) also discuss the *Odyssey*.

SAPPHO OF LESBOS

Backgrounds

In some ancient texts Sappho is referred to as a teacher and the girls whose names recur so often in her poems are said to be her pupils; a papyrus fragment published in 1974 (it was written in the late second century A.D.) speaks of her as "teaching in peace and quiet the noble girls not only from the local families but also from families in Ionia." A fragment of one of her poems, addressed, we are told by the writer who quotes it, to an "uneducated woman," begins with the words: "But when you die, you will lie there in the grave and no one will remember you afterwards or long for you..." All this seems to suggest that the context of her poetry may have been a sort of aristocratic finishing school in which girls were given instruction, in music and the dance, for example, to prepare them for their later career as wives of the nobility.

Many of Sappho's poems were *epithalamia*, marriage songs, composed presumably for her favorite pupils; others were heart-broken laments for the loss of a loved companion. "'Honest, I want to die,'" runs one fragment. "That's what she said to me, when in tears she was leaving me. 'Oh, what we have suffered, Sappho. It's not by my choice that I'm leaving you.' And I answered her: 'Go and fare well and remember me. For you know how we cared for you. . . .'" And the second poem in our selection sounds like a recreation of Sappho's passionate reaction to the sight of a beloved pupil visited by her future husband. But Sappho's poetry is not always so tensely passionate; she can also treat the pangs of unrequited love with an ironic wit. The first poem in our selection, for example, Sappho's invocation of the love-goddess Aphrodite, starts out as a conventional appeal to a deity to come to the suppliant's help. It employs the usual formulas—"you came before, now come again..."— but then it departs sharply from the established pattern. Instead of dealing with the present occasion, Sappho's need for help, it gives a vivid account of the goddess's previous visit. And we are told what Sappho's "grief and bitterness" are all about: she has been crossed in love, someone is rejecting her suit. On that previous occasion Aphrodite was gracious and promised her aid; Sappho now asks for the same promise: "accomplish all those things my heart desires to be done; appear and stand at my shoulder." The Greek for the final phrase means literally: "be my ally."

The poem is a brilliant example of self-mocking wit. The whole religious terminology of a hymn, the appeal to a god, including the epiphany of the goddess concerned, is put in motion so that Sappho can win the heart of some recalcitrant girl and furthermore, the poem shows us that this is not the first time Sappho has brought the goddess down from Olympus.

This light-hearted invocation of Aphrodite is, however, an exception; elsewhere Sappho is well aware of the awesome and terrifying powers of the goddess. "Once again," runs a fragment, "limb-loosening love makes me shiver, that bittersweet irresistible creature . . . " and another speaks of love that shakes the heart "like the mountain wind when it falls on the oak trees."

Further Reading

See also the suggestions in the anthology, p. 541.

Easterling, P. E., ed. *Greece*. Vol. I of *The Cambridge History of Classical Literature*. Cambridge, 1985. Pp. 202–209.
A critical survey of Sappho's poetry by David A. Campbell.

Greek Lyric. Vol. I. Cambridge, Mass. (Loeb Classical Library), 1982.
Contains the complete text of what remains of Sappho's work, with an English translation by David A. Cambell.

AESCHYLUS
The Oresteia

Backgrounds

The scene of the first two plays is the entrance to the palace of
Agamemnon at Argos; the time is the tenth year of the Trojan War. A
watchman on the palace roof sees the fire signal that announces the fall
of Troy. A chorus of old men comes into the orchestra (the circular
dancing floor in front of the stage area) and sings. They remember the
departure of the army ten years before; adverse winds delayed the sailing
and, at the command of the goddess Artemis, Agamemnon sacrificed his
daughter, Iphigenia, to release the fleet. Clytaemnestra enters and tells
the chorus the news—Troy has fallen. She describes the chain of signal
fires across the sea from Troy and speculates about what is happening in
that city now.

After her exit the chorus sings; the song begins as a hymn of victory
for the Greek success but ends on a note of fear and foreboding. Enter a
herald who has come to announce Agamemnon's arrival; he speaks of the
suffering of the Greeks at Troy and also reveals that Agamemnon will
come alone—Menelaus was blown off course and no one knows where
he is. Another choral song begins with a meditation on the name and
destiny of Helen but ends with a fearful vision of the recurrence of
violence in one generation after another, as Agamemnon enters in a
chariot. With him is a female figure who is not identified until later but
the audience knows, from Homer, that it is the Trojan princess Cassandra. Agamemnon, boasting exultantly of the destruction of Troy, is
welcomed by Clytaemnestra in a speech full of menacing ambiguity. She
invites him to walk into the palace on blood red tapestries; at first reluctant, he eventually does so, after recommending Cassandra to her care.
The choral song now is full of vague apprehension; they sense that
something is wrong. Clytaemnestra comes on stage again to order
Cassandra inside but meets only silence and departs.

Now Cassandra speaks. In a long exchange with the chorus she
prophesies, at first in riddling images and finally in clear statement, all
that is to come—her own death, the murder of Agamemnon, and even the
death of Clytaemnestra at the hands of her son. She has been given the
gift of prophecy by the god Apollo who loves her. But when she refused

him her love he added the proviso that though she could tell the future no one would believe her—as the chorus refuses to believe her now.

She goes off to her death and almost at once the chorus hears Agamemnon's death cries from inside the palace. As they discuss what action to take, the doors open and the bodies of Agamemnon and Cassandra are brought out; over them, Clytaemnestra makes a triumphant speech of self-justification. But as the chorus, recovering from its initial shock, rejects her defense and prophesies retribution, she retreats from the high confidence of her opening speech and appeals to the "savage ancient spirit of revenge" (1533) that plagues the house of Atreus to let it end here, shed no more blood. At this point, its very embodiment, Aegisthus, enters, with an armed bodyguard, and threatens the chorus. Clytaemnestra prevents their coming to blows with her plea—"no bloodshed now" (1693)—and ends the play with her hope to "set the house in order once for all" (1711).

The second play, *The Libation Bearers*, opens with the arrival of Orestes, now a grown man, from the north of Greece where his mother sent him as a boy while his father was at Troy. Accompanied by his friend Pylades, he has come to avenge his father, to whose tomb, onstage, he pays his respects. He is interrupted by the arrival of the chorus (who are slaves, perhaps captives from Troy) and his sister Electra. The two young men stand aside to hear the chorus sing about the nightmare of Clytaemnestra, who has sent Electra to Agamemnon's grave; she is to placate Agamemnon's angry spirit by pouring libations (liquid offerings of grain, honey, and oil) on his grave.

She sees the footprints of Orestes and a lock of hair he has laid as an offering on the tomb. He comes out of cover and identifies himself; brother and sister are reunited. Orestes tells her that he comes under direct orders from the god Apollo to avenge his father. And now brother and sister and the chorus, in a long lyrical scene, address prayers, demands, and finally reproaches to the body in the grave, calling for Agamemnon's help in what they are about to do. Electra tells Orestes what Clytaemnestra's dream was: she gave birth to a serpent that bit her breast when she suckled it. He interprets the dream: he is the serpent.

Electra goes into the house; Orestes and Pylades plan to knock at the door and kill Aegisthus when he comes out. The chorus sings about the "high daring spirit" of a man (579), but that is surpassed by the daring of women; they include Clytaemnestra's crime in a list of mythological female outrages. Orestes and Pylades knock at the door but it is Clytaemnestra who comes out. Orestes tells her that Orestes is dead; she welcomes him into the house. Orestes' old nurse Kilissa comes on stage; Clytaemnestra has sent her to summon Aegisthus and his bodyguards but the chorus persuades her to tell him to come alone. A choral song encourages Orestes not to flinch when he faces his mother—"When she cries 'Son!' cry out 'My *father's* son!'" (816)—and Aegisthus comes on stage on his way to the door.

He goes in and soon a servant comes out shouting to Clytaemnestra that Aegisthus has been killed. She comes on stage, sends the servant for a weapon, but too late: Orestes and Pylades come on stage to face her, Orestes with a drawn sword. Before his mother's appeal Orestes does in fact flinch; he turns to Pylades, who has not spoken yet but who now speaks, for the first and last time. He reminds Orestes of Apollo's orders. Orestes drives his mother into the house to kill her.

The choral victory song is followed by a repetition of the climactic scene of *Agamemnon*: the doors open and two bodies are laid on the steps; over them the murderer justifies his act. But as he goes on, Orestes loses control of his emotions and his words; he is, he says, a charioteer with his horses out of control. He starts to leave, bound for Delphi and Apollo's protection, but sees suddenly the Furies, the spirits of vengeance, "the hounds / of mother's hate" (1055–56). Only Orestes can see them now but in the final play we see them, too; they are its chorus.

The scene changes for the opening of *The Eumenides*: it is the temple of Apollo at Delphi. His priestess goes in to officiate but comes out terrified; she has seen, at Apollo's altar, a suppliant, Orestes, and the Furies sitting round him waiting. The audience now sees the scene she described: Apollo enters and sends Orestes off to Athens where he will find "judges of [his] case" (84). The ghost of Clytaemnestra (or is she a dream in the Furies' heads?) spurs the chorus to action and they exchange taunts and threats with Apollo before rushing off in pursuit of Orestes.

The scene is now Athens, where Orestes comes to clasp the statue of the goddess Athena; the chorus follows and after singing a song designed to "bind" and paralyze him, they move on to take their prey just as Athena arrives. After hearing both sides she determines to summon judges and set up a court; she has shown such fairness that the Furies accept this decision. They sing of their ancient duties, the punishment of criminals who would otherwise escape; they are confident they will win their case.

As the trial begins, Apollo arrives to speak for Orestes. Under the skillful questioning of the Furies Orestes breaks down and has to turn to

Apollo for help. Apollo proclaims the priority of the father over the mother: Orestes' duty to avenge his father outweighed his link to his mother. Athena addresses the jury, stressing the importance of this "first trial of bloodshed" (694) and repeats a theme of the Furies, that without fear there can be no order. She herself will vote for Orestes, since as a goddess born directly from her father, Zeus, without the intermediary of a mother, she favors the male.

The votes are evenly divided, which, under Athenian law, means acquittal; Orestes goes free, but the Furies now threaten to turn their rage against Athens itself. Athena finally wins them over by an offer of a home and worship in her city and the Furies, who have been outcasts even from the gods because of their function as executors of blood vengeance, accept her offer and become "Eumenides," kindly protectors of the institutions and lands of Athens.

Aeschylus (524?–456 B.C.) belonged to the generation that saw the establishment of democracy at Athens (in the last decades of the sixth century B.C.) and the heroic defense of that democracy against a Persian expeditionary force at Marathon in 490 B.C. as well as the decisive Athenian contribution to the defeat of a full-scale Persian invasion on the sea at Salamis in 480 B.C. and on land at Plataea in 479 B.C. Aeschylus fought as an infantry soldier at Marathon and, probably, in the naval battle at Salamis: on his tomb at Gela in Sicily, where he died, a verse inscription commemorated his combat service at Marathon and did not even mention his plays. Yet his plays so impressed the Athenian public that they were revived after his death, to compete with the offerings of his successors at the Dionysiac festival—an honor accorded to no other dramatist in the fifth century. In *The Frogs*, a comedy produced in the last decade of the fifth century, Aristophanes staged a contest in the lower world between the ghosts of Aeschylus and Euripides, old-fashioned patriotic virtue versus newfangled intellectual fashions, and, of course, Aeschylus was the winner.

How closely this nostalgic vision of Aeschylus the Marathon veteran as an arch-conservative corresponded to the reality we have no means of judging, but he was certainly an innovator in the world of theater. Aristotle, in the Poetics (this portion is not included in our selection), says that he was the first to increase the number of the actors from one to two, a move that "reduced the role of the chorus, giving first place to the dialogue." It also made possible dramatic confrontation instead of the predominantly narrative mode that must have been characteristic of performance with a single actor. Aeschylus was far from conservative, too, in his treatment of myth and especially in his manipulation of mythical material to give it contemporary resonance; in this field he had no equal.

The Eumenides, for example, put the court of the Areopagus on stage shortly after its status had been the key issue of a political struggle that threatened to lead to civil war. The Areopagus, its ranks filled by ex-magistrates, had become in the years after the Persian War a powerful political force, a sort of senate of elder statesmen that was an obstacle to reformists who wished to make Athenian democracy more radical and egalitarian. Just a few years before Aeschylus' play was produced, the reformers, led by Pericles and Ephialtes, had taken away all the court's powers except its legal right to try cases of homicide; feeling ran so high on both sides that Ephialtes was murdered. Hence when Aeschylus dramatized the foundation of the Areopagus by Athena he was treading on dangerous ground.

Modern critics are divided in their assessment of his position: was he acquiescing in the reform by emphasizing the solemn antiquity of the court's judicial function or was his reminder of the divine origin of the Areopagus a protest against the reforms? The fact that there is no agreement on this point suggests that in fact he did not take a position one way or another: the point he emphasized, in the song of the Furies and the speech of Athena (536ff.; cf. 709ff.) was moderation, the avoidance of extremes—"Neither the life of anarchy / nor the life enslaved by tyrants... / worship neither. / Strike the balance. . . "—and the civil war that extreme measures are likely to lead to. "Brutal strife," the Furies sing (988 ff.), "the civil war devouring men, I pray / that it never rages through our city... "

In *Agamemnon*, Aeschylus was dramatizing a story known to the audience from Homer (Cf. *Odyssey* I. 42ff.; III. 248ff.; IV. 535ff.; XI. 425ff.), but the climactic action of *The Libation Bearers*, Orestes' murder of his mother, is not explicitly mentioned there. The action of the last play, *The Eumenides*, has no Homeric model at all; in fact, it has been thought that Aeschylus may have invented the story of the trial of Orestes at Athens. Cassandra is mentioned in Homer (she is the first to see Priam coming back to Troy with Hector's corpse [*Iliad* XXIV. 819ff.] and is killed with Agamemnon by Clytaemnestra [*Odyssey* XI. 542ff.]), but in neither passage is there any hint of her prophetic powers. Aeschylus' adaptation of the standard version is very bold; the Attic dramatists, who worked almost exclusively with traditional tales, were allowed, perhaps even expected, to present the familiar figures and situation in a new light. Both Sophocles and Euripides, for example, wrote plays called *Electra*, that present the same action as *The Libation Bearers*, but though in both of them Clytaemnestra and Aegisthus are killed by Orestes, everything else is changed. Both dramatists, in contrast to Aeschylus, make Electra the central figure of the play, on stage throughout; but in Sophocles she is a heroic figure, while Euripides gives her a near-criminal mentality and has her collapse in bitter remorse after the murders. The fact that the poets used familiar stories did not rule out innovation and the element of suspense. The fact that the dramatists had to work with three actors was also not as much of a limitation on creativity as might appear. A change of mask and costume enabled an actor to reenter as a different character. *Agamemnon*, for example, has six speaking parts (Watchman, Clytaemnestra, Herald, Agamemnon, Cassandra, and Aegisthus) and *The Eumenides* five (Pythia, Apollo, Orestes, the ghost of Clytaemnestra, Athena). In addition the leader of the chorus could play an important speaking part, as he does in the trial scene of *The Eumenides*.

But the main function of the chorus is not the spoken word; it dances and sings. The word itself in Greek suggests dancing above all (our word *choreography* preserves this emphasis), and the long choral sections of our texts must be imagined as delivered by fifteen dancers whose movements emphasized their words. This movement, however, could not have been as athletic or complex as that of the modern ballet, for the chorus also sang, in unison, and their words, unlike those of modern opera, had to be intelligible to the audience, for they are vital for the significance of the dramatic action. Unlike the actors, who by the time the *Oresteia* was produced, were professionals, the chorus consisted of citizen volunteers, trained in their part, like the actors, by the playwright himself. The chorus is, as it were, the on-stage representative of the citizen audience; it observes and comments on the action and motives of the actors, reacts to their announcements and commands, opposes or supports them—above all, and this is especially true of the chorus in *Agamemnon*—it tries to understand, to interpret. It is rare to find a chorus that, like that of *The Eumenides*, assumes a decisive role in the action; this may have been a characteristic of Aeschylean drama, for we find it also in his *Suppliants*.

Classroom Strategies

Three assignments.

For the modern student perhaps the most disconcerting feature of the trilogy is the trial scene in *The Eumenides*, particularly the argument put forward by Apollo and approved by Athena, that "the woman you call the mother of the child / is not the parent, just a nurse to the seed. . . . " (666–67). This claim that the mother's role in the procreation of children is purely passive, that she is a mere incubator for the male seed, is the basis for Apollo's case that murder of a father is a more heinous crime than matricide.

This strange biology is not peculiar to Aeschylus; it appears also in the works of the philosopher Aristotle, who wrote a good hundred years after the death of Aeschylus. It is a theory that reflects the masculine bias of Athenian thought and feeling. The Greek city-state, and especially Athens, excluded women from political action and even in private life severely restricted their activities; they had no legal standing and were kept, in respectable families, out of sight in a special section of the house reserved for women and children. This male domination stemmed in part from the fact that most city-states, and especially Athens, were at war with their neighbors more often than they were at peace; treaties were always made with a time limit and even so, it was rare for the truce to last the full term fixed in the treaty. War, that in the ancient world meant close combat where physical strength was a crucial factor, was the exclusive business of men (compare Hector's speech to Andromache in the *Iliad* VI: "Go therefore back to our house, and take up your own work, / the loom and the distaff, and see to it that your handmaidens / ply their work also; but the men must see to the fighting" [490–92, not included in this anthology]). As combatants who were often called upon to risk their lives to save the city from destruction and its women and children from enslavement, men assumed the prerogatives of a ruling caste and developed an ideology of male supremacy to justify their dominance. (When Medea, in Euripides' play, makes her famous protest against a woman's subordinate position, she cites this military basis for male supremacy only to reject it.)

The goddess Athena explains her support for Apollo's position in mythological terms: she was born directly from the head of Zeus and had no mother. But it is understandable also in terms of contemporary realities. The goddess Athena, who was the guardian and protector of Odysseus in the *Odyssey* had another side to her nature: in the *Iliad* she is a relentless opponent of the Trojans, a warrior-goddess intent on the destruction of Troy and all its inhabitants. In Athens, the city that bore her name and worshiped her in the Parthenon on the Acropolis, she was thought of as the protector of Athens in war; her images in sculpture and painted on vases show her armed with a spear, shield, and helmet, sometimes actually in combat in the war with the Olympian gods against the Giants. "I honor the male," she says (752), as she casts her vote for Orestes, and later, when she urges the Furies to accept her offer of a home in Athens, she predicts a great future for her city: "As time flows on, the honors flow through all / my citizens. . . " (862–63). The source of such honor is made clear later in her speech: "Let our wars / rage on abroad, with all their force, to satisfy / our powerful lust for fame" (872–74).

Topics for Discussion

1. The theme of conflict between the sexes dominates the trial scene of *The Eumenides* but it is operative, sometimes openly, sometimes subtly, from the very beginning of *Agamemnon*. Trace its appearance and discuss its significance throughout the trilogy.
[In the opening scene the watchman calls Clytaemnestra "that woman" who "maneuvers like a man" (*Agamemnon*, 13), and in the scene in that she persuades Agamemnon to walk on the crimson tapestries we are shown how she works on his pride to bend him to her will. "Spoken like a man" (354) says the chorus to Clytaemnestra as she rounds off her vision of Troy's destruction with an ironic prayer for Agamemnon's safe return. Her lover Aegisthus plays the woman's part: "Coward," says the chorus, "why not kill the man yourself? Why did the woman...have to bring him down?" (1679–81) In *The Libation Bearers* the central choral ode (572ff.) rehearses the infamous female murderers of the past (killers of their sons, fathers, husbands) as Orestes prepares to kill his mother. Apollo, the male god *par excellence* champions the father's rights against the Furies, female deities, champions of the cause of Clytaemnestra.]

2. The question (which will recur in the discussion of *Oedipus the King*) of the independence of the characters: how far are their actions directed by the gods or by that Fate that seems even more powerful than the gods, until, at the end of the trilogy, "All-seeing Zeus and Fate embrace" (*The Eumenides*, 1059).
[The main question here is Agamemnon's responsibility for the sacrifice of Iphigenia. The goddess Artemis demands it as the price for the release of the fleet from adverse winds. But, as in so many

Greek stories of divine interference, Agamemnon is given a choice —he could abandon the expedition (indeed he mentions this possibility only to disregard it in *Agamemnon* 212–16). Aeschylus, in a paradoxical phrase, characterizes Agamemnon's decision to sacrifice his daughter as a free acceptance of destiny: "He slipped his neck into the strap of Fate" (217). Once he took this step, however, his heart hardened, "he stopped at nothing, / seized with the frenzy" (219–20) and gave the orders to gag his daughter and hold her ready for the knife in cold unfeeling words. Orestes too acts under orders from the oracle of Apollo and the threat, if he disobeys, of dreadful disease and a miserable death (*The Libation Bearers*, 285ff.). But he goes on to reveal that he has his own motives for action that would urge him to kill his mother even without the gods' command. There is not only "mounting sorrow for father" (306) but—a revealing detail—"the lack of patrimony presses hard" (307). His only route to the repossession of his father's kingdom and wealth lies through his mother's death.]

3. Many of the images of the *Oresteia* recur throughout the trilogy, gaining fresh significance with each new appearance (for an example see the discussion of the net imagery in the headnote, p. 547). Trace through the trilogy the pattern of images connected with (a) lions or (b) dogs.

[*(a) Lions*. The lion is the heraldic device of the house of Atreus as the lion gate at Mycenae reminds us. The choral parable of the lion cub that, brought up as a pet, turns savage when full grown (*Agamemnon*, 712–31), prepared for by the choral reference to Artemis as "so kind / to the ravening lion's tender, helpless cubs" (140–41) is the nexus of a widespread pattern of references to lions. This cautionary tale is offered by the chorus as a comparison with Helen and the destruction she will bring to the Trojans who welcomed her. But in *Agamemnon* the lion is used to characterize other figures as well: Agamemnon, who boasts of the slaughter at Troy as the work of "the beast of Argos . . . our bloody lion lapped its fill, / gorging on the blood of kings" (809, 812–13); Clytaemnestra appears in Cassandra's vision as "the lioness" who "rears on her hind legs" and "beds with the wolf / when her lion king goes ranging" (1275–77); even Aegisthus is "a lion who lacks a lion's heart" (1235). They all began as "a captivating pet . . . like an infant just born" (716, 719) and ended as "a priest of ruin"

(730). But the real lion cub is Orestes. His nurse, Kilissa, remembers him as a helpless baby (*The Libation Bearers*, 736ff.) but the chorus sees Orestes, full grown and with his mother's blood on his hands as the lion: "To Agamemnon's house returned / the double lion" (i.e., Orestes and Pylades; 924–25). In *The Eumenides* when Apollo orders the Furies out of his temple he tells them where they should be: "Your kind / should infest a lion's cavern reeking blood" (191–92). To which they might have replied that the House of Atreus, whose last male descendant they are in pursuit of, is just such a lion's den.

[*(b) Dogs.* The watchman on the roof in the opening scene of the play keeps his vigil "propped on my arms . . . like a dog" (*Agamemnon*, 3–4). He is a faithful dog, loyal to Agamemnon; we remember him when Clytaemnestra falsely claims that she is a "watchdog gentle to him alone, savage / to those who cross his path" (603–4) and salutes the king as "watchdog of the fold" (886) as she plans his death. When Cassandra sings of the crimes committed in the House of Atreus the chorus recognizes her as "a keen hound . . . trailing murder . . ." (1093–94); but when she foresees the king's death at the hands of "that detestable hellhound / who pricks her ears and fawns" (1240–41), the chorus cannot connect her word with Clytaemnestra. And Aegisthus, when the chorus defies him in the final scene of *Agamemnon*, calls them "insubordinate dogs" (1701): "We'll see if the world comes dancing to your song, / your absurd barking—snarl your breath away! / I'll make you dance, I'll bring you all to heel" (1666–68). Electra speaks of her imprisonment at the time of Agamemnon's murder: "I was an outcast, / worthless, leashed like a vicious dog in a dark cell" (*The Libation Bearers*, 433–34). Later she will play her part in the plot to kill her mother, like the "ruthless bitch," as the chorus later calls Scylla (605) who betrayed her father to his killers. It is when Clytaemnestra faces an Orestes who is determined to kill her that the Furies are for the first time evoked by this image: "Watch out," she says, "the hounds of a mother's curse will hunt you down" (911), and at the end of the play, when Orestes sees his vision of the Furies, they are "the hounds / of mother's hate" (1053–54). And in the final play when *we* see them too, they are indeed hounds, trackers of the scent of blood. Like hounds, they bay in their sleep (*The Eumenides*, 132) and like hounds they follow the prey: "Blood of the mother draws me on—

must hunt / the man for Justice. Now I'm on his trail!" (228–29). This is their exit line in the scene set at Delphi; their entrance speech, delivered by the leader of the chorus when they reenter now at Athens, uses similar language: "At last! / The clear trail of the man . . . / He's wounded— / go for the fawn, my hounds, the splash of blood, / hunt him . . . ." (242–46).]

Topic for Writing

Zeus, so the chorus sings, "lays it down as law / that we must suffer, suffer into truth" (*Agamemnon*, 178–79). Trace the steps by which the chorus of *Agamemnon* comes through suffering and a series of misapprehensions to a true vision of the situation.

[At the beginning of the play they believe that the war against Troy was just (66ff.); the kings are sent by Zeus. yet they are clearly disturbed by Agamemnon's sacrifice of his daughter (216ff.). They react with joy to the news of Troy's fall (269–70), which will of course mean Agamemnon's return. In their second choral ode they begin a victory hymn to celebrate the Greek triumph but as they describe the process by that men are led to "tread the grand altar of Justice down . . . " (384ff.), though they claim they are singing about the Trojan, Paris, their words are reminiscent of their description of Agamemnon's change of mind that enabled him to kill his daughter. They return to the theme of the righteous war with an indictment of Helen (403ff.) and expressions of sympathy for the grief of Menelaus (415ff.) but soon turn to the grief of mothers and fathers who have lost their sons at Troy, "all for another's woman." The image of the war god as a broker who exchanges living men for funeral ashes is in flagrant contradiction with the opening of the ode. They go on to speak of the "people's curse" that is "heavy with hatred" and the victory ode ends with a wish to be neither victor nor vanquished. But the sight of the herald who brings news from Troy raises their hopes again; they return to their illusion that Agamemnon's return will put an end to their doubts and fears. The herald's tale of victory renews their confidence and they sing (684ff.) of Helen and the destruction she wrought on the Trojans who greeted her arrival with such joy, and when Agamemnon enters they greet him with enthusiasm. They tell him they were against the war at first but "now from the depths of trust and love / I say Well fought, well won" (788–89). But when their king, whose sacrifice of his daughter they have almost forgotten in their joy at his return, goes into the palace treading the blood-red tapestries like some proverbial man of pride destined for a fall, they sing in fear of some unknown terror; they sense that something is badly wrong. Cassandra tells them, first in riddling, then in plain terms what they fear but dare not face: that Agamemnon must die, that according to that standard of Justice they themselves have often invoked (374ff., 751ff.) Agamemnon must pay for the blood of Iphigenia and perhaps for the blood of all those who fell at Troy (455ff.). Cassandra tells them the truth in plain terms but they cannot accept it; only as she goes into the palace to her death do they dare ask the question: "Now if he must pay for the blood / his fathers shed, and die for the deaths / he brought to pass..." (1366–68). The answer comes at once; it is Agamemnon's cry of agony from inside the palace. Confronted with the corpse of the king and the defiant boasts of Clytaemnestra, they try to lay the blame on Helen (1484ff.), a patent evasion, that Clytaemnestra bluntly rejects (1493ff.); they then cast the blame on the spirit of vengeance that plagues the House of Atreus from generation to generation, a view that Clytaemnestra accepts, for she sees it as absolving her of responsibility. To this the chorus reacts violently, but, reminded of the murder of Iphigenia, they lose their bearing: "The mind reels—where to turn?" (1562) In the end they recognize, at last, Agamemnon's guilt: "None can judge between them. Justice. / The plunderer plundered, the killer pays the price . . . the one who acts must suffer . . . ." (1592–93, 1595). They have learned, through suffering, to see the truth. But by that same law Clytaemnestra too must pay, and, stung to fury by the sight of Aegisthus lording it in the house of Agamemnon, they call on Orestes as their only hope for justice; they now understand, too late as always, the full meaning of Cassandra's vision of the future.]

Further Reading

See also the reading suggestions in the anthology, p. 547.

Aeschylus. *The Oresteia.* Translated by Robert Fagles. New York, 1975; New York (Penguin Classics), 1984.
Contains a long and stimulating introductory essay (pp. 13–77) by Robert Fagles and W. B. Stanford, as well as helpful explanatory notes (pp. 285–330) on selected passages.

Kitto, H. D. F. *Form and Meaning in Drama.* London, 1956.
In the first three chapters (pp. 1–86) Kitto discusses the trilogy in

an attempt to answer a series of questions, for example: "Why in the *Libation Bearers* and the *Eumenides* are Agememnon's sins entirely forgotten even by his adversaries? Why does Aeschylus so arrange *Agamemnon* that the events earliest in time, namely Atreus' feud with Thyestes, comes at the end of the play?" Kitto tackles these and many other puzzling aspects of the trilogy with probing analysis; his answers may not persuade everyone but his great merit is to have recognized and explored the problems.

Knox, Bernard. *Word and Action: Essays on the Ancient Theater.* Baltimore, 1979.
Contains an essay "Aeschylus and the Third Actor" (pp. 39–55) that deals in some detail with the Cassandra scene and also with the way the chorus comes to understand and face, too late, the truth (see *Topic for Writing*).

McCall, Marsh, Jr., ed. *Aeschylus: A Collection of Critical Essays.* Englewood Cliffs, NJ, 1972.
Includes an important article on freedom and its limitations by N. G. L. Hammond (see *Topics for Discussion* #2) and a brilliant essay on symbolism in the *Oresteia* by R. F. Goheen. There is also an interesting survey of "tradition and method" in translating Aeschylus by Peter Green.

Taplin, Oliver. *Greek Tragedy in Action.* Berkeley and Los Angeles, 1978.
A book on the ancient staging of Greek tragedy by a scholar who has become perhaps the foremost expert in this field. The book proceeds by subject rather than play by play, but discussion of passages in the trilogy can quickly be located from the index on pp. 199–201.

Winnington-Ingram, R. P. *Studies* in Aeschylus. Cambridge, 1983.
Contains interpretive essays by a recognized authority on Greek drama on "Agamemnon and the Trojan War," "Clytaemnestra and the Vote of Athena," "Orestes and Apollo," and "Zeus and the Erinyes" (pp. 78–174).

SOPHOCLES
Oedipus the King

Backgrounds

The city of Thebes is ravaged by a plague and in the opening scene of the play a delegation of its citizens comes to urge Oedipus, King of Thebes, to find some remedy. They have confidence that he can somehow help them, for he has been their efficient and benevolent ruler ever since, many years ago, he came to Thebes and rescued the city from the Sphinx, a creature with a bird's body and a human female head, that preyed on the city's young men. Those who encountered it and failed to answer its riddle were killed. Oedipus volunteered to face the Sphinx and answer this riddle correctly; the Sphinx died and Oedipus was given the reward proclaimed for the deliverer from the monster—the throne of Thebes and the hand in marriage of its recently widowed Queen Jocasta.

Her husband, Laius, had been killed on the way to Delphi in a quarrel over precedence at a junction of narrow roads; his killer was the young Oedipus, who does not realize that the man he killed in the fight was the King of Thebes. Nor does he realize that Laius was his father and Jocasta his mother. The play presents his discovery of this dreadful truth.

This situation is the result of a whole series of coincidences or perhaps the work of some power that guided the course of events. Laius and Jocasta heard a prophecy from the oracle of Apollo at Delphi that their son would kill his father and marry his mother. They sent a shepherd out to leave the newborn child on the mountainside to die of exposure; to make doubly sure that it would die, its ankles were pierced and fastened together. But the shepherd had pity on the child and gave it to another shepherd, one from the other side of the mountain range, the territory of Corinth. Knowing that his king and queen, Polybus and Merope, were childless, this shepherd took the baby down to them and they adopted it. Because his ankles were swollen from the wounds the boy was called Oedipus ("Swollen-foot").

Oedipus grew up in Corinth believing he was the son of Polybus and Merope. But as he grew to manhood rumors began to circulate about his legitimacy; in order to know the truth he went to Delphi to consult the oracle. All he heard there was a prophecy that he would kill his father and marry his mother; appalled, he resolved never to return to Corinth and set out in the opposite direction. At a place "where three roads meet" he was crowded off the narrow road by a man in a chariot; a fight broke out and he killed the man and (he thought) all of his companions. (But in fact one escaped and brought the news back to Jocasta.) Oedipus kept on his way and at Thebes defeated the Sphinx, married Jocasta and became king. Apollo's prophecy was fulfilled.

Now, many years later, the plague rages in the city and Creon, Jocasta's brother, comes back from Delphi where he was sent by Oedipus to ask what to do. The answer: find the killer of Laius, then kill or banish him. And Oedipus undertakes to find him. He puts a dreadful curse on the killer, cutting him off from all contact with his fellow citizens; he also sends for Tiresias, the blind prophet, who is believed to know all things. He does in fact know the truth but refuses to tell Oedipus; the king reacts with fierce anger, accusing him of betraying the city and then of conspiring with Creon to overthrow him. His anger blinds him to the truth that Tiresias, now angry in his turn, begins to reveal, although in riddling terms; he speaks clearly in the end, but Oedipus leaves in a fury, paying no attention.

In the next scene Creon is directly accused of conspiracy and sentenced to death; at the request of the chorus and Jocasta, who now comes on stage, Oedipus reluctantly retracts the death sentence. Wishing to calm Oedipus, Jocasta asks the reason for his rage; he replies that Tiresias accused him of the murder of Laius. She tells him to pay no attention to prophets, they know nothing more than ordinary men. To prove it she tells him of the prophecy that her son would kill his father and marry his mother. In fact the child, she says, died on the mountain and Laius was killed by a stranger at the junction of three roads.

This detail terrifies Oedipus; he now tells her the story of his encounter at such a place. He is afraid he may be the killer of Laius, the cause of the plague, the victim of his own solemn curse. (He does not connect the prophecy with the one given him by Apollo, for he is sure that his father and mother are Polybus and Merope at Corinth.) But he knows that he was alone, and Jocasta spoke of "robbers" as the assailants of Laius. He needs an eyewitness to reassure him, and there is one: the survivor of the fight, whom Jocasta has sent away into the country to be a shepherd. It is the same man who took the baby Oedipus to the mountains to die, and when he comes he will bear witness to more than the death of Laius.

But meanwhile a messenger comes from Corinth: Polybus is dead and the Corinthians want Oedipus to come back to reign over them. The news of Polybus' death is a great relief; Apollo's prophecy at Delphi was wrong—Oedipus did not kill his father—but he will not go to Corinth because the second half of the prophecy, that he would marry his mother, will best be falsified if he stays in Thebes. The messenger now tells him there is nothing to fear; Merope is not his mother. The messenger, when he was a shepherd, was given the baby by another shepherd; its ankles were pierced.

By this time Jocasta has realized the horrible truth; she tries to stop Oedipus, to make him give up the search. But he insists he will know the truth, whatever it is. Jocasta rushes off stage (to hang herself, as we find out later) and Oedipus waits for the shepherd Jocasta sent for in the previous scene. When he comes, the man from Corinth recognizes him and Oedipus forces the whole truth out of him. Then Oedipus too rushes off stage as the chorus sings a despairing ode about the nothingness of men.

A messenger comes on to tell of Jocasta's suicide and Oedipus' self-blinding; soon the blind king himself comes stumbling on stage. His laments turn to stubborn resolution as he demands that the chorus obey the oracle of Apollo and drive him out to die, on the mountain where he now wishes he had died as a child. Creon, now king of Thebes, comes on to take charge. Oedipus is allowed to embrace his two daughters, Antigone and Ismene, and then is ordered into the palace; about his eventual disposition Creon will consult the oracle.

The oracle of Apollo at Delphi was, in Sophocles' time, a powerful religious institution, that wielded considerable political influence. Greek states and foreign kings consulted it about the future, as did also private individuals; their sacrifices and offerings made it one of the greatest concentrations of art and wealth in the Greek world. Apollo, through his priestess the Pythia (compare the opening scene of *The Eumenides*) answered requests for advice; his advice was treasured because he was believed to know the future. During the last three decades of Sophocles' life, Athens was at war with Sparta; before declaring war the Spartans had consulted the oracle and had been told that they would win (as they did).

But this belief that the gods know the future was no longer universally held in Sophocles' day; like many other features of traditional religion it was subjected to critical examination by the new philosophers who speculated about the atomic constituents of matter and by the Sophists who applied the canon of probability to religious myth. The attack on the belief in divine prophecy was in fact the most dangerous of all the new attempts to reject tradition; if the gods do not know the future, they are no more in control of the universe than we are.

This intellectual conflict is reflected in the play. Jocasta sums up her argument that Oedipus should disregard the oracles with a contemptuous rejection: "So much for prophecy. It's neither here nor there. / From this day on, I wouldn't look right or left" (948–49). The reaction of the chorus is to call on Zeus, the supreme god, to make the prophecies come true, horrible as that will be for Oedipus; otherwise, they say, there will be no point in worshiping the gods at all: "Never again will I go reverent to Delphi . . . or Apollo's ancient oracle at Abae . . . unless these prophecies all come true" (985ff.). Prophecies are despised and "the gods, the gods go down" (997). Later on, when he hears of the death of Polybus, Oedipus echoes Jocasta's disbelief: "Why, why look to the Prophet's hearth . . . ? All those prophecies I feared . . . . They're nothing, worthless" (1054, 1062ff.). And Jocasta draws the ultimate conclusion, that human life is a meaningless chaos, a chain of mere coincidences: "What should a man fear? It's all chance. / Chance rules our lives . . . . Better to live at random, best we can" (1069–70, 1072). They do not know it, but the truth of prophecy is about to be revealed, to Jocasta before the end of this scene, to Oedipus in the next. The play uses the myth to present the most controversial religious and philosophical issue of the day; it comes down decisively on the side of prophecy, divine knowledge and design.

The Oedipus story was of course well known, but it is likely that Sophocles reworked it along lines suitable for his own artistic purpose (as all the Greek poets did when they handled mythical themes.) In Homer's *Odyssey* the hero Odysseus sees, in the lower world, the mother of Oedipus (she is called Epikaste); she married her son who had killed his father. The gods revealed the truth to mankind; Epikaste hanged herself but Oedipus, though he suffered from the sorrows that the Furies of a mother bring to pass, lived on as king of Thebes. (See *Odyssey* XI. 293–304.)

There is no mention here of Oedipus' children, of his self-blinding and expulsion from Thebes, of Apollo's oracle or the Sphinx. All these details presumably came into the story later, in other epic tales or lyric poems, now lost. But we do know that Aeschylus produced a trilogy dealing with the house of Oedipus (we still have the final play, *The Seven Against Thebes*); from that play and the fragments of the others we know that the Aeschylean trilogy referred to the story of the Apolline oracle and the exposure of the child, the encounter where three roads meet, the self-blinding of Oedipus, and the part played by the Sphinx. This suggests that Sophocles could rely on audience familiarity with the main elements of the story to ensure appreciation of this masterly use of dramatic irony in the first two-thirds of his play.

We have only a version of the riddle of the Sphinx that comes from sources much later than Sophocles' time, but there is good evidence that it was known in this form in the fifth century. It is in hexameter verse; here is a literal translation:

> There is a two-footed thing on this earth, four-footed (but only one voice) and three-footed. It changes its form and is the only thing to do so of all the creatures that move on land, in the air or in the sea. Now when it walks supporting itself on most feet, the speed of its limbs is at its weakest.

There may be an allusion to the text of the riddle where Creon says "The singing, riddling Sphinx / She . . . persuaded us to let the mystery go / and concentrate on what lay at our feet" (147–49). In any case, the fact that the answer is "man" is singularly appropriate for a hero who begins the play as a representative of humanity as master of its environment and ends it as a blinded outcast.

Classroom Strategies

One assignment.

Modern students will probably find themselves in difficulty when they move from the dramatic exchanges in the spoken scenes to the sometimes meditative, sometimes excited lyric poetry of the choral odes. Yet the choral poetry is not only, for most of its length, a profound meditation on the moral and religious themes of the play; it is also a reflection of the chorus's reactions to and interpretations of the dramatic action. As in *Agamemnon*, the attitude of the chorus is not fixed; it varies as the song expresses the hopes and fears of the citizens of Thebes before the words and deeds of their rulers. But whereas in *Agamemnon* the chorus learns through suffering to see, at last, the truth of the matter, the chorus of *Oedipus*, oscillating wildly between overconfidence and utter despair, serves Sophocles as a dramatic instrument for the creation of suspense, of irony, and of contrast.

The opening song (169ff.) is a desperate appeal to the gods for relief from the plague. The chorus does not yet know the message Creon has brought to Oedipus; they await the word from Delphi with apprehension. The vivid description of the sufferings caused by the plague in lines 190ff. reinforces the dramatic effect of the opening scene: Oedipus must act quickly and decisively if he is to save his city. As he comes out of the palace he hears the closing lines of the choral prayer and Sophocles gives him an opening line heavy with dramatic irony: "You pray to the gods? Let me grant you prayers" (245). He will indeed grant their prayers but only at the price of his wife's death and the loss of his own eyes.

The second choral song (527ff.) follows the scene between Oedipus and Tiresias. The first half of it develops a vision of the man responsible for the plague, the murderer of Laius, as a fugitive in flight from the gods' pursuit—an outcast in the wilds, in "bristling timber . . . rocks and caves" (542–43). Evidently they do not accept Tiresias' identification of Oedipus as the killer; as they go on to discuss the prophet's charge they confess to bewilderment. For all their respect for Tiresias, they can see no reason why a prince from Corinth should quarrel with and kill the king of Thebes. They reject this assault "without proof" on the reputation of the man who once before saved Thebes. Not that they reject prophecy "Zeus and Apollo know" (561). But a human prophet may err; they will not believe until they see "these charges proved" (568).

But their next choral ode (954ff.) comes after the quarrel between Oedipus and Creon (in which they intervened on Creon's behalf) and the revelations that followed; they have heard Oedipus tell how he killed a man at the crossroads and now fears that he may in fact be the killer of Laius—that Tiresias was right—and they have heard Jocasta reject prophecy altogether, including one that came from Delphi. They are deeply disturbed and sing of the immortal laws as they pray for reverence and purity; they denounce the tyrannical spirit that mounts too high only to crash in ruin. This seems to be a reference to political power (and so to Oedipus); they qualify it immediately as they pray that the god will never put an end to the "healthy strife that makes the city strong" (969). But dark thoughts return: they sing now of one who has no fear of justice, no reverence for the gods, who "lay[s] hands on the holy things untoucha-ble" (980). In that last phrase (and the suggestion is especially strong in the Greek) there might be a reference to incest. If such a man go unpun-ished, they ask, why join the sacred dance? The dance they are themselves performing as they sing is such a dance; the theater is a place of worship of the god Dionysus. If such crimes go unpunished, their words imply, why worship the gods at all? And they spell this implication out clearly in the final stanza. They will no longer go to

Delphi or any other sacred site unless "these prophecies all come true" (989). They are ready to abandon their king if the condition of his survival is the failure of divine prophecy.

But the next choral song (1195ff.) is a jubilant speculation about the birth of Oedipus. They know now that he is not the son of the royal pair at Corinth; as they wait for the arrival of the Theban shepherd who carried the baby Oedipus long ago to the slopes of Mount Cithaeron, they indulge in pleasing prospects: Oedipus may be the child of a god, of Pan by a nymph, of Apollo, Hermes, or Dionysus. It is not long before the dreadful truth is revealed, to Oedipus and to the chorus, that now sings despondently of the fate of man: "generations of men . . . adding the total / of all your lives I find they come to nothing" (1311–13). Oedipus is their example; in his rise and fall they find the proof of this gloomy estimate of the human condition. Yet the last scene of the play suggests that just as they went too far before in joyful expectation, they have now gone too far in despair. For in the last scene the blind Oedipus emerges from his initial abject misery to reassert himself as a man; he refuses to accept the chorus' condemnation of his self-blinding: "What I did was best—don't lecture me . . ." (1499). The imperious tone is certainly not that of a man who feels he is nothing, and he uses the same tone to Creon later: "I command you—I beg you . . ." (1583). This return to self-confidence is based on a feeling that his cruel destiny marks him as unique, that, for some purpose undeclared, he has been singled out among mankind: "I have been saved / for something great and terrible, something strange" (1596–97). That "something strange" is the subject of the last play Sophocles was to write, *Oedipus at Colonus*.

Topics for Discussion

1. The theme of sight and blindness; its importance in a play that turns on human ignorance of the truth.

    [Tiresias the blind prophet can see the truth (as Oedipus begins to fear [823]). Oedipus, who has the use of his eyes, moves blindly towards the revelation of the truth. He sees clearly only when he is physically blind. Compare the emphasis on Oedipus' sight throughout the first part of the play (17, 28, 70, 96, 119, 394, 427, 597, 830, 885, 1042, 1147, 1153, 1185, 1190) and contrast the references to the vision of Tiresias (323, 359–60). Also Oedipus' sarcastic references to the blindness of Tiresias (396, 423, 425ff., 440–42, 469) and Tiresias' references to the blindness of Oedipus

(419, 470–71, 517ff.; cf. 879, 1082, 1095, 1359, 1405ff., 1566, 1624ff.).]

2. Oedipus is a figure representative of human confidence that our intelligence makes us master of our world.

   [Oedipus is a man of action and experience (cf. 55–56) but he himself emphasizes that his action is based on thoughtful analysis ("groping, laboring over many paths of thought . . . painful search" [79–80]). And he boasts that he alone was able to answer the riddle of the Sphinx: "the flight of my own intelligence hit the mark" (453). Here he prizes his own human intelligence above the prophetic skills of Tiresias, that are the gift of the gods. His intelligence is displayed in the frequent cross-questioning to which he subjects witnesses in the course of his investigation, an investigation that starts as a search for the murderer of Laius and ends as a search for his own identity. His questioning of Creon (112ff.), Jocasta (804ff.), the messenger (1114ff.), and the shepherd (1229ff.) are models of logical pursuit of the truth. And it is through these intellectual efforts that he finally brings about the catastrophe, learns the truth about himself.]

Topic for Writing

Trace the pattern and discuss the significance of the following images throughout the play: (a) Oedipus as hunter; (b) Oedipus as plowman; (c) Oedipus as sailor-helmsman.

[All three of these images reinforce the central idea of Oedipus as the symbolic representative of human progress, for the conquest of the wild beasts, the discovery of agriculture, and the mastery of the sea are important stages in our long development from savagery to civilization. (That the Greeks were conscious of this historical view of human progress is clear from the choral ode in *Antigone* [376ff.] where mastery of the sea, the soil, and the animals are the first accomplishments of "man the skilled, the brilliant" [390].)

[(a) *Oedipus as hunter*. The investigator of the crime is easily seen as a hunter and this image is pervasive throughout the opening scenes of the play. "Where to find it now," he asks when Creon tells him that Apollo demands the punishment of Laius' murder, "the trail of the ancient guilt so hard to trace?" (123–24) "What stopped you," he asks Creon, "from tracking down the killer / then and there?" (146–47) He will take up the chase himself and later claims that if he had been present at the time "there would have been . . . no long hunt / without a clue in hand" (250–51). Later Tiresias will tell him "I say you are the murderer you hunt" (413), but it will be a long time before he realizes this is the truth. The chorus envisions the murderer of Laius as a hunted animal: "that man who left no trace— / after him, hunt him down with all our strength!" (540–41) They do not realize that Oedipus is both the hunter and the prey.

[(b) Oedipus as plowman. The agricultural images are heavily loaded with significance in this play because in the Greek language such words as "plow" and "sow" are familiar expressions for the begetting of children (as they were in the seventeenth-century English of the Bible—"the seed of Abraham," "the fruit of the womb," for example). Quite apart from their clear reference to the incestuous begetting of children by the royal pair, these images are strikingly appropriate to the dramatic situation. For the plague in Thebes affects the products of the soil as well as human beings (cf. "The fruits of our famous earth, they will not ripen" [196] and "the women cannot scream their pangs to birth . . . children dead in the womb" [197–98]). This sympathetic relationship between the fruits of the soil and the fruit of the womb is reflected in the transference of agricultural terms to the pollution of the marriage of Oedipus and Jocasta; what this suggests is the responsibility of that unholy marriage for the stunted crops and the plague. Oedipus' first statement about his relationship with Laius is made in terms of this metaphor. Not realizing the hideous ambiguities involved he says: "I hold the throne that he held then, possess his bed / and a wife who shares our seed" (295–96). What he means is simply that he and Laius have had children by the same wife, but the words suggest to the audience the hideous truth. The same image recurs when Tiresias prophesies that Oedipus will be revealed as his father's murder and his mother's son: "He sowed the loins / his father sowed" (522–23). After the revelation of the truth, the chorus asks in horror: "How, how could the furrows your father plowed / bear you, your agony, harrowing on / in silence O so long?" (1337–39) When Oedipus bursts into the palace, he asks, the messenger tells us, for "his wife, / no wife, his mother, where he can find the mother earth / that cropped two crops at once, himself and all his children" (1387–89). He explains his own polluted state to his daughters with this same image: "I fathered you in the soil that gave me life" (1626) and "Your father killed his father, sowed his mother, / one, one and the selfsame womb sprang you— / he cropped the very roots of his existence" (1639–41). The plowman has reaped a dreadful crop, the sower is not only the sower but also the seed.

[(c) *Oedipus as sailor-helmsman*. Oedipus as helmsman is a natural image, for as king he is thought of as guiding the ship of state (a common metaphor in Greek as in English). The city is compared to a ship in the opening speech of the priest—"our ship pitches wildly, cannot lift her head / from the depths" (29–30)—and Creon, bringing news from Delphi, speaks of the "plague-storm" (114) that afflicts the city; he also refers to Oedipus' rescue of Thebes in earlier days with the phrase "you came and put us straight on course" (118). The chorus takes up and elaborates this image when they assert their loyalty to Oedipus after his quarrel with Creon: "You who set our beloved land—storm-tossed, shattered— / straight on course" (765–66). And they exhort him to do the same thing now: "Now again, good helmsman, / steer us through the storm!" (766–67) But their wish is not to be granted; after Jocasta's mention of the three roads, Oedipus is distraught. The citizens, in Jocasta's words, are "passengers in the grip of fear, / watching the pilot of the vessel go to pieces" (1010–11). Oedipus has not yet discovered the full truth. When he does he will understand at last the riddling question Tiresias asked him. "What haven won't reverberate . . . . That day you learn the truth about your marriage . . . the lusty voyage home to the fatal harbor" (480ff.)? Oedipus, like a navigator, had plotted his course by the stars: "I abandoned Corinth, / from that day on I gauged its landfall only / by the stars..." (876–78). But it brought him to an unspeakable destination. "One and the same wide harbor," sings the chorus, "served you / son and father both / son and father came to rest in the same bridal chamber" (1335–37).

Further Reading

See also the reading suggestions in the anthology, p. 657.

O'Brien, Michael J., ed. *Twentieth-Century Interpretations of Oedipus Rex*. Englewood Cliffs, 1968.
Contains an essay by Eric Dodds ("On Misunderstanding Oedipus Rex") that with admirable clarity and concision draws on a lifetime of brilliant scholarship and teaching to deal with the difficulties students usually experience on reading this play. There are also essays by Francis Fergusson (on the play as theater), G. M. Kirkwood (on dramatic form), R. P. Winnington-Ingram (on the Old Testament and Greek archaic thought), and Bernard Knox (on

the ending of the play). The volume also contains useful short quotations from critics ancient and modern, including, for example, Plutarch, Voltaire, Bowra, Freud, and Marshall McLuhan.

Seale, David. *Vision and Stagecraft in Sophocles*. Chicago, 1982.
The title speaks for itself: the plays are explored primarily as theatrical performance (but with careful attention to content and imagery). Pages 215–60 deal with *Oedipus the King*.

Segal, Charles. *Tragedy and Civilization: An Interpretation of Sophocles*. Cambridge, Mass., 1981. Pp. 207–248.
A sensitive and rewarding reading of the play that makes use of modern structuralist approaches.

Sophocles. *Sophocles' Oedipus Rex*. R. D. Dawe, ed. Cambridge, 1982.
This is an edition of and commentary on the Greek text of the play but the introduction (1–22) is an especially useful discussion of the problems raised by the intricacy of the plot.

Winnington-Ingram, R. P. *Sophocles: An Interpretation*. Cambridge, 1980.
Pages 173–204 offer a profound and provoking exploration of the problems of fate in the play and of the moral implications of the "fall of Oedipus."

Antigone

Backgrounds

After the events dramatized in *Oedipus the King*, the blind man is eventually expelled from Thebes by Creon; his two sons, Eteocles and Polynices, do not protest, and Oedipus, accompanied by his daughter Antigone, becomes a wandering beggar. For their ingratitude, he lays on his sons a curse—that they shall kill each other in a battle for their inheritance. After Oedipus dies the curse comes to fulfillment. The sons quarrel over the exercise of royal power in Thebes; Eteocles seizes the throne and Polynices goes abroad to find allies who will help him regain it. With six allied chieftains and their forces (the besiegers afterwards known as the Seven against Thebes—one for each gate) he assaults the city; all seven are killed and Polynices and his brother, Eteocles, kill each other. Creon now resumes power; he orders an honorable funeral for Eteocles, who has died defending the city, and the exposure of the corpse of Polynices, who has led a foreign army against it. The corpse, under guard, is to be devoured by carrion birds and beasts; the penalty for interference is death.

This edict is proclaimed by Creon early in the play but before this happens, the audience has seen Antigone propose to her sister Ismene a joint attempt to bury their brother's body. Ismene is afraid to join her, so Antigone goes off alone to bury the corpse. No sooner is Creon's decree delivered to the chorus than a frightened soldier comes on stage; he is one of the guards posted to watch the corpse and he reports that during a dust storm, that made it impossible to see, someone has given the body a symbolic burial, scattered dust on it—enough, according to Greek belief, to ensure passage of the dead man's soul to the lower world. Creon suspects conspiracy at once, assumes the guard was bribed, and tells him that if he does not produce the culprit he will pay the penalty himself.

The chorus now sings the famous ode about human ingenuity, that has made us masters of the earth and sea, of the animals, fish and birds, as well as of the political arts of communal life; there seems to be no obstacle to our future development, except that human can go too far, be a force for evil as well as good. The sentry returns, leading Antigone on stage; she has been captured replacing the dust the guards had swept off the corpse and pouring libations on it as well. Interrogated by Creon she admits her responsibility, defies him contemptuously, claims the authority of higher, divine laws that override Creon's decree; she is condemned to death. Ismene enters; she now tries to associate herself with Antigone's action but Antigone denies her any share in what she sees as her glory.

In the course of the dialogue between Ismene and Creon we learn that Antigone is betrothed to Creon's son Haemon. After the choral ode (a lamentation for the doomed house of Oedipus) Haemon comes to reason with his father but Creon insists that Antigone must die, even though Haemon leaves in desperation, making vague threats.

Antigone is to be buried alive in a tomb (Ismene is released); after a choral song that celebrates the power of love, Antigone enters, led by guards on her way to the tomb where she is to die. In a lyric dialogue with the chorus she laments her premature death, unmarried; Creon orders her to be taken away at once and she makes her last speech, that is a declaration of her love for Polynices and that ends with a prayer that her persecutor be punished. The chorus sings of great men and women of the past who have suffered imprisonment (though the reference of the second half of the ode is obscure) and Tiresias comes on to warn Creon that the gods disapprove of his action. He sends Tiresias packing but then, in fear of the consequences the prophet has foretold (the death of "one born of your own loins" [1184]) he gives way; he goes to bury the body and release Antigone. He does bury Polynices but Antigone has anticipated him: she has hanged herself in the tomb. Haemon has found her, and after lunging with his sword at his father, kills himself. All this we learn from the messenger who is giving the news to Creon's wife, Eurydice; she goes into the palace and kills herself—she dies cursing Creon. At the end of the play he mourns over the corpse of his son, praying for death.

In *Antigone* Oedipus is spoken of as already dead (61); the plot of the play is taken from a later stage of the house of Laios than that of *Oedipus the King*. And yet it is almost certain that *Antigone* was written and produced before *Oedipus the King*. Ancient sources tell us that because of the great impression made by this play Sophocles was elected one of the ten generals the Athenians chose every year. We know that he was one of the generals in 441 B.C. and took part in the campaign against the large island of Samos that had tried to secede from the Athenian empire in wartime. Whether the success of the play had any influence on the election or not (and we know that Sophocles held other high political offices in the course of his long life) the story could only have started if *Antigone* had been produced before, but not too long before, 441 B.C.

For the date of *Oedipus*, on the other hand, we have no external evidence of any kind. But it is generally agreed that the graphic presentation of the plague in Thebes owes something to the real plague that swept through Athens in 430 B.C. and recurred intermittently until 425 B.C. In any case the reference to the death of Oedipus in *Antigone*— "think how our own father died, hated . . ." (61ff.)—is not likely to have been written after the production of *Oedipus*, that ends with Oedipus still alive and feeling that he had "been saved / for something great and terrible, something strange" (*Oedipus*, 1596-97).

The political concern of *Antigone* certainly reflects the career of Sophocles as a holder of high office in Athenian life. He was at various times elected to the Board of Treasurers of the Delian League (which was in fact the imperial treasury of Athens), to the Board of Generals at least once, and, after the Athenian catastrophe in Sicily in 413 B.C. to a board of emergency commissioners elected to deal with the situation. The play was famous in later times as a mine of quotations useful for political discussion; the orator Demosthenes, speaking a century after the first production of the play, quoted parts of Creon's opening speech (194-214) as a prime expression of democratic principle.

What tradition (if any) Sophocles was following when he wrote *Antigone* we do not know. We have no trace of the story in the fragments of Theban epic that have survived and there is no mention of it in Homer. The Aeschylean play *Seven Against Thebes* ends with a scene that presents in swift and summary fashion Creon's edict and Antigone's decision to disobey it. But the scene seems out of place as a kind of hurried epilogue to a play that comes to a fitting conclusion with the death of the brothers; scholars generally consider it a later addition, the work of a producer who, influenced by Sophocles' play, attached an epilogue to the old play of Aeschylus. The fact that Antigone story was not fixed by epic tradition seems clear from the fact that in Euripides' *Antigone* (now lost) the heroine, as we know from ancient accounts, was not put to death at all but married Haemon and bore him a son. It seems likely that Sophocles was presenting his audience with dramatic events with which they were not already familiar; *Antigone*, unlike *Oedipus*, makes little use of dramatic irony.

Classroom Strategies

One assignment.

The natural tendency of modern readers (especially students) is to see Antigone as all heroine and Creon as all villain and, though there is no doubt that Antigone *is* heroic and that she is right in the issue of burial, Creon, in the opening scenes of the play, is presented in terms that for Sophocles' audience suggested a patriotic, democratic statesman. His opening speech was quoted by a later orator as a model for democratic conduct (see *Backgrounds*), and some expressions in it recur in the great Funeral Speech of Pericles, a panegyric of Athenian democracy. In his insistence on the safety of the state as a consideration that overrides all ties of friendship and family he is simply stating what every Greek citizen believed. The small Greek cities, constantly at war with their neighbors, faced, in the case of defeat, not just loss of territory and property but the likelihood of massacre, enslavement, and even physical destruction of the city itself. This had happened to Mycenae in the fifth century; its powerful neighbor Argos reduced it to ruins. In the course of the thirty-year war between Athens and Sparta that raged at the end of the century, Athens three times killed the men and enslaved the women and children of cities that rebelled against her imperial rule. So that when the chorus sings of the enemy "thirsting for the kill" and ready "to glut his jaws with Theban blood" (134, 136) and Creon speaks of Polynices as one who came to destroy Thebes and the sanctuaries of its gods—"to burn their temples ringed with pillars, / their golden treasures—scorch their hallowed earth" (323-24)—the Athenian audience did not dismiss these phrases as rhetoric. The actor playing Creon would have the audience with him unanimously when he said: "whoever places a friend / above the good of his country, he is nothing" (203-4).

As the action develops, however, it becomes clear that for Creon the welfare of the citizen body is not an overriding concern. In the quarrel with his son Haemon he talks more like a tyrant than a democratic statesman: "Am I to rule this land for others—or myself . . . ? The city *is* the king's—that's the law" (823, 825). When Tiresias comes to warn him that his action offends the gods and will bring disaster on the city, he refuses to yield. He does yield in the end, too late to avoid the consequences of his obstinacy; Antigone, on the contrary, never gives an inch and goes to her death, true to her insistence on the right of her dead brother to burial. The nineteenth-century German philosopher Hegel, in a famous analysis of the play, saw it as a "collision between two moral powers"—the demands of the state versus the demands of the family—both of that were "one-sided." This is a valid estimate of the situation as presented in the opening scene, but Hegel, whose views on loyalty to the Prussian state were very much those of Creon, did not take into account the fact that the favorable impression created by Creon's first speech is quickly destroyed by his subsequent words and actions.

Topics for Discussion

1. The issue of the proper roles of the sexes, that was a major theme of *The Oresteia*, recurs in *Antigone* but seen from a different perspective.

   [Clytaemnestra played the man's part but she was repudiated by the Olympian gods and the court of the Areopagus, that was swayed by the arguments of Apollo and Athena for the supremacy of the male. But Antigone, who defies the power of the state first against the threat and then against the reality of death is vindicated in the end; Tiresias, speaking for the gods, condemns Creon's action and Creon's punishment comes immediately after his rejection of Tiresias' advice. Antigone's action is more unexpected and courageous than Clytaemnestra's, for Clytaemnestra was the ruling power in Argos while Agamemnon was away; she succeeded by cunning and concealment and she had Aegisthus and his guards to support her. Antigone is a young girl who has no position of power; all her male blood relatives are dead and her sister refuses to help her, yet she disobeys Creon's edict so openly that she gives the impression that she actually wants to be caught in the act. The attitude the Athenian audience expected to find in young women is proclaimed by Ismene in the first scene: "Remember we are women, / we're not born to contend with men" (74-75). Antigone does not even bother to argue the point; she simply repudiates Ismene as a traitor to the family and proceeds with her plan alone. For Creon, the fact that this edict was disobeyed by a woman ("What man alive would dare? " he says when told the news [281]) intensifies his rage; and when Antigone proudly proclaims her responsibility and defies him in the name of a higher justice than his, he takes it as a challenge to his manhood: "I am not the man, not now: she is the man / if this victory goes to her and she goes free" (541-42). At the end of the confrontation scene, as he confirms the death sentence, this tone recurs: "While I'm alive, / no woman is going to lord it over me" (592-93). He is sure, however, that Antigone (and Ismene, who has been condemned to death with her) will weaken when it comes to the point; after Antigone's proud speech about the higher laws, he speaks of "the stiffest stubborn wills" that "fall the hardest," of "the toughest iron" that cracks and shatters, of "proud, rebellious horses" that can be broken "with a light bit" (528ff). And as he orders the two girls inside he expects them to cave in: "From now on they'll act like women...even the bravest will cut and run, / once they see Death coming for their lives" (652, 654-55). Ismene is later released but Antigone shows no sign of willingness to surrender and this rouses Creon's anger to fever pitch. Three times in his argument with Haemon he sounds this same note: Men must not, he says, "let some woman triumph over" them, must "never be rated / inferior to a woman, never" (758, 760-61). When Haemon refuses to yield he is denounced as one who "is fighting on . . . the woman's side" (828), as "woman's accomplice" (837), and "woman's slave" (848). Creon speaks of surrender as the woman's part, but in the end the traditional roles are reversed. Antigone goes to her death defiant to the last and by her suicide brings down on Creon's head the death of his son and his wife. Creon, too late, gives in abjectly: "It's a dreadful thing to yield" (1219), he says, but yield he does. "What should I do?" he asks the chorus. "Tell me . . . I'll obey" (1223). This is Ismene's word—"I must obey" (79); what he feared has come to pass. By his own standards he is proved the woman, Antigone the man (cf. 541ff.).]

2. There is a conflict of religious views in the play. This is often overlooked because though Antigone's religious sanction for her deed is plainly exposed, Creon's religious point of view is hard for the modern reader to appreciate. Nevertheless, it exists, and as a matter of fact, it must have seemed more acceptable to the original audience than Antigone's devotion to the gods of the underworld and the dead.

[For Creon, the gods are the protectors of the city and so he can feel that in the measures taken to promote patriotic solidarity—honorable burial for the bodies of its defenders, exposure for those of traitors—he has the gods on his side. The Athenians, who considered themselves under the protection of the goddess Athena, whose temple, the Parthenon, dominated the city from the rock of the Acropolis, would certainly have felt that measures taken in the city's defense would have the approval and support of the goddess. Creon has no doubt that he has the gods of the city on his side; he mentions them at the beginning of his opening speech: "The ship of state is safe. The gods who rocked her . . . in the storm / have righted her once more" (180-82). And when he denounces the man who "places a friend / above the good of his own country," he calls on "Zeus who sees all things, always" to witness his stance (203ff.). His conviction that the gods share his attitude is so strong that when the chorus suggests that the burial may be "the work of the gods" he rejects the idea as "intolerable" (316ff.). "Was it," he asks sarcastically, "for meritorious service / they . . . prized him so?" Polynices "came to burn their temples"; it is "inconceivable" that they should intervene on his behalf. "When did you last see the gods / celebrating traitors?" This is an attitude most people shared, or at least sympathized with, but as in the case of Creon's devotion to the city (see *Classroom Strategies*) Creon abandons his announced principles as the action develops. When Tiresias, the representative of the gods Creon claims as his, comes to tell him that the altars are polluted by birds that have fed on the flesh of Polynices and that the gods demand the burial of the corpse, he rejects the prophet's advice. And he does so in blasphemous terms that reveal the falseness of his original claim. "You'll never bury that body in the grave, / not even if Zeus' eagles rip the corpse / and wing their rotten pickings off. to the throne of god!" (1151-53).

[Antigone's religious devotion is to the gods who represent a higher law than any the city can impose. Her claim of divine authority for her action turns out in the end to be justified, though she does not live to see that justification and, in fact, goes to her death in a despairing mood. "Why look to the heavens any more...?" (1014) It is remarkable that though Tiresias, the spokesman of the gods, condemns Creon, he does not praise Antigone—in fact he does not even mention her. Perhaps this divine coldness toward Antigone stems from a feeling on Sophocles' part that her loyalty to the rights of the dead and the divine law that she believed upheld them was so exclusive that she had no room for the loyalty to the city; her motives throughout are personal and private—the highest unit she feels loyalty to is the family (contrast the arguments which Haemon opposes to his father's decision; they are all based on the ultimate welfare of the community).

Topics for Writing

1. In the ode that sings of our progress from savagery to civilization (376-416) some of the triumphs of human ingenuity listed there find ironic echoes in the body of the play. Trace the recurrence and discuss the significance of references to or images drawn from (a) our conquest of the sea; (b) our mastery of the animal kingdom—snaring of the birds; and (c) our mastery of the animal kingdom—taming the horse and bull.

   [(a) *Our conquest of the sea*. Man as sailor, master of the sea (378-81), Man's city is a storm-tossed ship (180) now righted (182). Only when "she voyages true on course" (212), says Creon, can individual relationships prosper. Ismene, trying to associate herself with Antigone's action and die with her says: "I'm not ashamed /

to sail through trouble with you" (608-09). The chorus, brooding on the fate of the house of Oedipus, sees ruin as a "great mounting tide / driven on by savage northern gales" (661ff.)—contrast the picture of man who "crossing the heaving gray sea, / driven on by the blasts of winter . . . holds his steady course." (378-79, 381). Haemon opens his approach to Creon with conciliatory terms ("you in your wisdom / set my bearings for me" [709-10]) but later warns his father that he is headed for shipwreck: "Haul your sheets too taut, never give an inch, / you'll capsize . . . " (801ff.). Tiresias reminds Creon that he was right to follow the prophet's advice in time gone by, for "so you kept the city straight on course" (1097), and later, the messenger, about to announce the death of Haemon and the ruin of all Creon's hopes, speaks of former times when Creon "set us true on course" (1282). And when Creon, embracing the corpse of his son, learns that his wife, too, has committed suicide, cursing him, as his son did, he sees himself in the "harbor of Death, so choked, so hard to cleanse" (1413).

[(b) Our mastery of the animal kingdom—snaring of the birds. In the celebration of human skill and intelligence the chorus sings of the invention of nets to snare "the blithe, lightheaded race of birds," (386) but there is nothing blithe or lightheaded about the birds that are mentioned in the body of the play. The very first reference to them, in fact, is to the carrion birds that will feed on Polynices' corpse: "He's to be left unwept," says Antigone, "unburied, a lovely treasure / for birds that scan the field and feast to their heart's content" (35-36). Man is not seen as master of the birds here, nor is he in the chorus's image of the invading army threatening Thebes with destruction: "like an eagle screaming, winging havoc / over the land . . ." (127-28). The carrion birds recur, this time invoked not in indignation by Antigone but in exultation by Creon when he announces his decree; Polynices' corpse is to be "left unburied . . . carrion for the birds and dogs to tear, / an obscenity for the citizens to behold" (229-31). When Antigone finds the corpse of Polynices swept clean of the dust she had poured on it she "cried out a sharp, piercing cry, / like a bird come back to an empty nest . . . all the babies gone" (471-73). Tiresias first realizes that something is wrong when the birds, whose voices he understands, suddenly become unintelligible as they turn on each other "talons flashing, ripping . . ." (1105ff.); he realizes that the altars of the gods "are fouled, / one and all, by the birds and dogs with carrion / torn from the corpse . . ." (1124-26). And Creon, in his blasphemous rejection of Tiresias' warning, tells him the body will never be buried, not even if "Zeus' eagles rip the corpse / and wing their rotten pickings off to the throne of god . . ." (1151ff.). The birds do more than pollute the altars of Thebes; they will carry the infection back to the cities of the other champions whose corpses Creon has exposed—"a wheeling crow that wings the ungodly stench of carrion / back to each city, each warrior's hearth and home" (1204-5)—and so incite hatred abroad—"cities in tumult" (1202)—that, as the audience knew from the traditional story, would eventually result in a second attack on Thebes, this one successful.

[(c) *Our mastery of the animal kingdom—taming the horse and bull.* Man achieves his conquest of the soil with the aid of domesticated animals—"the breed of stallions turning up the furrows" (385)—but first he has to tame them—"training the stallion, clamping the yoke across / his shaggy neck, and the tireless mountain bull" (393-94). But in the body of the play, Creon talks of taming not animals for man's use but men as subjects of his rule. When he hears of the symbolic burial of Polynices he is sure it is the work of conspirators, "grumbling against me in the dark...never keeping their necks beneath / the yoke . . ." (330-31). Similarly, faced with Antigone's defiance he expects to break and tame her: "I've known spirited horses you can break / with a light bit—proud, rebellious horses" (532-33). When he orders the imprisonment of the two sisters, he says: "Tie them up, no more running loose" (653). When the chorus sings of other mortals who, like Antigone, were imprisoned, the image of the yoke recurs: Danaë was "wed to the yoke and broken" (1040) and "the yoke tamed him too / young Lycurgus flaming in anger . . ." (1051-52).

[Man may have tamed the animals but he himself is subjected to the yoke, of tyrannical power in the case of Antigone, of the gods in the case of Danaë, Lycurgus, and Creon. Creon bows his neck before it and submits; Antigone goes to her death untamed—"passionate, wild," as the chorus says of her, "she hasn't learned to bend before adversity" (526-27).]

2. Creon, Antigone and Tiresias all speak at different times and places of the issues at stake in terms of profit and loss, of monetary value.

Trace these terms through the language of the play and discuss the light the use of them throws on the attitudes and actions of the protagonists.

[Creon sees all opposition to his will as the product of bribery, as action for profit. The sentry who brings news of the burial is repeatedly accused of accepting bribes from conspirators (cf. 334, 341, 351, 355, 365, 370) and Creon sees in money the root of all evil in the community (335-41). Tiresias, too, is treated to a similar tirade; prophets, says Creon, have tried to sell him short and ship him off for years (1147-48). "Drive your bargains," he says to the prophet, "traffic . . . in the gold of India, silver-gold of Sardis" (1149-50, and cf. 1161 "for their own gain"). When Tiresias is driven to tell Creon that he must reveal the dreadful truth about his future, Creon replies contemptuously, "Spit it out. Just don't speak it out for profit" (1178), to which Tiresias replies, "Profit? No, not a bit of profit, not for you" (1179).

[Creon can think only in material terms. When the chorus tells him they will not obey his edict for "only a fool could be in love with death" (246) he rejoins: "Death is the price—you're right. But all too often / the mere hope of money has ruined many men" (247-48). It will prove beyond his comprehension that a girl can defy his edict and risk death for no material motive whatsoever; he can only think that she must be insane (633). Haemon tries to argue with his father by adopting his own terms: "Father," he says, "only the gods endow a man with reason, / the finest of all their gifts, a treasure" (764-65). But such arguments have no effect on Creon; treasures, for him, are of this world. So it is particularly appropriate that the messenger, announcing the death of Haemon and the ruin of all Creon's hopes—"he's as good as dead, I tell you" (1286)—offers the final comment on Creon's crass standards: "Pile up riches in your house, as much as you like . . . but if real delight is missing from the lot, / I wouldn't give you a wisp of smoke for it, not compared with joy" (1287-91).

[Antigone, too, though her standards are not Creon's, twice uses his language but to strikingly different effect. Speaking of Polynices' corpse, she calls it "a lovely treasure / for birds" (35-36), and the adjective suggests that she is not thinking of the birds but of herself—her "lovely treasure" is the brother for whose sake she will give her life. And that sacrifice she later refers to in the same terms. "And if I am to die before my time / I consider that a gain. Who on earth, / alive in the midst of so much grief as I, / could fail to find his death a rich reward?" (515-18). Between Antigone and Creon there is no common ground; though they use the same words, they are speaking different languages.]

Further Reading

See also the suggestions in the anthology, p. 657.

Goheen, Robert. *The Imagery of Sophocles'* Antigone. Princeton, 1951.
The title speaks for itself; the book analyzes in detail all the different sequences of imagery in the play. "The Money Sequence" discusses the question asked in *Topics for Writing* #2; "Images of the Sea and Sailing" will be found useful for #1. [Caution: Goheen is discussing the Greek text and often deals with nuances of imagery that do not appear in the Fagles translation.]

Knox, Bernard. *The Heroic Temper*. Berkeley and Los Angeles, 1964; paperback, 1983.
An attempt to define the characteristics of the Sophoclean hero. Chapters 3 and 4 (pp. 62–116) deal with *Antigone* with particular attention to the contrast in religious feeling, community loyalties, and heroic temper between Antigone and Creon.

Seale, David. *Vision and Stagecraft in Sophocles*. Chicago, 1982.
The title of Chapter 4 ("*Antigone*: Concrete Visualization") speaks for itself.

Segal, C. P. "*Antigone*: Death and Love, Hades and Dionysus." In *Oxford Readings in Greek Tragedy*, ed. Erich Segal. Oxford, 1983. Pp. 167–76.
An essay on the conflicting male and female elements in the play, developed along structuralist lines.

Segal, C. P. "Sophocles' Praise of Man and the Conflicts of the *Antigone*." In *Sophocles: A Collection of Critical Essays*, ed. T. Woodard. Englewood Cliffs, N. J., 1966. Pp. 62–85.
Useful for *Topics for Writing* #1.

EURIPIDES
Medea

Backgrounds

The background for the events of the play is briefly sketched by Medea's old nurse, who delivers the prologue. The romantic idyll of Jason and Medea (see ll. 1–10 and the explanatory notes on those lines) has long since come to an end; they are exiles in Corinth and Jason has married the daughter of the king, abandoning Medea and his two sons by her. She is desperate and the nurse is afraid of what she may do. The boys' tutor brings news that the king (his name is Creon but he has no connection with the Creon of the Sophoclean plays) intends to expel Medea and her children from Corinth; he is afraid of her.

That his fears are justified is made clear in the next scene; Medea wins over the chorus of Corinthian women by her famous speech lamenting the subordinate position of women and they promise not to betray her plans for revenge. Creon arrives to expel her but is talked into granting her one day's reprieve. That is all she needs, she says, when he is gone; she plans to kill him, his daughter, and Jason (370–71). At this stage she has not yet thought of killing Jason's sons. He now comes in to try to offer her financial help in her exile from Corinth, an offer she refuses with contempt in a speech of violent denunciation; he makes a cynical defense of his conduct but she sends him away with sarcastic wishes for his enjoyment of his marriage and with veiled threats.

One obstacle to her plan for revenge is the fact that if she does succeed in killing Jason and the king and princess of Corinth she will have nowhere to go for refuge; no city will take her in after that. The problem is solved by the chance arrival of Aegeus, king of Athens. He is childless and has been to the oracle at Delphi for advice, but Apollo's reply to his request was obscure and he is on his way to a wise man at Troezen to ask for an interpretation. Medea tells him her troubles and begs him for a refuge in Athens, promising that through her knowledge of drugs she can cure his sterility. He offers her a home in Athens and she makes him swear an oath to confirm this offer. (She does not tell him what she intends to do before leaving Corinth.)

Now she can plan her revenge. She will send the princess a wedding gift—a robe that will kill her and anyone that touches her. But she will

---

also kill the children (776). Jason will be left wifeless and childless (787ff.). She sends for Jason and with feigned humility she plays the part of the submissive wife; Jason, deceived, leaves with the children, who carry the poisoned gifts for the princess. When the tutor returns with the boys and announces that the gifts have been accepted, she prepares to kill her sons. In a famous monologue (995–1054) she struggles with her own soul, changing her mind and then returning to her original resolution. After the messenger comes to report the hideous deaths of the princess and the king, she goes into the house to complete her revenge; she kills the children.

Jason comes on to save the life of his boys (for the king's friends will kill them otherwise [1279–80]), but Medea appears above the house in a chariot sent her by her grandfather the Sun-god; with her are the bodies of the children. She and Jason exchange reproaches and curses (she prophesies the manner of his death); finally she leaves for Athens as Jason appeals to Zeus to bear witness to her slaughter of his sons.

Medea, with its concentration on the status of women, their sorrows and crimes, is not unique in Euripides' dramatic *oeuvre*; in fact he was famous (to some, infamous) for his emphasis on such themes. His *Hippolytus* deals with a stepmother, Phaedra, who falls in love with her stepson; in *Andromache* a barren, jealous wife plans to murder her husband's concubine and her son by him; the *Sthenoboea* had a plot similar to the story of Joseph and Potiphar's wife (Genesis 39, p. 59–60); *Aeolus* dealt with love of brother and sister, and *Auge* with a girl who bore her illegitimate child in a temple. The comic poet Aristophanes, in his *Frogs*, staged a debate between Aeschylus and Euripides in the lower world (Euripides died just before the play was written) and had "Aeschylus" denounce "Euripides" for his *Phaedra* and *Sthenoboea* and some of his plots in the lines: "His nurses go propositioning others / his heroines have their babies in church / or sleep with their brothers" (translated by Richmond Lattimore).

Long before Euripides produced *Medea* in 431 B.C. he had been attracted by the tragic possibilities of her story; his first offering at the festival of Dionysus (in 455 B.C.) included a play called *The Daughters of Pelias*, which dealt with Medea's role in the death of Pelias, King of Thessaly. (See *Medea*, lines 9–10 and the explanatory footnotes, also lines 474, 492). This incident was part of a long saga, the story of the Argonauts, which was well-known to the audience that saw *Medea*; it is the background against which the drama of *Medea* is played out.

Jason's father, Aeson, was the rightful heir to the kingdom of Iolkos, in the north of Greece near Mount Pelion (3) but the throne was usurped by his half-brother, Pelias. Jason, who had been sent off to safety, came to Iolkos when fully grown to claim his rights. Pelias, who had been told by a prophet that his death would be brought about by one of his own kin, persuaded the young man to set off in quest of the fabulous golden fleece, which was guarded by a dragon in the eastern kingdom of Colchis (2), beyond the Hellespont, on the southern coast of the Black Sea. The King of Colchis, Aietes, was a son of Helios, the sun god (403, 930); he had a daughter, Medea, and a young son, Absyrtos.

Jason assembled a company of heroes (called Argonauts after the ship Argo, the first long-range ship that was ever built) and set off on his adventurous journey to the east; one of the many dangers he faced was a passage through the Clashing Rocks (the Symplegades [2, 423]) which may be a mythical representation of the narrow passage of the Dardanelles, the entrance to the Black Sea. In Colchis, Jason had to face a series of ordeals before he could take possession of the fleece. He had to yoke a pair of fire-breathing bulls (466–67), plow a field with them, and sow dragon's teeth. The crop would be armed men whom he would then have to fight. Medea, who had fallen in love with Jason, gave him an ointment that would make him invulnerable and he came through successfully; the armed men he provoked into killing one another by throwing a stone which each side thought had been thrown by the other.

Aietes suspected Medea's complicity and planned to attack Jason and the heroes in the night. Medea came to warn them, led Jason to the dragon's lair, killed the dragon (468ff.), and embarked with Jason and the heroes in the night. When Aietes' ships came close in pursuit she killed her brother (165) and threw his limbs overboard one by one; Aietes' ships stopped to pick them up. After a long voyage Jason and Medea came to Iolkos, where Medea tricked the daughters of Pelias into killing their father, persuading them that he would be rejuvenated by the process which in fact caused his death. Jason did not, however, reap the reward of Medea's action; Pelias' son drove Jason and Medea out of Iolkos and they came to Corinth as refugees.

Classroom Strategies

One assignment.
Medea repeatedly refers to Jason as her husband (260, 227, 254, 259,

etc.) and herself as his wife (580), and Jason calls himself her husband (1312) and says she was married to him (1311). Yet he can abandon her and marry the princess of Corinth; though Medea protests passionately, Creon and the princess find nothing objectionable in Jason's conduct and there is apparently no violation of law on his part.

For the Athenian audience this would not have been seen as a contradiction; it was perfectly understandable as a reflection of conditions in their own society. At the time the play was produced an Athenian citizen's sons could be recognized as citizens themselves only if born of an Athenian mother; "marriage" was a contract entered into by two Athenian families, the bride brought her husband a dowry (which had to be restored if he separated from her) and the purpose of marriage was officially defined as "the procreation of legitimate children." A marriage with a foreign woman was not a marriage in this sense at all; many Athenian men had, in addition to their legitimate wives, concubines who might well be of foreign birth and had no rights. What sort of a marriage ceremony Medea and Jason went through we are not told but in the eyes of Athenian law it was not binding. Medea can call Jason to witness "the gods whose names you swore by" and "my right hand, and the knees which you often clasped / In supplication" (481, 484–85), but though it is true that he has broken his word (483) she has no legal hold on him.

(Virgil will later make use of a similar situation in the *Aeneid*. Dido considers herself married to Aeneas by the pledge of his right hand [IV.246] but Aeneas does not recognize the bond as legal: "I never held the torches of a bridegroom, / Never entered upon the pact of marriage" [443–444].)

Medea has no legal recourse; she has to fall back on cunning and violence.

Topics for Discussion

1. Medea's plan for revenge is not clearly announced until fairly late in the play. Analyze the formation in her mind of the decision to kill the children.
   [The first formulation of Medea's revenge is vague; she asks the chorus to aid and abet her by silence if she can find a means or devise any scheme "To pay my husband back for what he has done to me, / —Him and his father-in-law and the girl who married him" (259–60). After she has won her day's grace from Creon, she clarifies her intention: to kill all three of them, "father, the girl and

my husband" (371). She does not know how yet; she talks of the sword (375) and of poison (381). But she cannot proceed without assurance of a refuge, a city to take her in after she has killed her enemies. When she is sure of such a refuge at Athens, promised by Aegeus and confirmed by an oath, her plan is complete. "I shall tell to you the whole of my plan," she tells the chorus (756). She will pretend to give way, ask Jason to let the children take gifts to the princess, poison gifts which will destroy her and "all who touch the girl" (772). She hopes presumably that both Creon and Jason will do so. But her revenge now includes the murder of the children. She speaks of this as specifically aimed against Jason; Jason, she says, "will pay me the price . . . For those children he had from me he will never / See alive again, nor will he on his new bride / Beget another child . . ." (786–89). Jason, that is, will remain alive, to suffer the loss of his hopes—his sons who would prolong his line and preserve his name and memory; he will suffer also the loss of the hope of new children from his bride.

[There has been no overt preparation for this drastic change of plan; Medea gives no reasons nor does she explain, as Euripidean characters often do, the psychological process by which she arrived at this decision. Yet Euripides has in fact prepared the ground carefully, so that the audience can accept this new and dreadful resolve. Right at the beginning of the play, when the audience hears her hysterical outbursts offstage, she wishes first for her own death (96ff.) but then, when she sees the children brought into the house, she turns her despairing rage against them, Jason's sons. "I hate you, / Children of a hateful mother. I curse you / And your father. Let the whole house crash" (112–14). And the nurse fears for the children's safety (117ff.). When Medea speaks rationally and persuasively to the chorus, her wild rage against the children is forgotten.

[In her fierce exchange with Jason, however, she hears him speak with pride of his sons, of the plans he has for their future (which do not, of course, include her). He has left her, he says, in her best interests (and the children's). He wants to bring them up "worthily / Of [his] position (550–51), give them royal step-brothers by his new wife, a royal progeny to be brothers for the children he has now, "a sure defense to us" (584–85). Jason sees the future of his house in these sons. The point is brought home sharply to Medea and the audience by the appearance of Aegeus, an old man who has no sons and who goes from the oracle at Delphi to the wise man at Troezen in search of some remedy for his childlessness, who will promise Medea a refuge in Athens when she offers to cure his sterility.

[It is immediately after this scene that Medea announces her intention to kill the children. She will make Jason a man with no future in his line, a wreck of a man, like Aegeus. She does not announce this motive; she speaks instead of her inability to save the children after she has destroyed the king and his daughter (777). But when the chorus asks her if she can really have the heart to kill them, she reveals her true motive: "Yes, for this is the best way to wound my husband" (801). In the false submission scene, the children's fate is sealed. For Jason shows how much he loves them, how much he counts on their future: "And of you, children, your father is taking care. / He has made, with God's help, ample provision for you. / For I think that a time will come when you will be / The leading people of Corinth . . ." (890–93). At this point Medea turns white and bursts into tears (898); Jason cannot understand why. "I was thinking about these children," she says (901).

[We know what she was thinking. Jason's devotion to them, his rosy vision of their future career, to be men of influence and his support in old age—all this confirms Medea's feeling that this is in fact the best way to wound her husband. She wavers momentarily from her purpose (1030ff.) but not for long; she kills the boys. And she savors her revenge in her last interview with Jason. She has left him childless, he says, (1301), "my life is over!" (1325). And she turns the blade in the wound: "The children are dead. I say this to make you suffer" (1345). And she reminds him that he will suffer more as time goes by. "I go," he says, "with two children to mourn for" (1370). And she replies: "Not yet do you feel it. Wait for the future." (1371).]

2. Some critics (Denys Page, for example) refuse to see the play as, in part, a comment on woman's subordinate role in Athenian society; they point out that Medea is a dealer in supernatural poisons, who escapes the consequences of her action on a magic chariot, that she is, in fact, an oriental witch who cannot be regarded as representative of Athenian women. Is such a view justified?

[It is certainly expressed in the play; it is Jason's view: "There is no Greek woman who would have dared such deeds," he says

(1314), and he calls her "A monster not a woman" (1317). It is true that she has at her disposal a poison which seems more magical than real and that she escapes in a chariot that flies through the air. It is also true that she swears by the goddess Hecate, "my mistress, / Whom most I honor and have chosen as partner . . . who dwells in the recesses of my hearth" (392–94). Hecate is the mistress of witches in Renaissance literature (she appears on the stage in this role in an interpolation made to Shakespeare's *Macbeth*, for example) and appears in Greek literature from the Alexandrian age (third century B.C.) on as the patron goddess of sorcery. But there is no text from Euripides' time or before to connect her with sorcery. She was a goddess particularly associated with women (and is often identified with Artemis, the protector of women in childbirth) and there was an image of her outside every Athenian house. Medea's invocation of Hecate carries no suggestion of witchcraft.

[As for the robe and crown that burst into flames when put on, the audience is not likely to have read any hint of sorcery into it, since such devices are commonplace in mythical tales. In Sophocles' *Women of Trachis* the wife of Heracles sends him a similar robe (she does not realize its potency, but thinks it a love charm) which causes his death by fire, and in Euripides' *Ion* the Athenian princess Creusa uses a poison that is equally magical—a drop of the Gorgon's blood. Poison was in any case the natural recourse of a wronged wife driven to desperate action, for she could not hope to prevail in a contest of strength. The flying chariot is, of course, a gift from Medea's divine grandfather and points up the fact that the Odyssean figure with whom Medea is compared by the proponents of witchcraft, namely Circe, is not a witch at all but a goddess (cf. *Odyssey* X.245).

[It is true that in other plays of the period, a lost play of Sophocles for example, Medea is portrayed as a woman who works her will through drugs and poisons. But Euripides has been careful to avoid giving such an impression. It is noticeable that though his Jason, in the quarrel scene and in their final confrontation, pours out his contempt and loathing for her, he never uses this particular line of invective. Euripides did not want to undercut the effect of Medea's great speech on the position of women by any suggestion that she was not herself a wronged, abandoned woman. She tricks Creon into giving her an extra day, Aegeus into offering her a refuge, and

Jason into accepting the false gifts for his bride not through witch-craft but through purely human cunning and resolution.]

Topics for Writing

1. Medea is a woman, but Euripides has presented her as a figure previously thought of as exclusively male—a hero. Analyze her character in the play as an amalgam of the salient qualities of Achilles and Odysseus.
   [She expresses the heroic creed in lines 791–93: "Let no one think me a weak one, feeble-spirited, . . . but rather just the opposite, / One who can hurt my enemies and help my friends." Such a reputation ensures what Achilles values most—glory. "For the lives of such persons are most remembered," she says (794); so Achilles came to fight and die at Troy because his glory would be everlasting (*Iliad* IX. 500ff.). When he goes to kill Hector even though he knows his own death will follow, he says: "Let me seize great glory" (XVIII. 144ff.). Like Achilles (I. 201, IX. 791), Medea feels dishonored ("slighted" [20, 26]; "scorned" [1329]; "insulted" [591]). Like Achilles (I. 330, IX. 310, IX. 828) she reacts with "anger," "rage," (94, 99, 174) which makes her, like Achilles, impervious to advice, to appeals to reason or pleas for moderation (cf. Achilles in Book IX and Medea at 29, 827ff.). To others her rage seems like that of a wild beast ("wildness" [103]); she is "Like a lioness guarding her cubs" (188). So Achilles makes his spirit "savage" (IX. 769) and refuses to bend, "like some lion / going his own barbaric way . . ." (XXIV. 48–49). Both Medea and Achilles sacrifice the lives of their own people in their fury for revenge (Medea the children, Achilles his fellow Achaeans) and both become inhuman in their rage (Achilles: "Would to god my rage, my fury would drive me now / to hack you flesh away and eat you raw . . ." [XXII. 408–409]; Medea: "O your heart must have been made of rock or steel," sings the chorus [1254], and "A monster not a woman, having a nature / Wilder than that of Scylla in the Tuscan sea," says Jason [1317–18]—cf. *Odyssey* XII. 331ff.).
   [The resemblances between Medea and Odysseus are clear and abundant. She from the beginning of the play and he from the moment he loses his crew are absolutely alone, dependent on their wits and courage; no help comes from their protecting gods either,

until Odysseus reaches Ithaca and is met by Athena, and until Medea, her purpose accomplished, is given the winged car. Both play on the gullibility of their enemies, who do not realize that they are being deceived; Odysseus fools Cyclops as Medea does Creon and Jason. Both assume humiliating disguises: Odysseus as the beggar in his own house, Medea, in her second scene with Jason, the role of fulsomely flattering obedient wife. Both of them triumph over their enemies in a bloody revenge that more than compensates for their sufferings—seems, in fact, to go too far.]

2. Medea is a foreigner, an oriental princess, and Jason, as well as some modern critics, attribute the ferocity of her revenge to the fact that she is a "barbarian." How does the contrast between barbarian and Greek function in the play?
[The idea that Medea is a "barbarian" is in fact peculiar to Jason; even Creon, who fears her, does not speak of her in such terms. Jason, in the quarrel scene, reminds her that she owes him the privilege of living in a civilized society: "instead of living among barbarians, / You inhabit a Greek land and understand our ways, / How to live by law instead of the sweet will of force" (524–26). Medea, of course, has no reason to congratulate herself on living "by law," a law that allows her husband to abandon her; she later reproaches herself for trusting "the words of a Greek" (785). And Jason will later lament the day he brought her to Greece. "Now I see it plain, though at that time / I did not, when I took you from your foreign home / And brought you to a Greek house . . ." (1304–6). He should not have married a barbarian: "There is no Greek woman who would have dared such deeds" (1314).
[The chorus, however—who are appalled at her intention to kill the children (795ff., 827ff.) and pray to Earth and Sun to stop her (1236ff.)—never for one moment speak of her as a barbarian. When she makes her opening appeal for their sympathy (212ff.) she speaks as a Greek wife addressing Greek women; her problem is theirs. And though they reject the murder of the children (but not that of the King and his daughter) they understand the desperate rage that prompts it. Far from saying that no Greek woman would have done what Medea did, they mention one, Ino, who "laid her hands on her children" (1258). She was, they say, the only one, but the audience would have thought of others, too: Agave, of the royal house of Thebes, who under Dionysiac possession, helped

tear her own son Pentheus to pieces; Procne, who, to punish her husband who had raped her sister, killed her son Itys and served his flesh to his father.

[Medea, who sacrificed family and country to save Jason's life, is labeled a barbarian—called unfit for civilized Greek society—by the very man she tried to help. His cynical betrayal raises grave doubts about the civilization he claims to speak for.]

Further Reading

See also the reading suggestions in the anthology, p. 740.

Conacher, D. T. *Euripidean Drama: Myth, Theme and Structure.* Toronto, 1967. Pp. 183–98.
A challenging analysis of the play which is discussed as "realistic tragedy" as opposed to "mythological tragedy" which is concerned with "the individual in relation to the gods."

Euripides' Medea. Introduction and commentary by Denys L. Page. Oxford, 1938.
This is a Greek text and commentary which contains an eloquent introduction putting the play in the context of its time (viii–xvii) and stating the classic case for Medea as barbarian witch (xvii–xxi).

Schlesinger, Eilhard. "On Euripides' *Medea.*" In *Euripides: A Collection of Critical Essays*, ed. Erich Segal. Englewood Cliffs, N. J., 1968. Pp. 70–89.
An essay (translated from the German) that deals especially with the problems posed by the ending and uses a comparative approach (Goethe, Corneille, and Anouilh, for example, are cited) to throw light on the Euripidean play.

ARISTOPHANES
Lysistrata

Backgrounds

Lysistrata, an Athenian wife whose name means "disbander of armies," comes on stage expecting the arrival of other Athenian women whom she has summoned to an important meeting. She also expects some women from Sparta, a city with which Athens has been at war for twenty years. When everybody has arrived she announces her plan: a sex strike of the women on both sides to force the men to make peace. In spite of their initial reluctance she persuades them to swear an oath to refrain from sex with their husbands.

Meanwhile, another group of Lysistrata's women friends has seized the Acropolis in Athens; the Athenian women on stage leave to join them while the Spartan women go home to organize the strike in Sparta. A chorus of old men enters; they are on their way to the Acropolis to force an entry, or if repelled, to smoke the women out with the timber and fire pots they are carrying. They are met, however, by a chorus of women carrying water to put their fire out; the contest between the two choruses is interrupted by a magistrate who takes charge of the operations against the Acropolis gates.

But Lysistrata comes out to parley and in a spirited exchange with the magistrate she gets the better of the argument. After another rowdy altercation between the two choruses, Lysistrata comes on again; her troops are trying to desert under various pretexts—what they really want is to go home to their husbands. She restores their morale and they go back to the Acropolis.

At this point an Athenian husband, Cinesias, arrives; he is in a visibly excited state and demands his wife Myrrhine. In a ribald, comic scene Myrrhine teases Cinesias with the prospect of sexual enjoyment but in the end leaves him still frustrated. As he goes out a Spartan herald arrives, also visibly excited, looking for the Athenian magistrates; evidently the Spartan women have not let the side down. The Athenian magistrate tells him Athens is ready to make peace; Sparta is to send ambassadors with full powers to negotiate.

After some more choral song the ambassadors enter; they too are in desperate condition. Under the guidance of Lysistrata, who prevents disputes over small points in the treaty from becoming major problems, peace is made and the end of the war celebrated with a banquet.

When this comedy was produced in 411 B.C. there was considerable war-weariness in Athens. The war which began in 431 ended in a truce in 421 but this was not, in fact, the end of hostilities; Athens and Sparta fought each other indirectly through and sometimes directly with their allies, and in 415 Athens had launched a huge expedition westward with the aim of conquering the rich Greek colonies in Sicily. This expedition ended in disaster and inflicted huge losses in ships and men; the Spartans soon resumed hostilities against Athens as her subject allies in the Aegean tried to secede from her empire.

This was not the first Aristophanic comedy to deal with the folly of the war and to express, in fantastically comic terms, a serious wish for peace. In 425 he had produced a play called *The Acharnians*, in which a citizen who is fed up with the war makes a separate peace with the Spartans and proceeds to enjoy, in the midst of the Athenian war shortages, an abundance of luxury imports not to mention exemption from military service. In *The Peace* (421), produced as the first ten years of hostilities came to an end, an Athenian citizen flies up to heaven on a giant dung beetle to demand that Zeus put an end to the war. *Lysistrata* plays on the same wish, which must have been widespread in Athens, for a return to more peaceful days.

Nevertheless the war went relentlessly on; even when the Spartans, on several occasions, proposed a truce on unexpectedly favorable conditions, the political leaders of the democracy rejected them and Athens finally went down to complete defeat in 404 B.C.

Aristophanes' comedies are not to be regarded as political propaganda on behalf of a particular group or party. It was the function of comedy to provide a momentary relief from everyday cares through fantastic visions of freedom, abundance, and self-indulgence. The action was always something that could not possibly happen in real life: the private citizen making a separate peace, a ride to heaven on a dung beetle, or concerted political action on the part of Athenian women, who had no public function at all and played a subordinate role in private life as well. Athenian comedy was a safety valve, not an instrument of political protest or a forum for advocacy of change.

Classroom Strategies

One assignment.

The sexually explicit jokes and action (the Cinesias scene, for example) should not mislead the modern reader into thinking of the play in terms of pornographic shows or "adult movies." Comedy in Athens was part of a religious festival; the low jokes and obscene gestures of the comic actors were just as much a part of the celebration of the god Dionysus as the dignified language and formal movements of the tragic stage. Dionysus was originally a god of vegetation (and not just of the vine); tragedy perhaps represented the flowering and inevitable death of all things, comedy the fertility of the natural world.

The comic actor wore, as part of his costume, the ancient symbol of fertility, the *phallos*, a leather replica of the male sexual organ. The joking remarks about the excited state of the Spartan ambassadors at the end of the play had their visual corroboration on stage, and it is not hard to imagine what a comic actor could do with this apparatus in the Cinesias scene. This kind of horseplay was native to the comic genre. In Aristophanes it is used with keen wit and to dramatic and thematic effect.

Topics for Discussion

Both *Medea* and *Lysistrata* deal with, among other things, a conflict between men and women and exploit the contrast between their situation and aspirations. But though the two dramatists develop many of the same major themes (and even sometimes coincide in choice of minor details) the two plays are worlds apart: the same basic material from which Euripides produces his shocking tragic effect serves Aristophanes for a series of comic scenes culminating in a happy ending—conciliation and a return to normality.

[Both protagonists are women of courage, determination, and keen intelligence. Medea's speech to the chorus, appealing to their consciousness of woman's unhappy condition, is as perfectly adapted to the situation as the repudiation of her reputation as a woman of intellect (290ff.) in her plea to Creon, or as her assumption of the role of repentant wife in her deception of Jason. Lysistrata displays the qualities of a leader in her organization of the conspiracy in the opening scene and in her argument with the magistrate, especially when she gives her recipe for managing the affairs of Athens and "unsnarling the war" (p. 788) shows a statesmanlike intelligence beyond anything the fatuous magistrate she opposes could even imagine. Both heroines lament the subordinate lot of women—Medea in 228ff. and Lysistrata when she details the effects of war on the women of the city ("we bear children and send off our sons as soldiers..." [p. 788])—but Medea's speech ends with her plea to the chorus to abet her in her bloody revenge while Lysistrata's argument leads up to a ribald joke on the part of the magistrate, in return for which Lysistrata and the women's chorus dress him up like a corpse. Both Medea and Lysistrata speak of woman's nature as centered on love and sexual passion. "Once she is wronged in the matter of love," says Medea, "No other soul can hold so many thoughts of blood" (263–64), and Jason sees woman's nature in the same terms: "You women have got into such a state of mind / That, if your life at night is good, you think you have / Everything; but, if in that quarter things go wrong, / You will consider your best and truest interests / Most hateful" (557–61). He does not realize the meaning the audience will attach to these words: Medea will sacrifice her "best and truest interests"—her children—to punish him. In *Lysistrata* the same Greek cliché about woman's nature has no such tragic overtones but is instead the base for coarse innuendo ("something big . . . and stout" [p. 775]), for the wholesale desertion on the part of Lysistrata's supporters when she tells them her plan, and for the series of preposterous excuses the women give as they try to escape from the Acropolis and go home to their husbands ("my best wool is being devoured by the moths"; "my flax . . . all unpeeled"; "I'm going to have a baby—right now!" [p. 792]).

[Both plays have a scene in which the heroine administers a solemn oath. Medea makes Aegeus swear by Earth and Sun, repeating the words after her, that he will give her refuge in Athens when she leaves Corinth (730ff.). Lysistrata binds the women, by an oath on a flask of wine, to repeat after her a series of promises to refrain from all manner of sexual enjoyment (lovingly described in detail, p. 779) until their husbands consent to make peace.]

Topic for Writing

In an earlier comedy Aristophanes has one of his characters draw attention to the underlying seriousness of the action by claiming that even comedy (in spite of its buffoonery) can deal with questions of right and wrong. What serious issues are being explored beneath the ribald surface of *Lysistrata* and how are they expressed?

[The main issue, of course, is the folly of continuing a war between

Greeks which has gone on indecisively for so many years. There are serious obstacles to making peace and Aristophanes, right in the middle of the burlesque scenes of the women's oath-taking, brings them to the fore. The Spartan woman Lampito is sure that she and her friends can "persuade the Spartans" to make a fair and just peace but she says, "what about the Athenian rabble?" (p. 778) It will be difficult, she says, to convince them "while their ships are rigged so well and they have that mighty treasure in the temple of Athene." Lysistrata has already seen to the seizure of the Acropolis and the treasures stored there—the tribute from the subject cities of the Athenian empire. This, of course, is a joke; the fears of Lampito, however, do raise a serious issue.

[Though Athens had been reduced to a position of military inferiority by her catastrophic losses of men and ships in Sicily, the Spartans on several occasions showed a willingness to negotiate a peace. The Athenian democratic leaders ("the rabble," as the Spartans thought of Athenian democracy) were unwilling to make the necessary concessions; they still considered their resources in ships and money sufficient to win them victory or at least a position in which they could negotiate from strength. It was in fact this attitude that brought them in the end to defeat and unconditional surrender. Later in the play Lysistrata answers the magistrate's question—"What business have you with war and peace?" (p. 786) She tells how the women would ask their husbands what they had decided in the assembly; they would ask about "writing on the treaty-stone," that is, about making peace. But all they heard was news of one stupid measure after another. The political content of all this is plain, and when Lysistrata is asked how women can "stop all the confusion in the various states and bring them together" (p. 788), she makes her brilliant speech about "unsnarling the war" as if it were a tangled ball of wool and then goes on to give a recipe for cleaning up Athenian politics, including carding out "those who conspire and stick together to gain office" (p. 788).

[The play ends in fact with a sermon delivered by Lysistrata to both sides, reminding them that they are all Greeks and that as they destroy each other, the barbarians "stand by waiting with their armies" (p. 801). And so negotiations for peace begin and, although the give and take of territory between Spartans and Athenians is made wildly and obscenely funny by a series of *double entendres*, the fact is that the comic stage is presenting to the audience an image of a negotiated peace—something that no politician dared do in the Assembly.]

Further Reading

See also the reading suggestions in the anthology, pp. 773–774.

Easterling, P. E., ed. *Greece.* Vol. I of *The Cambridge History of Classical Literature.* Cambridge, 1985. Pp. 355–414 (E. W. Handley).
Contains a masterly assessment, written for the classical scholar and the literate general reader, of the whole genre; pp. 370–91 focus on Aristophanes.

McLeish, K. *The Theatre of Aristophanes.* London, 1980.
This is "an attempt to examine the plays from the point of view of a dramatic critic and to try to discover . . . what their effect may have been on their original audience." The approach is by subject, not by individual play but the index lists all the relevant passages under useful headings.

Whitman, C. H. *Aristophanes and the Comic Hero.* Cambridge, Mass., 1964.
An analysis of Aristophanes' achievement as the creator of "a new kind of hero, the comic hero, who parodies his two solemn older brothers of tragedy and epic, but at the same time challenges their supremacy in expressing human aspirations in the face of the world's dilemma." Chapter 6, "The War Between the Sexes" (pp. 200–227), deals with *Lysistrata*.

PLATO
Apology

Backgrounds

"Apology" is the Greek word for "defense"; this speech is Plato's version of the one in which Socrates defended himself in court against the charges brought by his adversaries. It is divided into three sections, which correspond to the three stages of the trial. The first (pp. 807–22, ending ". . . to be determined by you as is best for you and me") is the defense proper; at that point the jury decides on a verdict. It is "Guilty"; it is now up to the prosecutors and the defendant to propose what they think an appropriate penalty. The jury will choose one or the other; no compromise will be made. The prosecution asks for death; Socrates, in the second part of his speech, instead of proposing exile or imprisonment for a few years, makes the outrageous suggestion that he be rewarded as a public benefactor. But he then offers a small fine. He is condemned to death. The last section of his speech (p. 824, beginning "Not much time will be gained . . .") is his final address to the court.

In the first and longest part of the speech he deals with the general prejudice against him: the widespread impression that he is a philosophical agnostic and that he is a "sophist"—one who teaches new ideas and rhetorical techniques for high fees. None of this is true. The real reason for his unpopularity, he suspects, is that he has confounded so many Athenians in argument, shown them up as confused and ignorant. In doing so he claims that he was simply trying to test the truth of the god Apollo's statement that Socrates was the wisest of men. He found that men who thought they knew something did not, so he was wiser than they, since he knew that he knew nothing.

So much for the general prejudice; he turns then on his accusers, who have claimed that he corrupts the youth of Athens, disbelieves in the gods of the state, and introduces new divinities of his own. He cross-questions Meletus, his main accuser, and shows that the charges are invalid. He then announces that he will continue, as he has always done, to question the Athenians about justice and knowledge; this is, he says, his mission in life, imposed by Apollo. This announcement evidently causes an outcry in court, for he asks those present not to interrupt (p. 818); the jury brings in a verdict of guilty. Socrates' refusal to bargain about the death penalty leads to his death sentence. Socrates prophesies that the Athenians will silence him but will have to listen to younger men who will carry on his mission. He accepts his death calmly, secure in his belief that "no evil can happen to a good man, either in life or after death" (p. 827).

Plato belonged to an aristocratic Athenian family (he was related by his mother's second marriage to Critias, the leading spirit of the "Thirty Tyrants" who ruled Athens for a short time after the surrender to the Spartans in 404); while still young (he was born in 429) he became one of the group of Athenian men who spent their time listening to and arguing with Socrates. Though Socrates did not, like the sophists, assume the role of teacher, Plato and his companions were in a real sense his pupils. The execution of his beloved teacher in 399 B.C. left an indelible mark on Plato's thought and writing; in all his philosophical dialogues except the last (*The Laws*) Socrates figures as one of the principals and, in most of them, as the protagonist. The *Apology* is Plato's version of the speech Socrates made before the Athenian court in 399. He was present at the trial (see p. 824) and though his version is hardly likely to be a verbatim transcript of Socrates' remarks on that occasion Plato could not afford to make radical additions or subtractions; he was writing for an audience that included the crowds who attended the trial, not to mention the 500 members of the jury.

The speech defies the conventions of Athenian legal procedure and the rules recommended by the Sophists, the professional teachers of rhetoric. Instead of a "set oration duly ornamented with words and phrases" (p. 807), Socrates proposes to defend himself in his "accustomed manner"—in other words in the deceptively simple but actually disconcerting manner that has made him so many enemies among those whose ignorance and intellectual confusion he has often exposed. In fact, after disposing of the popular caricature of him as an atheistic philosopher who teaches immorality for high fees—the Socrates of Aristophanes' comedy *The Clouds* (423 B.C.)—he proceeds to defend the very thing his audience finds most aggravating about him: his habit of arguing with all the experts and proving them wrong. He knows that this has made him many powerful enemies but insists that it is a mission imposed on him by the god Apollo. So much for the actual charge brought against him by his accusers—that he does not believe in the gods the city believes in; to these charges he now turns and in a skillful cross-examination of his chief accuser Meletus he demonstrates in his "accustomed fashion" that Meletus doesn't know what he is talking about when he claims that Socrates is corrupting the younger generation. From this point on, instead of trying to win the good graces of the jury, he alienates them by insisting, at great length and with unmistakable sincerity, that since what he has been doing all these years is by command of the god, he will continue to do so as long as he lives. To cease would be impious; it would also be dishonorable.

In the course of this defiant speech he also takes time to answer another unstated charge: that though he is so interested in other people's opinions he never speaks up in the Assembly, never plays his part, like a loyal citizen, in the discussion of public policy. His defense is that if he had done so he "would have perished long ago," for he would never have acted against his conscience, as a man in political life has to do. He cites two cases in which he had to defy in one case public opinion and in the other tyrannical power. Under the democracy, serving—as every Athenian had to sooner or later—on the steering committee of the assembly, he refused to vote for what would otherwise have been a unanimous (and illegal) resolution, in spite of threats of impeachment. And under the dictatorial rule of the antidemocratic regime set up in Athens after the defeat in 404 he refused to obey an order to arrest a fellow citizen and escaped with his life only because the regime was overthrown soon after.

Plato does not mention the fact that there was a strong popular feeling against Socrates precisely on political grounds. Socrates mentions in his speech the fact that "young men of the richer classes, who have not much to do, come about me of their own accord" (p. 812); this innocuous phrase masks the fact that many of these rich young men were hostile to the democratic regime and one of them, Critias, was later the leading figure among the Thirty Tyrants who, backed by the Spartan victors, imposed a reign of terror on Athens. This regime had been overthrown by the democrats in 403 but, to avoid a counter-terror, the Athenians declared an amnesty (the survivors of the Thirty excepted); no prosecutions for political offenses prior to 404 were to be permitted. The resentment at what many saw as Socrates' responsibility for the education of such men as Critias could not express itself as a political charge; hence the vague indictment under a law against "impiety" which could be interpreted in more ways than one.

Socrates' defiance of the court in his apparently arrogant refusal to bargain by suggesting an acceptable penalty is not hard to understand, since the only penalty the court would have been likely to accept was exile: Socrates would leave Athens for some other city and the Athenians would have been rid of him without having to put him to death (p. 824). This he refuses to do, just as later, in prison awaiting death, he will reject the offers of his friends to help him escape from Athens. He will remain true to his mission: "the difficulty . . . is not to avoid death, but to avoid unrighteousness" (p. 825).

Classroom Strategies

One assignment if possible; otherwise, divide at page 816: "there is no danger of my being the last of them."

The student may well get the impression from the *Apology* that Socrates' philosophical contribution is purely negative, that all he does is to convince people that they do not understand the words they are using when they talk about morality; he himself has no definition to offer, but claims only to know that he himself knows nothing. In the other books of Plato which, unlike the *Apology*, are cast in the form of dramatic dialogues, Socrates emerges in a different light. It is true that he rarely proposes a solution to the dilemmas he uncovers by his questioning, but the dialogues show that his probing questions about the nature of piety, justice, bravery, and all the other moral qualities people think they know the nature of are the necessary preliminary to a definition. Previous philosophers have simply announced their doctrines to the world; the world could take them on or leave them, read them or not. Socrates insisted that true knowledge could not be simply proclaimed and accepted (or rejected); learner and teacher had to find their way, through hard-won agreement on point after point, to definitions they could both accept and act on. This process—"dialectic," to give it its Greek name— is the so-called Socratic method and it was, in its time, a startling contrast to the standard procedure of the Sophistic teachers, who gave lectures and wrote books but did not expect to be questioned.

But Socrates' contribution was not merely a revolution in method. He was also responsible for a decisive shift in the area explored by philosophy, which had begun, in the Greek city of Miletus, as an attempt to understand the material universe (Thales, the first philosopher, thought that water was the basis of all matter). Some later philosophers had proposed more sophisticated and complicated answers (two philosophers almost contemporary with Socrates had in fact invented atomic theory) and others wrestled with the philosophical problems inherent in such concepts as being, becoming, and motion. But it was Socrates who brought philosophy to bear on the moral problems of human life, especially on the problem of justice in individual and collective conduct.

Philosophy would after him still deal with cosmological, physical and metaphysical problems, but the question of human conduct would bulk large in the works of Plato, Aristotle (author of the *Ethics*), and of the later Epicurean and Stoic schools.

Though Socrates is no aristocrat (in fact his father was a stonemason and he himself, at the time of his trial, was penniless [pp. 819, 824]), he cites the example of Achilles for his refusal to be intimidated by the threat of death (p. 817) and, after his condemnation, looks forward to meeting, in the lower world, the heroes Palamedes and Ajax (p. 826). These epic figures seem at first glance strange company for a philosopher whose constant concern was to establish the primacy of justice and righteousness in human conduct but, in fact, in spite of the pride and violence such heroic names conjure up, they are not inappropriate in the context of the speech.

Palamedes was the cleverest of the Greek chieftains at Troy; he was credited with the invention not only of the alphabet and numbers but also of a game resembling checkers with which the Greeks amused themselves when all was quiet on the Trojan front. But he incurred the enmity of Agamemnon and Odysseus by speaking out against the long drawn-out war and calling for immediate return home. Odysseus framed him: Trojan gold was buried in his tent while he was away and a forged letter from Priam produced to convict him as a Trojan agent. In spite of a brilliant defense at his trial, he was condemned and executed. The story was well known to Socrates' audience; both Sophocles and Euripides (and perhaps Aeschylus as well) had written tragedies on the subject.

The other sufferer from an unjust court cited by Socrates is, however, a very different case. Ajax was the best man among the Achaeans while Achilles was away, Homer tells us in the *Iliad*, and even his enemy Odysseus calls him the noblest of the Danaans after Achilles. When Achilles was killed and the Achaeans decided to award his arms and armor to the bravest among them, Ajax naturally expected to be chosen, but the judgment went to Odysseus instead. After an unsuccessful attempt to murder Agamemnon, Odysseus, and others whom he regarded as responsible, Ajax killed himself.

When Socrates speaks of talking to Ajax in the next world he is of course recalling to the minds of his hearers the famous passage in the *Odyssey*, Book XI, where Odysseus addresses Ajax but gets no answer. Socrates, as a fellow sufferer, will not be treated so contemptuously. Yet it is a little disconcerting to find the gentle philosopher, whose sharpest weapon was the cut and thrust of his dialectic, associating himself with the primeval violence of Ajax. Just as surprising is his citation of Achilles, whom he actually quotes as an example to follow. Achilles would not let the prospect of certain death deter him from his purpose, which was, of course, to kill Hector and avenge the death of Patroclus: "Let me die forthwith and be avenged of my enemy, rather than abide here . . . a laughingstock" (p. 817). Socrates will not retreat in the face of death either: "Wherever a man's place is, whether the place which he has chosen or that in which he has been placed by a commander, there he ought to remain in hour of danger" (p. 817). Socrates remained in his place as a soldier, obeying the orders of the generals elected by the Athenians; now he will remain steadfast in the place ordained for him by the god Apollo, or rather, since this depends on his interpretation of the word of Apollo, in the place that he has chosen himself.

The snub-nosed, poorly dressed old man of seventy, facing adversaries determined to drive him out of Athens or kill him if he will not go, defies them and sees himself, not without reason, as one of the company of heroes whose memory all Greeks held in respect and whose burial places they recognized as holy ground. When he refuses to follow the usual practice of defendants in Athenian courts, to beg for mercy, to produce weeping children and relatives, he speaks in heroic terms, as a man who must be true like Odysseus, to his reputation, to what the world expects of a hero: "Whether this opinion of me be deserved or not, at any rate the world has decided that Socrates is in some way superior to other men" (p. 822).

Topics for Discussion and Writing

Behind the actual terms of the indictment lay a real prejudice against Socrates as an opponent of democracy, and this was not due solely to his association with such figures as Critias. Can you find in his speech any grounds for such a prejudice?

[His abstention from political activity under a democratic regime which encouraged and depended on full participation by all the citizens. In his defense on this point he actually uses clichés of the opponents of democracy: "The truth is, that no man who goes to war with you or any other multitude, honestly striving against the many lawless and unrighteous deeds which are done in a state, will save his life" (p. 819).

[Among the prominent figures he examined and found ignorant were politicians (pp. 810–811), that is, the orators whose speeches in the assembly shaped public policy (cf, Lycon who has a quarrel with Socrates "on behalf of the rhetoricians" [p. 812]).

[When he examines the artisans, he finds them, too, wanting: "because they were good workmen they thought that they also knew all sorts of high matters" (p. 811). In Athenian democratic theory an artisan was supposed to have just as much understanding of public policy and therefore just as strong a claim to direct it as, for example, a landed aristocrat.

[When he proposes that he be rewarded instead of punished he speaks of himself as the man who "has been careless of what the many care for—wealth, and family interests, and military offices, and speaking in the assembly, and magistracies, and plots, and parties" (p. 823). There is clearly a certain dislike for the political life of Athens expressed in that list and in fact he continues: "Reflecting that I was really too honest a man to be a politician and live . . ."

[Plato himself was no admirer of the democracy that had put Socrates to death; his picture of Socrates may have been influenced by his own feelings. But it is quite understandable that a man with Socrates' insistence on universal moral standards should have been disgusted with the politics of Athens in the last years of the war; it must indeed have seemed as if the politicians and the assembly that supported them were bent on self-destruction.]

Further Reading

See also the reading suggestions in the anthology, p. 807.

Guthrie, W. K. C. *A History of Greek Philosophy*. Vol. IV. Cambridge, 1975. Pp. 70–93.
  An authoritative discussion of the historicity, organization, and ideas of the speech. See also Vol. III (1969) on Socrates and the Delphic response (pp. 405ff.) and his political views (pp. 409ff.).

West, T. G. *Plato's Apology of Socrates*. Ithaca, N. Y., 1979.
  A new translation with interpretation. A careful analysis of the speech section with helpful chapters on Socrates as a Public Man and Socrates as a Private Man.

West, T. G., and G. C. West. *Four Texts on Socrates*. Ithaca, N. Y., 1984.

Translations of *Euthyphro, Apology, Crito,* and Aristophanes'
Clouds. The introduction deals with the *Apology* (pp. 16–24).

ARISTOTLE
Poetics

Backgrounds and Topics for Discussion

Our short selection from the work deals with tragedy. It begins with the famous definition of tragedy (for an explanation of the term *catharsis* see note 2, p. 831) which is explained, section by section, in the following paragraphs. Aristotle recognizes the importance of character in tragedy—the persons represented "must necessarily possess certain qualities of Character and Thought" (p. 832)—but places greater emphasis on the action, the plot. "It is not for the purpose of presenting their characters that the agents engage in action, but rather it is for the sake of their actions that they take on the characters they have" (p. 832). The plot has to have unity (which is not necessarily attained by telling the story of one individual) and the right "magnitude"—a length "sufficient to permit a change from bad fortune to good or from good fortune to bad to come about in an inevitable or probable sequence of events." Plots can be simple or complex; in complex plots the change of fortune involves a reversal or a recognition or both. (The prime example of change of fortune with both is the *Oedipus* of Sophocles.) Furthermore, the change of fortune should be from good to bad, and the victim of this reversal should not be a wholly bad man or a completely good one (for in the one case we would be pleased and in the other merely disgusted) but one "whose place is between these extremes . . . the man who on the one hand is not preeminent in virtue and justice, and yet on the other hand does not fall into misfortune through vice or depravity, but falls because of some mistake; one among the number of the highly renowned and prosperous, such as Oedipus . . ." (p. 834). (For the word translated "mistake" see note 7, p. 834.)

Aristotle's *Poetics* is the first treatise ever written on literary composition (the Greek word *poietes*—poet—means, literally, "maker"); many before him, Plato especially, discussed the nature and effect of poetry but a systematic treatise on the subject was unprecedented. It has had an enormous influence on modern critical approaches to tragic drama; particularly influential in the European Renaissance was the idea of the "tragic flaw," derived from the Greek word *hamartia*, which our translation more correctly renders as "mistake." A classic version of this doctrine can be found in Shakespeare, in Hamlet's speech about the Danish nation and their penchant for drink: "So, oft it chances in particular men, / That for some vicious mole of nature in them . . ." (1.4.23ff., p. 1906).

The *Poetics*, however, was written long after the deaths of the three great tragic dramatists of the fifth century B.C. And Aristotle's view of the tragic character, as one who "falls by some mistake" is, in most cases, not easily applicable to the plays of Aeschylus, Sophocles, and Euripides. This is a possible theme of discussion with the class: how far does *Oedipus*, for example, Aristotle's famous example of the well-made tragedy, fit the definition? Is Oedipus a man "not preeminent in virtue and justice" who "on the other hand does not fall into misfortune through vice or depravity, but falls because of some mistake"? If so, what is the mistake? His whole life seems to be a series of mistakes. Does Antigone fit the formula? Hardly. But perhaps Creon does: his mistake is to underestimate Antigone's heroic stubbornness. It is hard to see how Medea can be understood along these lines, or Clytemnestra either, but perhaps a case could be made out for Agamemnon.

Also essential to Aristotle's conception of tragedy is the recognition, which in what he considers the best type of plot is identical to the reversal of the protagonist's fortune. Oedipus is the classic example: he recognizes himself as the murderer he is searching for and also as a patricide and incestuous son; but recognition plays a part also in the *Oresteia*: when Clytemnestra recognizes her son's identity her death is only moments away. Recognition of identity, though it frequently occurs in other Greek tragedies, plays no part in *Antigone* or *Medea*; but in a metaphorical sense (one that Aristotle does not express but which he may have realized) recognition *is* essential to the tragic process. The tragic hero in the end is forced to dispense with illusions of power and claims to godlike superiority; in the reversal of fortune—often brought about, as Aristotle says, by his own actions which produce the opposite of what he intends—he is forced to recognize the mortality and fallibility which is the condition he shares with all mankind. Achilles in the tent with Priam comes at last to see himself as others see him; Antigone in her last speech recognizes that the motive for the action that has brought her face to face with death was in the last analysis purely personal and Creon recognizes, but too late, that there are laws superior to those imposed by dictatorial power.

The class might also be asked to discuss the plays in the light of Aristotle's concept of unity—the avoidance of plots "in which episodes follow one another in no probable or inevitable sequence" in favor of a "plot so organized that if any one of [the events which are part of it] is displaced or taken away, the whole will be shaken and put out of joint." *Oedipus* has the most closely logical plot; comparison with *Medea* (how organic is the arrival of Aegeus?) should prove interesting and all the plays can be examined to see if there is adequate motivation for new entries and developments.

Further Reading

See also the reading suggestions in the anthology, p. 831.

Aristotle's Poetics. Translated by S. H. Butcher. New York, 1961.
The introduction, by the outstanding modern critic Francis Fergusson, is a full and brilliant interpretation of Aristotle's work for the modern reader.

Aristotle. *Poetics.* Ed. by D. W. Lucas. Oxford, 1968.
An edition, with commentary, of the Greek text. The introduction contains a survey of Greek literary theory before Aristotle and valuable appendices on "Pity, Fear and *Katharsis*" and "*Hamartia.*"

Aristotle on Poetry and Style. Translated by G. M. A. Grube. New York, 1958.
A translation of the *Poetics* and selections from the *Rhetoric.* The introduction, "Aristotle as a Literary Critic" (ix–xxx), deals succinctly and clearly with the problems raised by the text.

CATULLUS

Backgrounds

We know very little about Catullus; almost all that we do know is based on inference from the poems themselves. Luckily the full collection of 116 poems which has survived the centuries contains many references to identifiable persons and events of his time. Many of them are addressed to men who were prominent in the cultural and political life of the Roman capital; it is clear that Catullus, though born in a provincial city, was well-connected and fully at home in sophisticated society. He was also the leading figure in a literary movement, one of a group of young poets the orator and statesman Cicero refers to as "the moderns"; they turned their backs on what had so far been the characteristic media of Roman poetry, national epic and tragedy, to produce shorter poems, modelled on the work of the Greek poets of Alexandria, full of learned allusions, elegant, witty and compact. Catullus himself, however, surpasses his models; he can, on occasion, be learnedly allusive, even slightly pedantic, but he can also write about the humors and passions of everyday life with an energy and directness which have their equal only in the poetry of Sappho.

That the real name of his "Lesbia" was Clodia we know from the statement of a later writer, Apuleius (2nd century A.D.). What is not entirely certain is whether this Clodia was the famous—or rather, notorious—daughter of Appius Claudius Pulcher, a former consul and a member of one of the oldest patrician families of Rome. Clodia was married to another Roman aristocrat, Metellus Celer, but during his absence abroad as governor of a province her scandalous behavior was the talk of Rome. She took many lovers; there was even a rumor that she had an incestuous affair with her brother Publius Clodius Pulcher, who, in the last violent years of the Roman Republic's collapse into anarchy and civil war, distinguished himself as the most audacious and dangerous of the political gangsters who terrorized their opponents. When Clodia's husband died in 59 B.C. there were many who suspected she had poisoned him. Three years later she was instrumental in having one of her lovers, Caelius, who had broken with her, prosecuted for a series of illegal actions. He was defended by Cicero, from whose speech in his defense, *Pro Caelio*, we know the details of the rumors which were circulating in Rome about Clodia's morals. Cicero was delighted to accept the case, since he was one of the principal targets of Clodia's brother and had suffered much at his hands. At one point in his speech he imagines that one of Clodia's most famous ancestors, Appius Claudius, has come back from the dead to reproach her. "Was it for this that I built the first aqueduct to bring water to Rome, so that you could use it to wash after your debauches? Was it for this that I built a road [the Via Appia] so that you could travel on it with packs of other women's husbands?" Cicero does not forget, either, to make good use of the rumors that one of her lovers was her brother.

This trial took place in 56 B.C.; Clodia's liaison with Caelius had lasted about two years. The latest event mentioned in Catullus' poems occurred in 55 B.C.; it seems probable that he died in that or the next year. His affair with Clodia must then have taken place before 54 B.C. Though we cannot be absolutely certain of the identification, some of the things Catullus says about *his* Clodia (for example, the adulterous emotions described in our sixth selection, the accusations of promiscuity in 12, 13, and 14) correspond well with Cicero's picture of the woman.

Further Reading

See also the suggestions in the anthology, p. 836.

Cicero. *The Speeches. Pro Caelio etc.* Cambridge, Mass. (Loeb Classical Library), 1958.
Contains a translation of *Pro Caelio*; for Clodia, see pp. 445–453.

Kenney, E. J., ed. *Latin Literature.* Vol. II of *The Cambridge History of Latin Literature.* Cambridge, 1982. Pp. 198–200.

VIRGIL
The Aeneid

Backgrounds

Aeneas, a Trojan prince in flight from the Greek sack of Troy with his father, his young son, and the statues of his household gods, sails west in search of the new home promised him by the gods in a score of prophecies. Virgil opens his narrative at a moment when Aeneas has almost reached his goal—the plain of Latium in Italy where he will eventually found a city, Alba Longa, from which will come after his death the founders of Rome. Aeneas and his fleet are off Sicily, almost in sight of their destination, when Juno (the Roman equivalent of Hera), who hates even the survivors of ruined Troy, sends a storm to scatter the ships.

Aeneas, with his one ship, is driven south to the African coast, to the territory of Dido, queen of Carthage, a new city for which Juno plans a glorious future as master of the Mediterranean world (the same destiny Jupiter [Zeus] and Venus [Aphrodite] plan for Rome). Dido welcomes Aeneas, as well as the crews of his scattered ships who also come ashore; she offers Aeneas and the Trojans a partnership in the city that she is building. At a banquet she gives for them, Aeneas is prevailed upon to tell the story of his wanderings since he left Troy.

He begins (Book II) with the fall of the city: the Greek stratagem of the wooden horse, the lying story of Sinon that tricks the Trojans into admitting it to the city, the fate of Laocoön who warned against it, and the night assault of the Greeks, led into the city by the Greek warriors concealed in the horse. Aeneas fights but in a losing battle; he sees Priam killed at the altar of his palace by Neoptolemus, son of Achilles, and returns to his own house, where he collects his father, Anchises, his wife, Creusa, and his son, Iulus, and leads them out of the burning city. On the way, Creusa is lost; her ghost appears to him urging him on and promising him a kingdom in the west. From Troy, Aeneas sets sail and, after a series of adventures like those of Odysseus (one of them in fact is a meeting with a Cyclops), reaches Sicily, where his father, Anchises, dies. (These travels, the material of Book III, are not included in our selection.)

Book IV opens with Dido passionately in love with Aeneas; during a hunt they are overtaken by a storm and shelter alone in a cave. There they become lovers but, though Dido regards her union as a marriage, Aeneas will later insist that it is not binding. For meanwhile the gods who have imposed on Aeneas the responsibility for Rome's future have become impatient with his long stay at Carthage and his cooperation with Dido in the foundation of Carthage, a city that will one day be Rome's mortal enemy.

Jupiter sends Mercury (Hermes) to order him to put to sea. As he prepares to obey, Dido summons him, pleads with him, denounces him, and threatens him—all to no avail; he must obey the commands of heaven, think of his son and the kingdom he is to inherit in Italy. As Aeneas puts out to sea, Dido, after cursing him and promising unceasing war between her descendants and his, kills herself. In Book V (not in our selection) Aeneas, back in Sicily, holds funeral games for Anchises (like those Achilles held for Patroclus in the *Iliad*) and then sails for Italy. There he is led by the Sibyl down to the realm of the dead, where he sees, as Odysseus does in Book XI of the *Odyssey*, the great sinners and great men of the past but also, unlike Odysseus, the great men of the future, who will impose Roman dominion on the whole of the known world.

In books VI and VII (not in our selection) the Trojans become involved in a war with the Italians, who are roused to battle by Juno, anxious to forestall the foundation of the city that will be the rival and conqueror of her favored Carthage. At the end of Book VIII Venus brings to her son Aeneas, as Thetis brought to her son Achilles in the *Iliad*, armor newly forged by Vulcan (Hephaestus); on the shield (cf. the shield of Achilles) Vulcan has depicted the glorious exploits of the Roman descendants of Aeneas. Books IX–XI (not included in our selection) follow the ebb and flow of battle which ends (Book XII) with the death of Turnus at the hand of Aeneas and Juno's acceptance of the Roman destiny. She accepts on the condition that the Trojans, whom she still hates, abandon their language and nationality and merge their identity in the new Roman nation which is to conquer the world.

In Book XX of the *Iliad* (not included in this anthology) the Trojan prince Aeneas, whose mother was the goddess Aphrodite, fights with Achilles; he is rescued from certain death by the god Poseidon because "it is destined that he shall be the survivor." He is to found a royal house that will reign over the Trojans in time to come. Later poets developed this mysterious prophecy into a story of Aeneas' escape from Troy, carrying his old father Anchises on his back, and other poets made him the leader of a westward voyage with his family and his household gods in search of a place to found a new Troy. When in the third century B.C. the Romans came into contact with Greece, they admired and imitated its arts and literature, but had to subdue the Greek cities by force of arms. The Roman wish to find a place for themselves in the Greek epic and historical tradition without claiming kinship with the subjected and despised Greeks of their own day was granted by the creation of the legend that Aeneas the Trojan was the founder of the Roman nation. This story was given literary form in the epics (now lost) of the Latin poets Naevius and Ennius (third century B.C.) and was in Virgil's time the authorized version of Rome's origins. Augustus, the first Roman emperor and Virgil's patron, had the temple of Athena at Troy rebuilt on a magnificent scale.

Virgil was recasting the traditional Roman story in what was to be its enduring form, a restatement of national ideals, for the new age of peace and prosperity under the rule of Augustus, who had finally brought peace to a world that had been racked for over a century by civil war.

Augustus was intensely interested in Virgil's poem; we know that parts of Book VI (the visit to the underworld) were read aloud to him by the poet himself and when Virgil, dying before he could put the last touches on the work, ordered his friends to burn it, Augustus intervened to preserve the poem.

The poem is, in a sense, officially inspired, but it does not read like propaganda. The sacrifices Aeneas has to make in order to fulfill his god-given mission are so great that some readers have even seen the poem as a muted repudiation of imperial Roman values. This is an exaggeration but there is no question about the sacrifice the imperial mission involves, both for the hero and for the Roman people. Aeneas has not only to abandon the great love of his life; he will also die before he has time to enjoy the promised reward, the city from which will come the founders of Rome. Dido's dying prayer to her gods will be answered. If, she says, he is indeed destined to land in Italy,

> yet all the same
> When hard beset in war by a brave people,
> Forced to go outside his boundaries
> And torn from Iulus, let him beg assistance,
> Let him see the unmerited death of those
> Around and with him, and accepting peace
> On unjust terms, let him not, even so,
> Enjoy his kingdom or the life he longs for,
> But fall in battle before his time and lie

Unburied on the sand!
(IV. 823–832)

Aeneas does indeed find himself hard beset in war; books VII to XII are a Virgilian *Iliad* in which Aeneas and his Trojans fight against Turnus, a new Achilles. He does indeed have to leave his son, Iulus, and go begging for help from neutral Italian tribes. He loses allies in battle, chief among them young Pallas, for whose death he takes revenge on Turnus in the last lines of the poem. He accepts a peace that, if not unjust, is at least a compromise: the bargain made by Jupiter with Juno that the Trojan name will vanish in the fusion of Aeneas' people with the Latins. And after a few years at the head of his new kingdom he is to be killed in battle; his body will not be found. Greatness, Virgil is suggesting, calls for almost unbearable sacrifice. And the Romans who later carry on Aeneas' line will have to make sacrifices, too. Anchises, in the world of the dead, spells out the Roman destiny for Aeneas:

> Others will cast more tenderly in bronze
> Their breathing figures, I can well believe,
> And bring more lifelike portraits out of marble;
> Argue more eloquently, use the pointer
> To trace the paths of heaven accurately
> And accurately foretell the rising stars.
> Roman, remember by your strength to rule
> To pacify, to impose the rule of law,
> To spare the conquered, battle down the proud.
> (VI. 848–57, not included in the anthology)

The "others" who perfect the creative arts and sciences of peace are the Greeks; the Roman destiny is war and rule over peoples. The contrast is more emphatically expressed in the original Latin: the address to the Roman begins, *At tu Romane memento* ("But you, Roman, remember"). The imperial destiny excludes the arts of peace. Virgil himself was an intellectual who studied philosophy, a poet steeped in the literature of Greece and Rome; his heart was with those "others" and he above all men realized what had to be given up if men were to become Romans.

Classroom Strategies

Suggested assignments:
1. Books I and II
2. Book IV

3. Books VI, VIII, and XII
   or:
1. Books I, II, and IV
2. Books VI, VII, and XII

Virgil, unlike Homer, thinks always in terms of history, of the rise and fall of nations and in particular of the rise of Rome. His characters and incidents have not only their dramatic present intensity, they are invested also with a wealth of symbolic correspondences to history, past and future. The student will need some background in Roman history to appreciate the significance, to take one example, of Dido's great curse on Aeneas. She appeals to her people, the Tyrians, the Carthaginians,

> ...besiege with hate
> His progeny and all his race to come:
> Make this your offering to my dust. No love,
> No pact must be between our peoples; No,
> But rise up from my bones, avenging spirit!
> Harry with fire and sword the Dardan countrymen
> Now, or hereafter, at whatever time
> The strength will be afforded. Coast with coast
> In conflict, I implore, and sea with sea,
> And arms with arms: may they contend in war,
> Themselves and all the children of their children!
> (IV. 834–844)

Every Roman who read these lines remembered the history of the wars that, after threatening the existence of Rome itself, extended Roman power overseas from Italy and launched the city on the path to world empire. They were called the Punic (that is, Carthaginian) wars, and there were three of them.

The first began in 264 B.C. as a Roman attempt to restrain Carthaginian expansion in Sicily. In order to win the war, however, the Romans, who had never had a navy, found themselves compelled to become a seapower in order to deal with Carthaginian control of the sea between Italy and Africa. They did so and, in what was mainly a naval war ("Coast with coast / In conflict . . . sea with sea"), they eventually forced Carthage to evacuate Sicily and pay an indemnity.

The war lasted twenty-three years; a little over twenty years later the Second Punic War began. In the interim, the Carthaginians had built up a base in Spain; when the Romans tried to check their expansion there, the Carthaginian general Hannibal led his forces through Spain and southern

France, over the Alps, and down into Italy. He defeated one Roman army after another and laid waste Italy with fire and sword ("rise up from my bones, avenging spirit! / Harry with fire and sword the Dardan countrymen . . ."). But he was unable to assault the fortified city of Rome itself, or to break the loyalty of the Italian fortified cities to Rome and in the end, when the Roman general Scipio drove the Carthaginians from Spain and then invaded North Africa, Hannibal came home to Carthage, only to be decisively defeated by Scipio in 202 B.C.

Carthage was forced to give up Spain (which became a Roman province), surrender her fleet, and pay an indemnity. But in the next few decades she began to gain strength again, and in 149 B.C. the Romans began the Third (and last) Punic War. Carthage was invaded, the city stormed, and then utterly destroyed; the Romans ran plows over the ruins of the city. Africa became a Roman province.

All this, and more besides, was evoked for the Roman reader by the lines of Dido's curse, and this is typical of Virgil's poetic practice throughout. Dido herself, for example, would recall to the Roman reader another African queen, Cleopatra of Egypt, who had ensnared with her love Mark Antony, Augustus' rival for supremacy in the Roman world. Aeneas, abandoning his mission and helping to build Dido's Carthage, would remind the Roman readers of Antony, who, reveling in the delights of Cleopatra's Alexandria, lost a world for love; this would deepen their sense of the danger Aeneas was courting by his delay at Carthage. The subdued reference comes clearly to the surface when, on the shield of Aeneas in Book VIII, we see Augustus, the descendant of Aeneas, facing in battle Antony, the renegade Roman who marshals against Rome the power of the East "And in [whose] wake the Egyptian consort came / So shamefully" (VIII. 106–7).

Topics for Discussion

Virgil deliberately models his poem on Homer; the first six books are Aeneas' *Odyssey*, the last six his *Iliad*. Sometimes specific incidents from Homer are imitated, yet though the relation to the model is in every case clear; Virgil makes the material serve his own, different purpose. Discuss the nature and effect of the Virgilian adaptation of:

1. Odysseus' interview with Ajax in Book XI of the *Odyssey* for Aeneas' interview with Dido in Book VI of the *Aeneid*.
   [In both cases the hero makes an appeal for reconciliation with a

suicide who has reason to feel wronged by him, but the appeal is rejected in silence. In Odysseus' case, however, he does not really admit that he was responsible; he wishes the Greeks had not given him the arms of Achilles as his prize but does not say that in fact they should have gone to Ajax. He blames the whole thing on Zeus ("no one bears the blame but Zeus" [*Odyssey* XI. 666]). Aeneas too puts the responsibility on the gods (*Aeneid* VI. 245) but in this case we know that he did indeed have direct orders form Jupiter, brought by Mercury, and furthermore that the fate and future of a great nation rested on his decision. For Odysseus the silence of the shade of Ajax is a minor matter: "Who knows if in that darkness he might still / have spoken, and I answered? But my heart / longed, after this, to see the dead elsewhere." (*Odyssey* XI. 673–676). Odysseus and Ajax in life were fellow soldiers, rivals for rewards and glory, but Aeneas loved Dido, and her silent, hostile rejection of his plea brings him to shed the tears he held back when they parted at Carthage. Unlike Odysseus who let Ajax go, "Aeneas still gazed after her in tears, / Shaken by her ill fate and pitying her" (*Aeneid* VI. 263–64).]

2. Homer's description of the shield of Achilles in the *Iliad* (XVIII. 565ff.) for Aeneas' shield in the *Aeneid* (VIII. 24ff.).
   [The parallelism of the contexts is close; the mother-goddess in each case brings armor made by the divine smith for her son to use against his enemy (Hector, Turnus),and each hero delights in the splendor of the arms. But the shields present two different worlds. Achilles' shield is an image of human life as a whole, of cities in war and at peace, of work on the land and the dance at the palace—a world that has no past or future, a human condition that will never change. On Aeneas' shield the god has figured episodes from the early history of Rome—the three generations of Ascanius (Iulus, Aeneas' son) and the wolf suckling Romulus and Remus, the builders of Rome. On goes the historical procession, through the early kings, to the expulsion of Tarquin the last king and the heroic defense of the city against his Etruscan allies. An incident from times still further in the future, the Capitol attacked by the Gauls, is followed by scenes from the lower world, the conspirator Catiline in torment, the virtuous Cato giving laws. These two men lived and died not too many years before Augustus established his imperial regime; the prelude to that period of peace and recon-

struction was the defeat of Mark Antony and his eastern allies at the Battle of Actium in 31 B.C.—the central scene on the shield. All this lies far in the future and it is beyond the comprehension of Aeneas, though "He felt joy in their pictures, taking up / Upon his shoulder all the destined acts / And fame of his descendants" (*Aeneid* VII. 165–67).]

3. Odysseus' story of his wanderings at the court of Phaeacia for Aeneas' account of the fall of Troy and his subsequent wanderings, at Dido's banquet.

[Odysseus at the court of Alcinous is alone, a shipwrecked naked sailor befriended by a princess and cautiously concealing his identity until, moved by the song of the bard Demodocus, his tears betray him as one of the heroes from Troy. His tale, a spell-binding story of encounters with giants, monsters, and hospitable goddesses, of visits to strange lands, even to the land of the dead, wins him rich gifts and a passage home and, though the princess Nausicaa, with her father's consent, would obviously like to keep him as a husband, he insists on returning to Ithaca. Aeneas does not conceal his identity but reveals it to Dido, as she offers his ships' crews the choice of passage to Italy or a share in the new city she is building in Africa. At the banquet where he tells his tale, the queen, through the machinations of Venus, is already falling in love with Aeneas and the tale of his sorrows and adventures wins her heart completely. But it is a very different story from that of Odysseus. The first half of it is the account of the destruction of Troy, the hideous death of Priam, the loss of his wife, Creusa, and, in what follows, he is wandering—not like Odysseus to find his way home—but in search of a site to found a new city. His tale is not romance but the tragic history of a great defeat, the end of a civilization, and of the painful search for a place in which it can be recreated. Nausicaa's gentle hints to Odysseus become, in the Virgilian version, Dido's passionate pursuit of Aeneas, and Odysseus delicate rejection of Nausicaa's offer (*Odyssey* VIII. 495–500), Aeneas' "marriage" with Dido in the cave. Odysseus on his travels becomes the lover of Circe and Calypso but these are incidents with no consequences; Aeneas' love for Dido endangers the future of his race and of the world and when he renounces it to follow his destiny he sows the seeds of the great Punic Wars of the future.

Topic for Writing

Discuss the character of Aeneas, which has often come in for harsh criticism (Charles James Fox, the eighteenth-century English statesman, found him "either insipid or odious" and William Butler Yeats speaks of an Irishman who thought Aeneas was a priest). The implied comparison is of course with epic heroes such as Achilles and Odysseus. How far is such an attitude justified?

[There is sufficient material in *Backgrounds* and *Classroom Strategies* to suggest an answer. The main line of defense of Aeneas is of course that, unlike Achilles and Odysseus who have no responsibilities other than the maintenance of their own heroic reputation, Aeneas carries the burden of a nation's destiny. He is a man devoted to duty (this is the basic meaning of the word *pius* which Virgil applies to him so often), and this does not make him as attractive a figure as the rebellious and wrathful warrior Achilles or the unscrupulous and calculating adventurer Odysseus. Yet he can, on occasion, act with the wild passion characteristic of the heroic temper of an Achilles (or a Medea); in the last book, where everything leads us to expect that he will spare Turnus, his defeated enemy, the sight of Pallas' belt worn as a trophy by his killer inflames Aeneas with rage. The poem closes not on the note of reconciliation that the divine agreement seemed to promise but with a typically heroic act of revenge.]

Further Reading

See also the reading suggestions in the anthology, p. 842.

Commager, Steele, ed. *Virgil: A Collection of Essays.* Englewood Cliffs, N. J., 1966.
Contains essays on "Basic Themes" by Victor Poschl, "The Imagery of the Second Book of the *Aeneid*" by Bernard Knox, and a brilliant essay by Adam Parry, "The Two Voices of Virgil's *Aeneid*," which deals with the imperial theme and the contradictory theme of human suffering and sadness.

Kenney, E. J., ed. *Latin Literature.* Vol. II of *The Cambridge History of Latin Literature* Cambridge, 1982. Pp. 331–69 (R. D. Williams).

An up-to-date discussion for the modern reader. It covers the Augustan background, the literary background, composition and structure, the chief characters, destiny and religion, and style and meter.

OVID
Metamorphoses

Background

Ovid's account of "bodies changed / To different forms" (I. 1–2) runs, so his proem announces, "from the world's beginning to our own days" (4). The transformation which occurred in his own day was the metamorphosis of the soul of Julius Caesar, assassinated in 44 B.C., into a star. Augustus was the adopted son of Julius Caesar, so the poem ends with a compliment to the reigning emperor, which is deftly capped by the wish that many years may elapse before Augustus too ascends to heaven and becomes a god.

Ovid starts with the creation of the material world (the transformation of "rude and lumpy matter" [7] into an ordered universe), and proceeds to the birth of man and the history of his four ages—Gold, Silver, Bronze, and Iron—a tale of change from good to fair to bad to worse. The men of the Iron Age are so wicked that Jove (Jupiter) begins to fear for his throne; he tells a council of the Olympian gods the story of Lycaon.

Jove had gone down to earth to see how bad things actually were; when he came to the kingdom of Lycaon in Arcadia and revealed his divinity, the king decided to test the truth of his statement by offering him human flesh, to see if he could detect it. Jove brings down lightning on the house and turns Lycaon into a wolf—the first metamorphosis described in detail (204–43).

Jove then decides to wipe out the human race and sends the flood. Deucalion and Pyrrha, the sole survivors, receive an oracular command to throw their mother's bones behind them; they finally understand that they are to throw stones (bones of mother earth). When they do so the stones are changed into men and women and life comes back to the world.

Among the forms of life are serpents; one of them, Pytho, is killed by the god Apollo, who falls in love with Daphne, the daughter of the Peneus river. A virgin huntress, Daphne flees the god's advances. About to be overtaken, she prays for help to her father, the river god, who changes her into a laurel tree. The rivers of Greece come to console Peneus, all except Inachus, whose daughter Io is missing; he does not know whether she is alive or dead.

She has, in fact, caught the roving eye of Jove, who has pursued and caught her. When Juno catches him in the act, he changes Io into a white heifer. Juno, pretending not to know what has happened, begs for the heifer as a gift, and Jove must give way. Juno puts Io under the surveillance of Argus, who has a hundred eyes. Io finds her father and manages to identify herself by scratching her name in the dust, but there is nothing he can do. Jove takes pity on them and sends Mercury to kill Argus. He first lulls Argus to sleep with his magic wand, meanwhile playing on his reed pipes and telling a story.

It is the story of Syrinx, pursued by the god Pan but rescued from his embraces by being changed into a reed. Once Argus falls asleep, Mercury kills him. Juno takes his hundred eyes and sets them in the tail of the peacock. She also sends a fury to drive Io all over the world. Io's prayers to Jove induce him to swear to Juno that he will never touch the girl and Juno changes Io back again to human shape.

Our selection breaks off here (almost at the end of Book I) and proceeds to Book XV. Numa, the second king of Rome, goes to the Greek town of Croton in southern Italy to study the doctrines of the Greek philosopher Pythagoras. Pythagoras explains the creation of the natural world, and the causes of natural phenomena. He speaks out against the consumption of animal food. He recalls the Golden Age, when food grew abundantly on trees and in the earth, when birds flew and animals ran unharmed. Some "innovator" decided to kill in order to eat; so steel and violence came into the world. It is permitted, he says, to kill animals that endanger us or our livelihood (but not to eat them); but there are no grounds for killing sheep which give us clothing and milk, or cows, or oxen which help us till the soil.

The connection of all this with metamorphosis becomes clear when Pythagoras reveals that human souls, when they leave their earthly bodies, find other homes, perhaps in other humans, perhaps in animals— the spirit passes "to ever-changing bodies" (XV. 131). Pythagoras' doctrine of *metempsychosis*, transmigration of souls, is another kind of metamorphosis. He goes on to point out that change of form is universal: night becomes day, the seasons of the year turn into each other, our bodies change with age, even the elements, earth and air, are not stable, land becomes sea and vice versa. Pythagoras goes on to cite even stranger changes of shape: rotting carcasses that breed insects, eggs that hatch birds. Change is a universal principle, its variety endless: "The day will end . . . Before I have the time I need to tell you / All of the things that take new forms" (XV. 371, 373–74).

Ovid, whose reputation as a poet had been built on his playful, witty, and at times licentious love poetry, turns in the *Metamorphoses* to the epic genre; the meter of his verse, the hexameter, is the same as that of Virgil's *Aeneid* and the opening lines of the poem announce the theme in solemn strains. This dignified tone is maintained through the account of the creation and the four ages, the Lycaon story, the account of the flood and the recreation of mankind by Deucalion and Pyrrha; but with the episode of Apollo and Daphne we are back in Ovidian territory, as we are also in the story of Jove and Io (not to mention the story within a story, that of Syrinx).

But it is not only the subject matter that has changed; though the stories still deal with gods, the style modulates toward the playful wit that will be characteristic of Ovid's narrative for the bulk of the poem. The dialogue between Apollo and Cupid, for example (I. 456ff.), makes no attempt at epic seriousness. Apollo's detailed appreciation of Daphne's charms as he pursues her (502ff.) recalls the poet of the *Art of Love*. The embarrassment and subterfuges of Jove when caught red-handed by Juno (627ff.) suggest social comedy rather than epic grandeur. Daphne is rescued from what she feared most, and Io is restored to human shape.

Ovid's poem pursues its course through more than 12,000 lines; this "epic of the emotions," as it has been called, rings the changes on all the genres—comedy, tragedy, pastoral, didactic—as it creates a brilliant anthology of mythological tales (most of them Greek). Most of the mythical stories that have become household words in Western culture through their re-creation in later art and literature—Pygmalion and Galatea, Midas and the golden touch, Pyramus and Thisbe—owe their form to their appearance in Ovid's *Metamorphoses*.

In the second part of our selection, however, Ovid returns to the serious tone of the opening. Pythagoras' teachings—the doctrine of eternal change, the impermanence of all things human and material, the transformations brought by time—impart a solid moral to the kaleido-scope of changing forms which, sometimes gruesome, sometimes comic, but always memorable, justifies Ovid's claim to immortality: "I shall be read, and through all centuries / If prophecies of bards are ever truthful / I shall be living always."

Classroom Strategies

One assignment. Book I first, and the Pythagoras section later.

It should be pointed out that Pythagoras was a historical figure and that Ovid's account of his teaching, although it is a poetic adaptation, has some basis in fact. Pythagoras was a native of the Greek island of Samos, who sometime early in the sixth century B.C. emigrated to Croton in southern Italy and there founded a sort of philosophical and religious brotherhood, which observed strict vegetarian dietary rules. His doctrine of metempsychosis and his claim to remember his previous incarnations are well attested and so is his concentration (not mentioned by Ovid) on mathematics as a key to understanding the universe. (Some students may have come across Pythagoras' theorem.)

Ovid's treatment of the gods may puzzle some students. In the *Aeneid* the gods, though subject to human passions—Juno's hatred of Troy for example—are figures of immense dignity. Virgil's Juno may be simply jealous but she is also terrifying in her wrath; Venus may trick Dido into falling in love with Aeneas, but her purpose is serious and the fate of empires is involved. In Ovid, however, these same gods are treated with lighthearted humor; even Jove himself appears in the likeness of an embarrassed husband caught philandering by his wife. Ovid's attitude toward the gods is not really a religious one at all; in the two parts of the poem that sound deeply serious—the creation story and the teachings of Pythagoras—the Olympian gods play little or no part. In his *Art of Love*, in fact, Ovid had expressed a cynical view: belief in the existence of gods is advantageous for society, so, he says, let us believe in them (*Expedit esse deos, et, ut expedit, esse putemus*). In that same passage, however, he goes on to recommend conformity with ritual—incense should be burned and wine poured on the altars. For Ovid the Olympian gods had become material for poetry, and lighthearted poetry at that; but there is no reason to think that his attitude was unusual. Pagan religion, in the early centuries of the Roman empire, was for most people a question of conformity to custom, not of belief. It had little spiritual force with which to confront the new religions, Christianity in particular, which commanded fervent belief in their new visions of divine power and man's life in this world and the next.

Topic for Discussion

In the opening sections of the *Metamorphoses*, the account of creation

(5–80) and the story of the Flood (262ff.) bear remarkable resemblances to the biblical stories of creation and flood in Genesis. Compare and contrast them in detail and in the fundamental ideas underlying them.

[The resemblances are many and obvious. The main difference is the spiritual and intellectual sources from which the accounts derive. Genesis expresses a profound religious idea, the creation by God not only of the universe but also of mankind; in the Ovidian account, which owes much to Greek philosophical speculation, our origin is not so clearly defined and our position in the hierarchy of being seems more exalted. The accounts differ, too, in their explanation of the origin of evil. In Genesis human weakness and willful curiosity yield to a tempter to produce disobedience and from "that first disobedience" came death and all the sorrows of this world. In Ovid, the wickedness that compels Jove to decide on the destruction of the human race is presented as a process of gradual degeneration through the Four Ages, a kind of moral evolution in reverse. In both respects, Ovid's account reflects the anthropocentric bias of Greek thought whereas the Hebrew texts emphasize human subordination to the will of an all-powerful and omniscient God.]

Topic for Writing

Ovid drew on the rich mythological literature for his stories of transformation but he added a new element to these tales of changed forms. "By . . . fleshing out the story, by inspecting the emotions and psychological problems of the characters, . . . by weighing the reasons for the metamorphosis and the feelings of the human spirit inside the changed body, Ovid gave new life and meaning to the myth" (W. S. Anderson). Discuss this analysis of Ovidian technique for the transformation of (a) Lycaon; (b) Daphne; (c) Io.

Further Reading

See also the reading suggestions in the anthology, p. 918.
Anderson, W. S., ed. *Ovid's* Metamorphoses, *Books 6–10.* Norman, Okla., 1972.
An edition of the Latin text with introduction and commentary. Although it does not deal with the books contained in our selection, the Introduction (pp. 3–22) gives many useful insights into Ovidian style and technique.

Duff, J. Wight. *A Literary History of Rome from the Origins to the Close of the Golden Age.* London, 1909. Pp. 598–605.
A venerable but still suggestive discussion of the Metamorphoses and its place in Latin and European poetry.

Fränkel, H. *Ovid: A Poet between Two Worlds.* Berkeley and Los Angeles, 1969.
Pages 73–79 discuss the transformations in Book I of the *Metamorphoses.*

Kenney, E. J., ed. *Latin Literature.* Vol. I of *The Cambridge History of Classical Literature.* Cambridge, 1982. Pp. 430–41.
A sensitive critical analysis of the poem which places it in its literary context and presents a revealing estimate of Ovid's achievement. (All quotations from the Latin translated.)

Wilkinson, L. P. *Ovid Recalled.* Cambridge, 1955.
Pages 190ff. discuss the gods and pp. 203ff. mortals in the *Metamorphoses.*

THE NEW TESTAMENT

Backgrounds

Our selection (from the Gospels according to St. Luke and St. Matthew) begins with the birth of Jesus (from St. Luke) and the famous story of the "good tidings of great joy" brought by the angel of the Lord to the shepherds in the fields. This selection ends with the picture of the twelve-year-old Jesus questioning and answering the learned interpreters of the scriptures and the laws. There follows St. Matthew's account of the Sermon on the Mount, which contains Christ's basic doctrines and also the words of the Lord's Prayer. The next selection (from St. Luke) contains the famous parables of the lost sheep, the lost piece of silver, and the prodigal son. The rest of our selection comes from St. Matthew: the Last Supper, the agony in the garden, the betrayal and arrest of Jesus, his denial by Peter, and then the trial before Pontius Pilate and the crucifixion; finally, the resurrection and Christ's command to the disciples to "teach all nations."

When Alexander died at Babylon in 323 B.C. after conquering the whole of the immense land empire of the Persians, his generals divided the spoils between them; Ptolemy took Egypt (his descendants ruled it until the last of them, Cleopatra, went down to defeat with Mark Antony in 31 B.C.), and Palestine, together with most of the Middle East, came under the control of Seleucus and his descendants the Seleucids. Over the whole area Greek became the language of administration and in the cities, at any rate, Greek culture took firm hold; the ruins of its typical buildings—temple, theater, and gymnasium—still testify to its wide dissemination.

In Palestine, however, the attempts to impose Greek culture ran into the stubborn resistance of the Jews, who after a long war succeeded in retaining the right to practice their own religion and observe their own laws. Eventually, in the first century B.C., the area came under Roman control; it was before a Roman official, Pontius Pilate, that Jesus was tried and condemned to death.

While the governing officials conducted their business in Greek or Latin, the Jewish population spoke a Semitic dialect called Aramaic (though the scriptures that their rabbis expounded were written in classical Hebrew). Jesus' native tongue was Aramaic (some of his last words on the cross—*Eli Eli lama sabachthani*—are in that language), but he must have learned classical Hebrew to be able to dispute with the rabbis in the temple, and it is quite likely that he knew enough Greek to speak to and understand Roman and Greek officials. But his preaching to the crowds that came to hear him was in Aramaic, and when he died on the cross in A.D. 30 it must have been in that language that his disciples remembered and perhaps began to record his words.

He had given them the mission, however, to "teach all nations" and if his message was to go outside the narrow confines of Aramaic-speaking Palestine, it would have to be in a Greek version. And it is in that language, the "common" Greek of the Middle East (not the highly wrought literary Greek of the Athenian writers), that the four gospels were written, probably in the last third of the first century A.D. In that language the message was accessible to anyone in the Middle East and mainland Greece who could read at all; later, as Latin versions were made, the gospels (the word means "good news") could be read all over the Roman empire.

The translation in our selection is the so-called Authorized Version of the Old and New Testaments which was published in A.D. 1611; it was made on the authorization of King James I of England by the leading scholars of the English Protestant Church. It drew heavily on earlier translations but received its final form in a great age for the English language, the age of Marlowe, Shakespeare, Spenser, and Jonson. It has been a classic of English literature ever since, a text that for many centuries has been the common property of all English speakers and that has enriched the language of all who have written in English since the book first appeared.

Classroom Strategies

One assignment.

One aspect of the gospel narratives, especially that of St. Matthew, that may puzzle students, is the frequency of reference to the Old Testament, often to cite a prophecy that is being or is about to be fulfilled. Many of these references are made by Jesus himself, as, for example, when he predicts that his disciples will desert him in his hour of need and cites the prophet Zechariah (13:7— "For it is written, I will smite the shepherd and the sheep of the flock shall be scattered abroad"), or by the narrator, as in the case of the potter's field bought with the thirty pieces of silver paid to Judas—a fulfillment, says St. Matthew, of a prophecy made by Jeremiah (in our text it is in Zechariah 11.13— "And they took the thirty pieces of silver, the price of him that was valued, whom they of the children of Israel did not value, and gave them for the potter's field . . .").

The purpose of these references is to establish Jesus' claim to be the promised Messiah, a Hebrew word which means "anointed" (the Greek word for which is *christos*, hence our word "Christ"). A king was anointed with holy oil (a king or queen still is in the British coronation ceremony), but this king, the Messiah, was to be one appointed by God to deliver his people, the Jews, and establish his kingdom in righteousness. Jesus' claim to be that Messiah was one of the reasons for the hostility of many of the Jews, for they expected the Messiah to deliver them from the Romans, while Jesus, announcing that his kingdom was not of this world, renounced violent action of any kind. It is with reference to this claim to be the Messiah that the Roman magistrate Pilate, not understanding its theological nature, can ask Jesus, "Art Thou the King of the Jews?" (Matthew 27:11) and that the mocking legend can be fixed to the cross: "THIS IS JESUS THE KING OF THE JEWS"(27:37).

By the end of the gospel of St. Matthew (the one that is clearly aimed especially at a Jewish, as St. Luke's is at a Greek audience), the mission of the Messiah has become worldwide. The resurrected Jesus tells his disciples: "Go ye therefore, and teach all nations . . ." (28:19).

Topic for Discussion

All three of the parables in our selection—the lost sheep, the lost silver piece, and the prodigal son—emphasize the lesson that the redeemed sinner is more precious to God than the righteous person who never sinned. This implies a conception of God unlike that found in the Old Testament (cf. the Genesis stories of the Garden of Eden and the Flood) or in Greek literature and thought (cf. the gods of the *Iliad*, the *Odyssey*, and the *Oresteia*). The parables emphasize the entirely new emphasis that Christian doctrine was to place on human repentance and divine mercy.

Topic for Writing

Compare the recommendations for human conduct offered in the Beatitudes (Matthew 5:3–11) and those that are implied in the Greek texts you have read.

[The contrast is striking in the case of the heroic values of an Achilles or Odysseus; perhaps the only one of Jesus' commands that one can imagine Achilles accepting is "Blessed are the pure in heart" (which he would probably have understood as meaning "Blessed are they who speak the truth and hate a liar"— cf. *Iliad* IX. 378ff.). With Socrates, on the other hand (who was also put to death), many of the commands of Jesus seem perfectly compatible.]

Further Reading

See also the reading suggestions in the anthology, p. 948.

Barrett, C. K. *The New Testament Background: Selected Documents.* London, 1956; reprinted New York, 1961.
Documents illustrating the period of the origin and rise of Christianity translated from Greek, Latin, Hebrew, and other languages.

Cook, Stanley. *An Introduction to the Bible.* Harmondsworth, Middlesex, 1945; reprinted 1950.
Useful chapters are: 1, The English Bible; 5, The Books of the Bible: The New Testament (pp. 69–72); and 6, The Messiah and the New Age (pp. 116–28).

May, H. G., and B. C. Metzger. *The New Oxford Annotated Bible.* Oxford, 1965; reprinted 1977.
Besides presenting an annotated edition of the Old and New Testaments in the Revised Standard Version, this volume contains excellent chapters on modern approaches to Biblical study (pp. 1519ff.), literary forms in the Gospels (pp. 1530ff.), and a historical account of Palestine during "the invasion of Hellenism" and the rule of Rome (pp. 1543ff.).

Metzger, B. C. *The New Testament: Its Background, Growth, and Content.* Nashville, 1965.
An up-to-date survey of the historical and doctrinal problems presented by the New Testament, written for the nonspecialist by one of the most prominent Biblical scholars of our time. Especially recommended are Chapter 4, on the sources of our knowledge of the life and teachings of Jesus, and Chapter 6 on his teachings.

PETRONIUS
The Satyricon
(Dinner with Trimalchio)

Backgrounds

Our selection is an account of a dinner given by a vulgar profiteer
called Trimalchio; the narrator, Encolpius, is an educated man, a student
of rhetoric. The dinner proceeds with one wildly extravagant course after
another as the guests, most of them tradesmen with Greek names, talk
business and cheap philosophy in language that has a scurrilous vitality
unequaled in all Latin literature. Trimalchio tells the story of his life and
with the late arrival of Habinnas (a man in the funeral monument business who is building Trimalchio's tomb according to his specifications)
the party gets wild: Fortunata, Trimalchio's wife, arrives and shows off
her jewelry but when Trimalchio makes a pass at a handsome boy slave,
she bawls him out and is treated, in turn, to a vicious stream of vulgar
abuse from her husband. Finally, maudlin drunk, Trimalchio orders his
burial shroud to be brought in for the guests to admire; the band he has
ordered to play a funeral march makes so much noise that the neighbor-
hood is aroused and the fire brigade, thinking Trimalchio's house is on
fire, breaks in with water and axes, thus giving Encolpius and his friend
Giton a chance to escape in the confusion.

The *Satyricon* has come down to us as a collection of fragments (the
banquet of Trimalchio is the longest); we have only remnants of what
was originally an immense narrative of perhaps twenty books (our
fragments seem to come from books XIV–XVI). It was a sort of picaresque novel: the amorous and disreputable adventures of its young
narrator, Encolpius. He is a penniless student of rhetoric, living by his
wits (and occasionally by the lightness of his fingers) in the cities of
southern Italy. He has a young companion-lover, Giton, who is a perpetual bone of contention with another of his shady companions, Ascyltus,
who from time to time takes his place in Giton's affections.
    The literary origins of such a work are hard to seek; it may have
drawn on licentious Greek narratives (the so-called Milesian tales) and
does owe much to Roman satire (the Augustan poet Horace, for example,

describes a rich upstart's banquet much like that of Trimalchio in one of his *Satires*), but the vitality and realism of Petronius' fiction is something new in ancient literature.

Its author was almost certainly an aristocratic member of the court of Nero (emperor, A.D. 54–68), Gaius Petronius, whose life and death are described by the historian Tacitus, writing some fifty years after the events he records. Petronius, he says,

> was a man who spent his days sleeping and his nights working or enjoying himself . . . He was thought of as a refined artist in extravagance. His conversation and actions had a freedom and an air of carelessness which appealed to people by its lack of affectation. Yet as governor in Bithynia and later as consul he showed that he was a man of energy and fully equipped to deal with business. Later, returning to loose habits (or perhaps pretending to do so), he became a member of the inner circle of Nero's companions where he was known as the Arbiter of Elegance; Nero's jaded fancy would find charm and finesse only in what passed Petronius' scrutiny.

This position of influence aroused the jealousy of the powerful commander of the praetorian guard and as a result of his intrigues Petronius was arrested on suspicion of treason. Rather than wait for Nero's sentence, he committed suicide by cutting his veins. But his suicide was a spectacular event:

> He had the veins, once severed, bandaged up, when he felt like it, and then opened them again, meanwhile talking to his friends, not on a serious note or with any intention of winning a reputation for a brave end. The conversation was not concerned with the immortality of the soul or philosophical doctrines but consisted of amusing songs and frivolous verses. Some of his slaves he gave rewards to, others he had whipped. He sat down to a banquet, drowsing a little, so that his death, though forced on him, would look natural. In his will he did not follow the usual routine of flattering Nero; instead he listed the names of Nero's sexual partners male and female, and followed that with detailed descriptions of the emperor's activities, specifying the novel features of each sexual encounter. This document he sent to Nero.
>
> Tacitus, *Annals* XVI. 18–19

Classroom Strategies

One assignment.

The student may wonder about the social position of slaves in Roman imperial society; on the one hand Trimalchio owns a great many of them—there are at least forty "divisions" of slaves in his household (p.

971)—but he himself was a slave once and so were some of his rich friends (one of them takes it upon himself to reproach Ascyltus for laughing at Trimalchio [p. 972] and proclaims his pride in his status of "freedman," that is, liberated slave). There seems to be a certain social mobility in this society, and this does correspond to the facts of Roman history.

In Greece we hear very little about the transition from slave to free status; the one thing we do know is that a freed slave remained an alien in the city—he could not acquire citizenship. In Rome, however, he did. His status as *libertus*, "freedman," gave him citizen rights, and in the next generation his son would not even be a freedman but a citizen on a level with all comers. The Augustan poet Horace was, in fact, a freedman's son and yet he moved easily in the exalted circle of the emperor Augustus.

Trimalchio's account of his rise from rags to riches (pp. 978–79), though Petronius' satiric intent is plain, has a ring of truth to it. He came from Asia—probably a Greek city in the Middle East—and was a slave for fourteen years, during which time he was the sexual favorite of his master (and incidentally obliged his mistress too). He became, as he says, "boss in the house"; he learned accounting and became steward—the indispensable servant manager. He was left, at his master's death, not only his freedom, but a fortune. He bought freedom for his wife, Fortunata, too (p. 978) and went into business in the wine trade. With the proceeds he bought back all his master's old estates, built a house, and invested in slaves. Trimalchio's emancipation by his master's will was in fact a common occurrence; common enough so that the imperial government collected a tax on it.

Topic for Discussion

Although the *Satyricon* is unlike any other literary work that has come down to us from antiquity, it is nonetheless influenced by and conscious of its predecessors. In particular, since it is a long narrative, it frequently compares and contrasts itself with the noblest and most monumental narrative form in antiquity, the epic. The references are, of course, ironic; the business of the inhabitants of Trimalchio's world emerges in sharp relief from the implied comparison with Achilles and the heroes of the Trojan saga.

The name of the rhetoric teacher, Agamemnon, is one among the many deliberate references to the heroic past; the point is emphasized by the name of his assistant, Menelaus. But this Agamemnon is a flatterer who dignifies Trimalchio's inane remarks by admiring their "wit" (p. 971). The mural in Trimalchio's house includes representations of "The *Iliad*, and *Odyssey*, and the gladiatorial show given by Laenas" (p. 964), and in the conversation of the guests that goes on when Trimalchio has left to go to the toilet the heroes of past time who are held up to admiration are not warriors but, for example, Chrysanthus, who "started out in life with just a penny" and "left a solid hundred thousand" (p. 967) and Safinius who kept the price of bread down by terrifying the bakers: "he used to wade into some of them—no beating about the bush . . ." (p. 980).

As for the heroes of the present day, chief among them is Titus who, his friend Echion the rag merchant says, is about to give a gladiatorial show that will be "the best ever . . . cold steel, no quarter and the slaughterhouse right in the middle where all the stands can see it" (p. 969). Echion's son is "ahead with his Greek, and he's starting to take to his Latin," but his father wants him to pick up some legal training for home use: "There's a living in that sort of thing" (p. 972).

Trimalchio too has pretensions to culture; he has "two libraries, one Greek, one Latin" (p. 971), but he doesn't seem to have read the books. He remembers a story of Ulysses (Odysseus), "how the Cyclops tore out his thumb with a pair of pincers" (p. 972)—which he claims to have read in Homer. The only time he gets an allusion to the great literature of the past even remotely right is when he calls Fortunata, who has objected to his dalliance with a boy slave, a "Cassandra in clogs" (p. 978).

Topics for Writing

1. Discuss the following statement:

Trimalchio is a complex character; he now wallows in luxury and self-deception, but was once resilient and faced a hard world on its own terms. For all his coarseness and ostentation, he is not utterly unlikeable.

F. D. Goodyear

2. The same critic says of the characters who speak at the banquet when Trimalchio is absent: "they are characterized by what they say as well as by the way they speak." Discuss with specific examples.

Further Reading

See also the reading suggestions in the anthology, p. 962.

Kenney, E. J., ed. *Latin Literature*. Vol. I of *The Cambridge History of Classical Literature*. Cambridge, 1982. Pp. 635–38 (F. D. Goodyear).
A short discussion of the *Satyricon* as a whole, with some perceptive remarks on the banquet of Trimalchio.

Petronius. *The Satyricon*. (With the *Apocolocyntosis*, by Seneca.) Translated by J. P. Sullivan. Harmondsworth (Penguin Classics), 1977.
This is the translation from which our selection is taken; from it you might like to get an idea of the rest of the work. Especially recommended is the famous story of the widow of Ephesus (pp. 120–22).

Petronius. *The Satyricon*. Translated by William Arrowsmith. Ann Arbor, 1959; reprinted New York (Meridian Classics), 1983.
The introduction (pp. vii–xix; in the reprint, v–xviii) is a brilliant discussion of the work as literature.

ST. AUGUSTINE
Confessions

Backgrounds

Augustine begins with a reconstruction of the first months of his childhood, based on the "word of others," then describes his own earliest memories; they include a fascinating analysis of the process of learning to understand his parents' speech. He continues with an account of his boyhood, his education, and later his adolescence; one incident from this period, his participation in the theft of fruit from a pear tree, remains in his memory as an example of malice—"My soul was depraved" (p. 987).

At Carthage, where he was a student, he fell victim to the lusts of the flesh; he also frequented the theater and was one of a gang of rowdy and rebellious students at the university where he studied law and rhetoric. He read for the first time the gospels (in Latin) but found the style inferior to that of Cicero and was "repelled by their simplicity" (p. 990). He became professor of rhetoric at Milan in the north of Italy, at that time (late fourth century A.D.) the administrative center of the western Roman empire.

His mother, Monica, came to live with him and was distressed to find that he was not yet a Christian. He had great worldly ambitions (conversion would have interfered with them) and was also living with a mistress by whom he had a child. He did not wish to give her up and so resisted the force that drew him toward Christianity but was finally converted when a voice he heard in a garden said: "Take and read" (p. 995).

He took up the Bible that was on his knees, opened it at random, and found the words of St. Paul which begin, "Not in rioting and drunkenness . . ." (Romans 13:13). He went in and told his mother he had made up his mind; he left his mistress, resigned his professorship at Milan, joined the church there which was headed by St. Ambrose, and eventually became a priest. His mother died as she was about to return home to Africa; Augustine records what she had told him about her early life and paints an affecting picture of a simple but devoted woman who lived in the Christian faith through all the trials of a hard life and a difficult marriage.

Augustine wrote his *Confessions* around A.D. 397, a few years after he had become bishop of Hippo, a town second in importance only to Carthage, the capital city of the Roman province of Africa. Although no other example of autobiography survives from classical antiquity, we know that he had predecessors; the Roman statesman Sulla, for example, had written his memoirs in the first century B.C. But, judging from the examples of Greek and Latin biography that have survived—the lives of the famous Greeks and Romans by Plutarch, for example, or the lives of the Roman emperors of the first century A.D. by Suetonius—Augustine's book must have been very different from any of its predecessors. The biographers, for example, hardly mention the childhood and youth of their subjects; they are concerned with the public career and, though they may give lurid details of the subject's private life (especially in the case of Suetonius), they do little to explore the psychology behind the virtues and vices they chronicle.

Augustine's work, however, is a spiritual biography, an account of a man's long and troubled journey toward his final conversion to the Christian faith that his mother had lived by and was to die in, an account, furthermore, pervaded by that sense of sin that is the particular contribution of Christianity to the western mind. Augustine's genuine regret and shame for his part in the robbery of a neighbor's pear tree is something a classical Greek or Roman would have found incomprehensible.

This concentration on the spiritual life, rather than on the life of activity or the intellect, is the real novelty of the work and from that stem many of its most remarkable innovations. The account of his childhood, for example, the first in all ancient literature, with its remarkable analysis of the process by which babies learn their parents' language, owes its genesis to Augustine's conviction of the basic sinfulness of man, even children. "In your sight," he says to God, "no man is free from sin, not even a child who has lived only one day on earth." This conviction that sin is innate in human nature and that without God's grace human beings cannot hope for salvation is a world away from the Greek anthropocentric vision of man's capacity for heroic action, as warrior, inventor, legislator, or poet, with or without and sometimes in defiance of the gods who are like us in shape as well as in their passions, different only in their overwhelming power.

Classroom Strategies

One assignment.

See *Backgrounds* for a discussion of the main difficulty the modern student will encounter—Augustine's sense of sin. You might add to the discussion of this subject the relevance of the form Augustine employs. The work is not presented as an autobiography; the title *Confessions* is accurate, since all through the work Augustine is speaking directly to God, confessing his sins. This, again, is something unparalleled in the ancient world, one more sign of the transition from the ancient to the medieval world that is visible in the pages of Augustine's book. No Greek or Roman would "confess" to a god; prayers, sacrifice, worship by hymns or dance, consultation by oracle—these were the pagan approaches to the gods. The very idea that a god would be interested in an individual's confession of wrongdoing is alien to the ancient mentality; the gods, for one thing, are not so closely concerned with human feeling and conduct. Augustine's sense of sin is oppressive, but, on the other hand, his conviction that God is interested in him is a comfort that the pagan could not enjoy.

Topic for Discussion and Writing

Compare Augustine's evaluation of his own conduct with that offered by Socrates in the *Apology* and the complete lack of self-criticism or evaluation by Achilles the *Iliad* (until, in Book XXIV, he does for a moment see himself through the eyes of others).

Further Reading

See also the reading suggestions in the anthology, p. 981.

Brown, P. *Augustine of Hippo*. Berkeley and Los Angeles, 1970.
A full and brilliant biography that covers the whole period of Augustine's life as well as his voluminous writings. Pages 158–81 deal in depth with the *Confessions*.

Marrou, H. *St. Augustine and His Influence through the Ages*. New York, n.d.
An introduction to the life and works, lavishly illustrated, with selections (translated) from other works than the *Confessions* and an estimate of his importance for later centuries.

Masterpieces of the Middle Ages

The Koran

Backgrounds

About the year 570 A.D. a young man was born into the Quraish tribe of Mecca. He was given the name Muhammad, and, since his father had died before his birth and his mother died while he was about six, he was raised first by his grandfather and then by his uncle, Abu Talib. In his early twenties he was married to the wealthy widow, Khadija, who was some years older than he. The marriage was prompted by convenience—he was a poor orphan, she a middle-aged widow—but by all appearances it was a happy and loving one. He had trained as a merchant by his uncle and had a talent for commerce. Their affairs prospered.

Muhammad had a serious, spiritual bent and often withdrew to meditate. One day in the year 610, while he was meditating in a cave outside Mecca, the Angel Gabriel appeared to him, ordered him to "Recite," and revealed the first verses of what became the Koran to him. Other verses followed and Muhammad gradually gathered a circle of believers around him. The first was his wife, and the second his nephew, Ali. (Ali was married to Muhammad's daughter, Fatima, and became the fourth caliph [successor] as leader of the community.)

Others followed, and the success of this fledgling community threatened the established order of Mecca. Mecca's success as a trading center rested on its importance as a center of pilgrimage. Muhammad's God demanded the destruction of the idols that were the objects of pilgrimage. He also challenged the tribal basis of the society, arguing that faith was more important than blood. He was abandoned by his own tribe but survived by being adopted into another. His situation was perilous, and some of his followers fled to temporary exile in Ethiopia. Eventually, in

622, he and his community made a flight (Arabic *hijra*) to the oasis center of Medina at the invitation of the local residents. There he established a Muslim community which he led until his death in 632. During this time he attracted many converts from all over Arabia. He also forced out the Jewish tribes that had been resident there so that Medina became wholly Muslim.

In 624 Muhammad initiated a war with Mecca that ended with a complete Muslim victory in 630. All the Meccans converted to Islam and the remaining tribes of Arabia followed their example in short order. Mecca became the center of the new religion, and a few months before his death in 632 Muhammad returned to Mecca to make a pilgrimage to the Ka'bah—now emptied of idols—a journey that established the pilgrimage ritual, a practice followed to the present day.

Shortly before his death, Muslim expeditions were sent against Islam's neighbors to the north. There was a brief pause after the Prophet's death while the question of his succession was settled, but then the Muslim conquests continued north, west, and east with astonishing success. Within a century Islam stretched from the Atlantic in the west to central Asia in the east, and from northern Syria to the southern shore of Arabia.

For those accustomed to the Bible, the Koran is a hard book to get used to. It lacks much of the poetry, narrative thread, stories, and rich variety of characters and incidents that reading the Bible has trained us to expect in a book of revelation. Although "the Merciful" and "the Munificent are the two most common epithets given to God by Muslims, the Koran seems to emphasize God's wrath and the punishments He inflicts on unbelievers, rather than His mercy and generosity. Personal tastes aside, it can be self-defeating to read the Koran simply as an inferior version of the Bible. Differences between the two works oblige us to read the Bible from a more comparative perspective. For example, contrast illuminates the extent to which the Bible is embedded in the history of a single nation and underscores its historical depth. There are so many layers to the Bible, so many voices have contributed to its composition, while the Koran is the product of a single moment in time and has an overall consistency of tone and emphasis.

Another point worth mentioning is that the fire and brimstone sermonizing of the Koran finds echoes in many eras of Christian history, such as the preaching of the fundamentalist Protestants who first settled New England. Even today, one would not have to travel far to hear sermons that promise a scorching in Hell to sinners who will not repent.

Classroom Strategies

Suggested Assignments:
Suras 1, 12, 19, and 71
Remaining Suras

Topics for Discussion

The most familiar portions of the Koran, and so the most accessible,
are probably the prophetic tales.

Joseph (Sura 12)

Islam is more accepting of human error than Christianity; it does not
acknowledge original sin. As a consequence, Joseph (Arabic *Yusuf*)
would have fallen if God had not warned him when Zuleikha (the name
given to his master's wife by Islamic tradition) tempted him. Zuleikha is
also treated in a more tolerant fashion. She is given a chance to show the
women of the city that they, too, would have been seduced by Joseph's
angelic beauty. In Genesis, the story of Joseph casts him as a hero who is
tested and then given the responsibility of leading his people into Egypt.
In the Koran, the story of Joseph has nothing of this epic dimension, but
focuses on the smaller but more general theme of the importance of
trusting in God.

Noah (Sura 71)

In the Koran, Noah (Arabic *Nuh*) is the first of the major prophets, a
step well above his position in the Bible. He establishes the pattern for
the role of the prophet in his community. It is a disheartening one and
probably reflects Muhammad's view of his relations with his fellow
Meccans. He is reviled and rejected for years. At last, however, he is able
to call down God's wrath on his tormentors. The emphasis is on his
prophetic role rather than upon the details of the ark and the salvation of
the animals. Some of these details occur in other Suras. Unlike the Bible,
the Koran does not tell the tales of any of the prophets in a continuous
narrative, but alludes to them in a number of suras; Jonah is a fine example.

Mary (Sura 19)

Islam does not accept that Jesus (Arabic *Isâ*) was the son of God. For them such a mixture of divine and human attributes is unthinkable. Jesus they account a great prophet, but no more. They also do not accept the martyrdom of Jesus, but believe that at the crucial moment a substitute was put in Jesus's place. The miracles surrounding the birth of Jesus do occur in the Koran, but in a very different form than in the New Testament.

Topics for Writing

Any of the questions raised in the *Topics for Discussion* and:

1. What is the Koranic attitude toward women as revealed in Suras 4 (Women), 12 (Joseph), and 19 (Mary)?

2. How do Islamic perceptions of Heaven and Hell differ from those of Christianity and Judaism?

3. What is the Koranic attitude toward previous revelations?

Further Reading

See also the reading suggestions in the anthology, p. 1011.

The Koran, translated by N. J. Dawood. Revised edition, 1990.
 The new edition is preferable to the earlier, both because of the revisions in the translation and because a useful subject index has been added.

Esposito, John L. *Islam: The Straight Path*. 1988.
 One of the most useful of recent introductions to Islam.

Gibb, H. A. R. *Muhammadanism: An Historical Survey*. 2nd edition, revised. 1962.
 A good, brief survey that has long been a standard work.

Peters, F. E. *Children of Abraham: Judaism, Christianity and Islam.*

1982.
A brief but enlightening discussion of the differences among the three religions.

Waldman, Marilyn R. "New Approaches to 'Biblical' Materials in the Qur'ân," from *The Muslim World.* Volume LCCV, No. 1 (January, 1985): pp. 1–16.
A practical demonstration of how to avoid reading the Koran as a defective translation of the Bible.

Beowulf

Backgrounds

No divisions are indicated in the Old English poem, but there is general agreement that it falls naturally into two parts. Part One tells the story of the hero's fight with Grendel and his mother. Part Two deals with the fight with the dragon. Raffel's translation divides the poem into a prologue followed by forty-three narrative units averaging some seventy lines each. This should be a convenience to the student coming to the poem for the first time, but the teacher may find an outline listing the sequence of topics (or groups of topics) helpful as well. Such an outline may be especially appropriate in view of the poet's fondness for including brief narratives not actually a part of the main story. These are sometimes called "digressions," but this term is inaccurate as well as unfriendly. The poet never loses sight of his theme and purpose; rather, a situation or event in the story of Beowulf often reminds him—by similarity or contrast—of a figure or an incident from Germanic tradition. The included narratives (as we shall call them) are sometimes closely related to the central plot: thus Beowulf's account of the swimming feat shared with Breca both refutes Unferth's disparaging remarks and reenforces his fitness to undertake the contest with Grendel. (It is a substantial item of his resumé!) And near the end of the poem, the gloomy forecast of a Geatish spokesman—now that the great king Beowulf is gone—is justified by references to earlier wars between the Geats and foreign nations. Nevertheless, it may prove helpful to recognize the distinction between Beowulf's exploits (and their context), and the other topics in the poem. The "included narratives" are enclosed in square brackets below:

1. (Lines 1–85) The ship-burial of the Danish king, Shild; his royal descendants down to Hrothgar, who builds the splendid hall named Herot. (Often called a prologue to the poem.)

2. (Lines 86–661) Herot ravaged by the monster, Grendel; arrival of Beowulf, a Geatish prince; entertainment in Herot; offer to await Grendel in the hall. [Included narrative: the swimming feat of young Beowulf and Breca.]

3. (Lines 662–1250) Beowulf's victory over Grendel; celebration with speeches and gift-giving. [Included narratives: Siegmund, the dragon-slayer; the story of Hnaf and Finn.]

4. (Lines 1251–1650) Herot invaded by Grendel's mother, who kills Esher; Beowulf's fight with her in the under-water room, and return to Herot.

5. (Lines 1651–1961) Renewed celebration in Herot; Beowulf's farewell to Hrothgar; return voyage of the Geats to Higlac's kingdom.
[Included narratives: Hermod's disastrous career as a warning to Beowulf; the taming of a "shrew" named Thrith.]

6. (Lines 1962–2199) Beowulf's report to King Higlac, his uncle.
[Included narrative: Ingeld and renewal of a Danish-Hathobard feud—represented as a prophecy by Beowulf.]

End of Part One at line 2199.

7. (Lines 2200–2591) Beowulf's fight with the dragon; the hero's wounds will prove fatal.
[Included narrative: Higlac's expedition against the Frisians and Franks, in which he was killed, his death avenged by Beowulf who killed Dagref, the slayer of Higlac; Beowulf supports young Hareth and succeeds him as king of the Geats when Herdred is killed in a battle with Swedes; Beowulf's autobiographical speech recounting earlier Geatish wars.]

8. (Lines 2592–2820) With Wiglaf's help, Beowulf finally kills the dragon; the hero gives directions for his funeral pyre and memorial mound; Beowulf's death.
[Included narratives: the herald's prophecy of wars between Geats and Swedes, Frisians, and Franks; he recounts episodes from times past, notably the deeds of the Swedish king, Ongentho.]

Classroom Strategies

Assignments will naturally depend on the length of time devoted to the poem. The list above may serve as a flexible outline of the possibilities: the area covered by each Arabic number could provide enough material for a single class period. In the event of time restrictions, combinations of these sections are possible.

The range of emphases in teaching *Beowulf* is wide indeed; each instructor is free to decide which focus is best suited for the course. The editor's view is indicated, more or less, in the Introduction in the anthology and in the *Topics for Discussion and Writing* below. Judicious use of visual aids—slides, photographs, etc.—have proved especially valuable in any approach to the poem.

Approaches to Teaching Beowulf, edited by Jess B. Bessinger, Jr. and Robert F. Yeager (from the Masterpieces of World Literature series, MLA, 1984) is a rich mine of materials and information. Pages 144–49 by Donald K. Fry offer an extensive list of visual materials. The book also contains, as its primary content, groups of essays by experienced scholars arranged according to particular focus: undergraduate and graduated classes in Old English, in translation, mixed undergraduate and graduate classes, etc. Along with the books mentioned in the anthology, this volume provides abundant guidance in both teaching focus and further reading.

Topics for Discussion and Writing

1. Do you find Beowulf more or less attractive than Homer's Achilles or Odysseus?
   [You should defend your preference by citing acts, situations, and speeches from the poems. Then try to form a comprehensive but concise statement of your view.]

2. Which is the more dangerous antagonist for Beowulf: Grendel or Grendel's mother?
   [Discuss specific features of each contest, for example, the killing of Handshew, the escape of Grendel from Herot, the fearsome head of Grendel which Beowulf brings back to Herot; and the fierceness of Grendel's mother's struggle with the hero, the lucky discovery of a sword at the essential moment.]

3. The poem has been described as a portrait of the ideal ruler, "a mirror for princes" of the age. What do you think of this view? [Consider the traits of character shown in the narrative—the motives of his acts; his treatment of Unferth, Hrothgar, Welthow, Higlaf, Higd, and Hrethric, including the similarities and contrasts suggested by reference to other figures of Germanic tradition.]

4. In a speech after the hero's death, Wiglaf expresses regret that his friends could not persuade Beowulf to leave the dragon alone. What do you think of this view? [Consider such aspects as these: what the dragon was doing; the apparent absence of anyone else to cope with the dragon; the hero's motives (the glory and the gold); the responsibility of the king for the welfare of his people. (If you have read Sophocles' play, *Oedipus the King*—in the anthology—you might compare Oedipus' refusal to follow the advice of others, especially Tiresias.)]

5. Choose a favorite passage—perhaps fifty lines or less—and tell why it is a favorite of yours.

Suggested Reading

See the reading suggestions in the anthology, p. 1051.

The Wanderer

Backgrounds

The Wanderer belongs, in part, to what has been called the elegiac theme in Old English poetry: the expression of regret for kindred or friends or happiness that were once enjoyed but have now been lost. Two passages in *Beowulf* might be so described. One is the farewell of the "last survivor" as he buries his treasure and prepares for death or exile (lines 2247–66); the other is the lament of an aged father whose son has apparently died a violent death (2444–62). Closely associated with this sentiment is the *Ubi sunt?* (literally, "Where are they?") motif found in European poetry at least from Boethius to Villon. In *The Wanderer* this pattern is properly adjusted to the situation of the speaker, i.e., an Anglo-Saxon thane who recalls the time when he had a lord who provided treasure and drink:

> Where now is the warrior? Where is the war-horse?
> Bestowal of treasure, and sharing of feast?
> Alas! the bright ale-cup, the byrny-clad warrior,
> The prince in his splendor—those days are long sped
> In the night of the past, as if they never had been!
> (84–88)

In other passages the poet seems to be thinking of ruined cities, their stone walls now crumbling, their inhabitants long gone. This may be based on the desolate remains of Roman buildings in England, some of them built originally during the period when Britain was a province of the Empire (between the first and fifth centuries A.D.).

In its scenes of recollection our poem vividly reflects the *comitatus* relationship between a king or chief and the members of his retinue which was basic in the Germanic Heroic Age. In return for faithful service in war the thane received from his lord both protection and reward—arm rings, neck rings, food and shelter in his chief's large hall. The relationship was deeply personal; a king's "men" were his *companions*, as the word *comitatus* indicates; reciprocal loyalty between them, rather than the later patriotic devotion to nation or land, was the strongest link of that society. This institution was older than Christianity in the life of the Germanic peoples; and it is interesting to see the difference or addition which the new religion brings. If this secular world can give no assurance of lasting security and happiness, then where can man turn? The answer of many a Christian in all ages has been trust in God; and it had a strong appeal to people in the troubled times of early medieval Europe. Some scholars have emphasized this dimension of our poem, and it is indeed the attitude expressed in the concluding lines. But *The Wanderer* (or "The Solitary [One]," Old English *Se anhaga*) surely derives also from the mood of reminiscence and regret for lost happiness in this world.

Topics for Discussion

1. Is the poem an indulgence in sentimentalism—does the speaker enjoy his misery? Or are there solid reasons for his regret—as he recalls lord, friends, happiness once enjoyed? Does the sharp realism of the scenes he recalls also convince *us*? Do the wintry weather and the (Roman) ruins harmonize with the theme and mood of the poem?

2. Students might be shown that *The Wanderer*, an extended monologue with a fairly rapid change of scenes, is much like the dramatic monologues of Browning and other later poets whom they may know. A written assignment might focus on a comparison and contrast of this kind.

3. You may wish to read a few lines of the original Old English in order to make clear the importance of alliteration. Here are the first five lines, spaced to indicate the metrical verses or half-lines of which each is made up:

Oft him anhaga   are gebideð
Metodes miltse,   þeah þe he modcearig
geond lagulade   longe sceolde
hreran mid hondum   hrimcealde sae,
wadan wrae clastas.   Wyrd bið ful araed!

[If you have studied Old English, you may wish to spend part of an hour pointing out the variety of metrical patterns in the original and the corresponding flexibility which the translator has employed to achieve broadly similar sound effects. You may decide to translate these lines more literally into Modern English prose, thus showing the adaptation necessary to maintain a definite metrical scheme. But these efforts should be regarded as optional and peripheral; the emphasis should be on the text which the students have before them.]

Topic for Writing

Trace the combination of reminiscence, daydreaming, and dreams in sleep.

[At line 30 the verb "dreams" must mean "remembers"; it contrasts with 35–36, where the dreaming is a part of sleep; line 39 records the awakening. But at line 45 his recollection becomes a daydream, apparently; and presently the images of "old comrades remembered . . . melt into air." Elsewhere in the poem the past is presented in a series of vividly recalled scenes.]

Further Reading

See also the reading suggestions in the anthology, p. 1124.

Scholarly editions of the poem, with discussion of themes, structure, and problems, are R. A. Leslie, *The Wanderer* (Manchester, 1965), and T. P. Dunning and A. J. Bliss, *The Wanderer* (London, 1969).

The Story of Deirdre

Backgrounds

The prose narrative tells us all the essential events of the story, and it is useful at some point to read it through and ignore the poetry for the time being. In this way it will be seen that the poetic passages add little or nothing to the *narrative*. Instead, they comment on the situations, characters, and events; they express emotions naturally arising out of the narrative.

The opening scene is as typical of Irish Heroic Age tradition as Homer's Troy or Phaeacia is typical of the corresponding phase of Greek civilization. A large company of warriors and counselors, along with their wives and daughters, are eating and drinking in a spacious, more or less public, room or hall. This is a part of the court of Conchubur, king of the Ulaid, a people living in modern Ulster; specifically, it is the house of Fedelmid, the official storyteller. With the latter we might compare the minstrels named by Homer—Demodocus, for example, in the *Odyssey* (VIII. 47ff.). After a long evening of food and drink, a bit more raucous than comparable scenes in Homer, members of the company have gone to their beds or pallets within the hall, perhaps near one of the walls.

To this broadly realistic and "natural" setting is now added a super-natural incident: the unborn child of Fedelmid's wife cries out from her womb. Evidently it is a loud cry, and it is not surprising that the warriors—who have been reclining or dozing in a place illuminated, probably, only by a central hearth fire, now doubtless dying out—should take alarm and get up to find out what is going on. The wise old counselor Senchae takes charge for the moment; the woman is questioned; Cathub, a druid, touches her womb; when the child murmurs, he declares that a girl will be born, her name Derdriu, who will cause great trouble. The apparent consensus is that the infant, now born, should not be allowed to live, a view not unusual in this pre-Christian age. (Because of a similar sinister prophecy the parents of the infant Oedipus ordered a servant to leave the child to perish on a mountain. [See Sophocles' *Oedipus the King*.])

At this point the king, Conchubur, intervenes; he will have the girl brought up in seclusion and intended as a royal consort. The narrative now skips an unstated number of years—until Derdriu has grown up. She announces her own adulthood suddenly and in a most striking manner: "I could love a man with those three colours: hair like a raven, cheeks like blood and body like snow" (p. 1131). The reader may be a bit startled at Lebarcham's prompt encouragement and her designation of Noisiu as a readily available lover. But female satirists were a well known feature of early Irish culture; and there was an element of verbal magic associated with satirists in general, whose invective was believed capable of causing bodily harm. That is why Conchubur did not dare exclude Lebarcham from the milieu of the growing child. The narrative now introduces Noisiu and his two brothers (their names, Arddan and Aindle, are given in a later poem). They are young men attached to the court (a rather anachronistic term for the circle of fighting men surrounding Conchubur). Both as musicians and as warriors their abilities suggest supermen rather beyond the limits of Homer's heroes.

The first encounter of Derdriu and Noisiu should not be expected to reflect the etiquette of "courtly" love or metrical romance, for these belong to a time much later than our story of the eighth century or earlier. Instead the woman overtly takes the initiative, and her challenge includes a threat of disgrace to Noisiu if he refuses to cooperate. But implicit in the situation is the narrator's premise of fatality or destiny and the related idea of love *before* first sight, both features found in other Old Irish stories. It should be noted that Noisiu resists at first because of the druid's prophecy of danger but also that his devotion to Derdriu is faithful and flawless once he is committed. Noisiu and his family belong to the military nobility or aristocracy of the Ulaid people, as is evident from the size of their retinue, even allowing for considerable exaggeration in the figures given. Escaping the power of Conchubur, they travel about in Ireland, receiving the protection of many of the rulers of the country, that is, petty or tribal kings, and living off the land (by hunting). But, threatened by Conchubur's people, they eventually leave Ireland and go to Scotland (Albu), entering the service of a king there. But Derdriu's peerless beauty renews the danger; the king resolves to have her by fair means or foul; and they are forced to take refuge in an unnamed island. The next step is the proposal by Conchubur's followers that Noisiu and his company be invited to return in safety; Conchubur assents but secretly plans treachery.

Our narrative omits some details. Thus Conchubur must have learned of Noisiu's vow to take no food or drink before reaching the king's court. That is why he arranges that Fergus, the most powerful of the guarantors of Noisiu's safety, shall receive a series of invitations which he cannot decline. We are not told why or how this taboo (the Irish word, not used in the text, is *geis*) was attached to Fergus, but the fact was evidently well known. A *geis* of some kind is a frequent feature of Old Irish stories. Conchubur is able to persuade Eogan, a petty king and a former enemy, recently reconciled, to kill Noisiu. But the guarantors honor their pledges and either lose their lives or join Fergus in a destructive attack on the royal headquarters, Emuin, which is burned. Then Fergus and his company—the figure given is three thousand—move to (the modern) Connaught and join the court of King Aillil and his queen Medb. That is where we find Fergus at the time of the great war between Ulaid and Connachta, as told in the *Tain Bo Cuailnge (The Cattle Raid of Cooley)*, the greatest and longest of the Old Irish stories.

With Noisiu and his brothers dead, Derdriu is now a helpless captive of Conchubur. She evidently resists all his efforts at reconciliation, and he finally becomes vindictive, as the dialogue of the last paragraph indicates (p. 1136). Condemned to spend a year with Eogan, the slayer of Noisiu, she leaps to death from the rushing chariot.

Topics for Discussion

1. What gives the narrative its extraordinary intensity and immediacy of impact?
   [A striking example occurs in the incident of the raven drinking the blood of the skinned calf on the snow (p. 1031). Deirdre's comment foretells and initiates the main action to follow; this is her first utterance in the entire story and it marks her arrival at adulthood: " . . . and she said to Lebarcham 'I could love a man with those three colours: hair like a raven, cheeks like blood and body like snow.'" Lebarcham says the man is available—and thus we meet the other chief protagonist, Noisiu. The suddenness of action and the vividness of images, though most notable here, are found throughout, as in the opening scene with the cry of the infant from the mother's womb and the ominous prophecy of the druid Cathub; in the first dialogue between Deirdre and Noisiu (about heifers and bulls); and, finally, in the report of her suicide.]

2. What part does the poetry play in this story? How much of the *story* would be lacking if the poetry were omitted? What about the verses spoken by Cathub at Deirdre's birth? How do the poems spoken by Deirdre express her character and personality?

Topics for Writing

1. A comparison of the Irish and the Greek Heroic Ages.
   [This should be based on the *Iliad* and *Odyssey* as represented in the anthology. It might include methods of warfare; government; attitudes toward the foretelling of future events; and communal life (as in a king's hall). Or the topic could be limited and focused; for example, was Irish life simpler and cruder in the time of Deirdre than Greek in the time of Helen of Troy?]

2. Deirdre and Helen of Troy as *femmes fatales*, women destined to cause catastrophe. Both Homer and the Irish author tell of prophecies of trouble; both link beauty and disaster. What differences are there in the reader's attitude toward the two? How account for these differences? (Obviously, there are no "right" answers; but the conclusions should be based on passages cited from the texts.)

3. A comparison of the treatment of the story here and in Synge's *Deirdre of the Sorrows* or Yeats's *Deirdre*.

4. For those familiar with Shakespeare's play, a comparison of Noisiu and Romeo, Derdriu and Juliet could be interesting.

Further Reading

See also the reading suggestions in the anthology, p. 1128–29.

Cross, T. P., and C. H. Slover. *Ancient Irish Tales*. 1936; reprinted with C. W. Dunn as editor, New York, 1969.
The largest collection of Old and Middle Irish stories in English translation.

Dillon, Myles. *Early Irish Literature*. Chicago, 1948.
A brief, attractive account of the several "cycles" into which the large body of stories has been traditionally divided; representative excerpts from each cycle (in English translation).

Dillon, Myles, and Nora Chadwick. *The Celtic Realms*. New York, 1967.
A comprehensive account of early Celtic culture.

Henry, P. L. *The Early English and Celtic Lyric*. London, 1966.
Illuminating in connection with the poems included in *The Story of Deirdre*.

Piggott, Stuart. *The Druids*. 1968; reprinted Penguin, 1974.
One of several books on this difficult and controversial subject. (Were the Druids primarily priests or [oral] scholars or magicians or prophets—or something else?)

The Song of the Seeress

Backgrounds

The *Voluspa*, as our poem is called in Old Norse, is the first and one of the longest of the poems in the collection known as the *Poetic Edda*. Like the rest, it is anonymous and undated; scholars have variously suggested dates between the eighth and the twelfth centuries. It seems to be the work of a poet nourished in the pagan Germanic (or at least Scandinavian) tradition, but one who knew something of the teachings of Christianity. Since the Icelandic people adopted Christianity in the year 1000, the poem was most likely composed within a century before or after that event. Presented as a series of utterances by a seeress of more than ordinary knowledge, it is a sequence of kaleidoscopic scenes displaying the history of the cosmos from the original "giant," or animated Nature, to the universal destruction in the war between gods and monsters—with a brief glimpse of renewal in the final strophes of the poem. It can be described as a concise, summarizing vision addressed to listeners or readers already familiar with the events and the contestants in the total story. In its "prophecy" of the end of the world it may be compared with the visions in the New Testament book Revelation.

Some general similarities with early Greek conceptions may be pointed out to students. The gods, even the greatest, are not ultimate creators of the world; they are at most administrators, rulers; they have ancestors as well as progeny. Again, although Odin, like the Greek Zeus, is represented as the principal deity, the religion is not monotheism but an abundant polytheism.

Classroom Strategies

You will do well to take advantage of the popularity of the imaginative cosmic narratives of J. R. R. Tolkien, especially the series that makes up *The Lord of the Rings*. The recent success of these books was phenomenal; some instructors doubtless shared the enthusiasm. Tolkien's cosmos is in part derived from the Old Norse tradition as set forth in *The Song of the Seeress* and elsewhere.

Another attractive focus could be our translator, the recently deceased Anglo-American poet, W. H. Auden. The name Auden is cognate with

Authun, a name frequent in Iceland. The poet was said to be fond of his Icelandic connection; in his youth he lived for a time in that country and he visited it in later life. Some students will know one or more of Auden's short poems.

Many details in *The Song of the Seeress* are not entirely clear; they are still the topics of controversy for modern scholars. But this does not seriously affect the scope and intensity of the poet's vision or its impact on the contemporary reader. You will do well to read aloud (at least some of) the majestic sequences (using the divisions summed up in the footnotes) and invite the class to see with the mind's eye.

Topics for Discussion and Writing

1. A comparison of the conflict between good and evil forces in *The Song of the Seeress* and in J. R. R. Tolkien's *The Lord of the Rings*. [As noted in the headnote (see p. 1137), Tolkien was greatly indebted to the Norse cosmogony and mythology, though for the most part he introduces new names for his monsters. But the representation of an essentially perpetual conflict—with periods of hot and cold war—is common to both. Tolkien creates an atmosphere of mystery and wonder surrounding the fate of the universe and mankind along with it. The poem is more vivid and more specific, but our only partial knowledge of the traditions which it employs may make the poem also mysterious.]

2. A comparison of the poem with either (a) one of the operas in Wagner's *Ring* cycle or (b) the design of the *Ring* as a whole. [Again, there was great indebtedness on Wagner's part, but the far greater role of human beings in the operas sets the two works apart. Yet it should be noted that the very anthropomorphic deities in the poem represent the *human* desire for order, stability, and justice in the universe. (This topic is suitable only for students with some fondness for Wagner.)]

3. A comparison of Homer's Olympian deities and the gods and goddesses in *The Song of the Seeress*. [In Homer the deities have favorites among men and women of this earth and they often intervene to help these or to hinder their foes. Thus the goddess Athena usually assists Odysseus, and this makes her—to that extent—an opponent of Poseidon, whom Odysseus

offended by blinding the sea god's son Polyphemus. But there is no alignment of one group of "good" deities opposed to a set of powerful, "evil" monsters, which is the situation in the Norse poem. In *The Song of the Seeress*, moreover, the very anthropomorphic gods represent our human interest in cosmic order and justice on earth. But the record of the gods is flawed: strophes 21–26 tell of their occasional strife and their violation of the contract made with the Giant who built Asgard for them. Eventually the present world order will end, along with the death of the gods in war against the monsters. But there is a final glimpse of a (better) restoration, perhaps strongly influenced by Christian teaching.]

Further Reading

See the reading suggestions in the anthology, p. 1137.

Thorstein the Staff-Struck

Backgrounds

The events of the story take place in northeastern Iceland, near the coast, and mostly at Thorarin's farm in Sunnudale or at Hof, the homestead of Bjarni, the head of a household including his wife Rannveig, his brothers Thorhall and Thorvald, who are his dependents or subordinates, and his chief servant Thord. Our story is a pendant to a longer saga (*Vopnfirdinga saga*) in which Bjarni is a principal figure; hence the allusions to his acts at Bodvarsdale, as well as the account of his descendants at the end of the story. The protagonists in *Thorstein the Staff-Struck* are old Thorarin and his son Thorstein on one side and Bjarni, with his family and household, on the other. But it is important to note the mixture—sometimes amounting to conflict—of motives *within* the several characters. Thus Thorstein, who surely knows that Thord's blow was intentional, would prefer to avoid further violence; one motive, implied rather than spelled out, is his aged father's precarious physical and economic condition. If Thorstein should be killed or forced to go into exile, old Thorarin would be left destitute and helpless. Knowing the old man's bellicose disposition, Thorstein tries to keep him from hearing of Thord's act; but he does learn about it and hence goads Thorstein to action by accusing him of cowardice. Now note the contrast between Thorstein and Thord. Thord, who surely knew that he had been the unjustifiable aggressor, is offered a way out: he can declare the injury unintentional and pay a fee. According to the code of that age and country, this would be an honorable settlement for both men. But it does not appeal to Thord, whose foolish arrogance costs him his life.

In this situation, Bjarni, the master and necessarily the protector of Thord, has no easy alternative to the step which he takes, namely prosecution of Thorstein for homicide, ending in a sentence of exile. We must remember that Iceland in the tenth century had no public means of enforcing judicial decisions; the plaintiff when victorious had to step in and see that the verdict was carried out. When Bjarni does nothing in this direction, malicious gossip, shared by the brothers Thorhall and Thorvald in his own household, ridicules him as a coward. It is a nice touch on the author's part to have Bjarni *overhear* this kind of talk; and the reader will think it a fit response when Bjarni sends Thorhall and

Thorvald to kill Thorstein—if they can! When he kills them instead, Bjarni is once again forced into the position of reluctant avenger. But now the major protagonists, Bjarni and Thorstein, must face each other. The teacher should point out the abundant detail with which their encounter is narrated—with time out for shoe-tying and a word with old Thorarin back in the house. All this enables us to understand the characters of the two men better; and a near-final surprise comes with the hopeless attempt of Thorarin to kill Bjarni (who has told him that he has killed Thorstein). Then the final reconciliation satisfies protagonists and readers alike.

Topics for Discussion

1. The authors of Icelandic sagas do not overtly declare their attitudes toward the characters. Usually much can be inferred, though sometimes a measure of doubt may remain. Students might be asked to attack or defend such a conclusion as this: "The author approves of Thorstein, admires Bjarni, disapproves of Thord, holds Thorhall and Thorvald in contempt, enjoys Thorarin with reservations, is amiably amused by Rannveig and the other (unnamed) female character."

2. The role of Rannveig, wife of Bjarni.
   [She goads Bjarni into going after Thorstein and then seems to discourage him from the act, at any rate without help. Their two conversations dramatize the conflict in Bjarni's own mind (although in the sagas women traditionally incite their kinsmen to vengeance).]

Topic for Writing

The reluctant avengers.
[Thorstein would prefer to treat Thord's blow as an accident both because he is "even-tempered" and because he fears for his aged father's welfare if he (Thorstein) should be killed. Bjarni is not eager to avenge Thord because he believes that Thorstein never attacks anyone without good reason. Yet both Thorstein and Bjarni ultimately feel compelled to fight in order to maintain their reputation as men of courage (essential to a satisfactory life in that civilization). Their final confrontation provides a happy solution in the form of reconciliation.]

Further Reading

See also the reading suggestions in the anthology, p. 1149.

Byock, Jesse L. *Feud in the Icelandic Saga*. 1982.

The Song of Roland

Backgrounds

In A.D. 777 Charles, King of the Franks, later known as the Emperor Charlemagne, concluded an agreement with a rebel faction of the Saracen rulers of Spain. In return for sending an army in support of that faction, Charlemagne was to be acknowledged sovereign of the entire country. But things did not work out as planned. The great city of Saragossa, which by the agreement was to welcome Charles's entry, kept its gates closed against him, and following a fruitless six-week siege he decided to withdraw. On August 15, 778, as it made its way home through the Pyrenees, his army was set upon in the manner described in the following passage from a life of Charlemagne, written about fifty years after the event:

It happened this way: as the army was proceeding, stretched out in a long thin column because of the narrowness of that defile, the Basques [*Wascones*] lay in ambush on top of a mountain—the place is thickly covered with woods and therefore well suited for such covert attacks; and they rushed down upon the end of the baggage train and upon those troops in the rear guard who were protecting the main army ahead, forced them down to the bottom of the valley, engaged them in battle and killed them to the last man; then they looted the baggage, and protected by the gathering night they scattered in every direction with all the speed they had. In what took place the Basques were favored by the lightness of their arms and the terrain in which they fought; and the Franks were put thoroughly at a disadvantage by the great weight of their arms and the unevenness of the ground. In this battle were killed Eggihardus, seneschal of the royal table; Anshelmus, count of the palace; and Hruodlandus [i.e., Roland], prefect of the marches of Brittany, among many others.

It is on this incident, altogether transformed by storytellers' imaginations that the *Song* is based. As the poem presents it, Charles's withdrawal from Saragossa is brought about by a trick. The Saracen king of Spain, Marsilion, seeing his country laid waste by seven years of French invasion and even Saragossa about to fall, sends Charles a deceitful message promising to surrender sovereignty if he and his forces will return to France. Marsilion and the other Arab leaders will, they promise, speedily follow him there, confess his rule, and convert to Christianity.

To Charles and his barons, worn by years of war, the offer looks attractive and is accepted, though one of their number opposes it: Roland. Now word of their acceptance must be sent to Marsilion, and the question is: who shall go? The last time ambassadors were sent to the Arabs, they were executed. Various stalwart heroes volunteer—Roland, Oliver, Turpin, and others—but Charles is unwilling to risk them. At last Roland nominates his stepfather Ganelon, a choice all immediately approve. All, that is, except Ganelon, who is outraged and plans revenge. Reaching Saragossa as Charles's ambassador, he tells Marsilion and the other Arab leaders that the surest way to be rid of the French forever is to kill their stoutest fighting men—Roland, Oliver, and the Twelve Peers—by a sortie against the forces that will be left behind to protect the army's rear as it makes its way through the mountain passes. He, Ganelon, will see to it that Roland and the rest are in that rear guard.

Returning to the French camp, Ganelon announces that the Arabs will behave as promised. Naturally, a rear guard will have to be established for security's sake, and who so suitable to command it as Roland and his dauntless friends? In the great battle that follows, twenty thousand French soldiers are slain with their leaders till only Roland remains— dying not because any Saracen has bested him but because he has burst his temples by his efforts to recall Charles's armies with mighty blasts upon the oliphant, the ivory horn.

Summoned, too late, by Roland's trumpet, the emperor Charles returns with his main army and destroys Marsilion and his allies. There follows a long episode telling of his later victory over the great Saracen leader Baligant, after which the scene changes to the headquarters at Aix. Ganelon is brought to trial; his claim that his acts against Roland involved no treason against Charles is finally disallowed. There ensues a "judicial combat" between the Emperor's champion Tierri and Ganelon's representative Pinabel; victory was left in the hands of God in the traditional view of such affairs. Pinabel is defeated and Ganelon is executed.

The poem itself offers abundant evidence that it has a background in the "oral" tradition of poetic composition. First, there is a pattern of repetition; for example, the idea that Charles will, or may, or should leave Spain and return to his capital at Aix is stated at ll. 36ff., 51ff., 134ff., and 187ff. The scene and the participants vary, of course, but the thought is expressed again and again in very similar phrasing. Entire scenes are often closely parallel: Charles and Marsilion hold assemblies, receive ambassadors, listen to counselors, and render decisions essentially in the same manner. The battles are series of single combats between notable fighters and the action as well as the language describing it is often much the same from one encounter to the next. And since the deeds and the skills remain essentially identical, it is natural that the words and phrases which describe them should do so as well. The result is a large number of more or less uniform phrases or short sentences. In the *Roland* and in the Greek epics and in the Old English *Beowulf* also the result is a body of *formulaic* diction (differing from one language to another) conspicuous in poems deriving from a background of oral tradition. These poems were meant to be listened to by an audience, rather than read by a solitary individual in silence. Hence the recurrence of set phrases, like the repetition of scenes, would reinforce the narrative and reassure (rather than annoy) the public for which the poems were composed.

Roland is by general consent the finest example of a popular genre of narrative poetry known in French as the *chanson de geste*. Poems of this kind dealt typically with great deeds done in war or warlike adventure; normally love is absent or unimportant, and this especially differentiates the *chanson de geste* from the romance (French *roman*). Again typically, *Roland* has a tenuous relation to actual history; the central background figure is Charles, king of the Franks (crowned Emperor by the pope in the year 800, the first head of the Holy Roman Empire). But comparison of the historical kernel, given on earlier pages, with the poet's narrative will indicate the extent of the transformation.

As intimated in the headnote in the text (see p. 1156), the attitude of the poet is emphatically "positive"; the story as he tells it is filled with enthusiasm for king, Charles, whom all his feudal vassals extol with complete sincerity; for country, "sweet France," almost a refrain in many a *laisse*; and for the Christian religion. Indeed, Charles feels an obligation either to annihilate the heathen religion of the Saracens by destroying or by converting its adherents. Neither the poet nor any of his Christian characters expresses the least doubt as to the rightness of this purpose. It may seem a bit strange to us that they know so little about the faith which they oppose; the poem makes them polytheists, worshippers, oddly enough, of the Greek god Apollo as well as the Arabic prophet Mahoun (Muhammad). Historically, of course, they have always been strict worshippers of one god, Allah, whose prophet was Muhammad. In short, the poet is an ardent partisan untroubled by qualms of any kind.

Once the modern reader understands and accepts this fact, he should be free to enjoy the unremitting energy deployed in the narrative, to delight in the brilliant pageantry of its assemblies, to "identify" with Roland and his comrades in the procession of military duels.

But *Roland* is not simply a narrative of straightforward action; the plot is complicated by the treachery of Ganelon and later by the disagreement between Oliver and Roland. The poet carefully shows us how Ganelon sets about his object, the destruction of Roland. This is no easy task. First, he must convince King Marsilion that Roland, not Charles, is an implacable enemy of the Saracens; and he must begin by convincing Blancandrin, the envoy who has come from Marsilion and who will return with Ganelon himself. Then he must persuade Marsilion to send hostages and false promises of submission to Charles and then to attack with overwhelming force the small army which Charles will leave behind as a rear guard under Roland's command. If we dwell for a moment on the several uncertainties in this plan—the number of things that could go wrong—we realize what a skillful diplomat Ganelon must have been. Thus his initial harshness in stating Charles's (alleged) terms is designed to anger Marsilion and his court, to get them in the mood to fight. Once that is done, the anger can be directed against Roland. The poet's lines make it clear that Ganelon took a deliberate risk; there were two moments at which he might have been struck down by an enraged Saracen. (This topic could be a focus of class discussion or written assignments.)

Oliver, whose sister has been promised in marriage to Roland, is also his closest friend and, apparently, second only to him in valor. From the beginning onward the poet calls attention to the difference between these devoted friends. When Roland offers himself as the envoy to Marsilion, it is Oliver who protests at once:

> "No, no, not you!" said Oliver the Count,
> "that heart in you is wild, spoils for a fight,
> how I would worry—you'd fight with them, I know."
> (255–57)

Later, when both see the huge Saracen army approaching the rear guard, Oliver pleads with Roland to blow the trumpet which will bring Charles to the rescue; Roland is adamant in his refusal. Finally, after the rear guard has suffered total defeat and death stares the survivors in the face, Roland wants to sound the horn; now Oliver objects, and his anger is evident when he breaks off the marriage arrangement between his sister and Roland. His reply to Roland, who asks why Oliver is angry with him, is important for the poet's characterization of Roland: it is judgment, not madness, that makes a good vassal; Roland had rejected (good) judgment when he refused to sound the horn while there was time. The reply occupies an entire *laisse* (no. 131, ll. 1722–36). The relationship between the two men (which need not be further rehearsed here) is one of the major foci of the narrative; it should receive due attention in the classroom. Nowhere else in the poem is there a relationship of friendship, then alienation, then misunderstanding, and finally reconciliation at death. As for the attitude of the poet, it seems clear that he uses the contrast of the two men to point to a flaw in the character of Roland. Immediately after Roland's rejection of Oliver's repeated pleas that the horn be sounded (before the battle), we find the line, "Roland is good, and Oliver is wise" (1093). (The word translated "good" is the French *proz*, which may best be rendered "valiant.") The distinction, made incidentally in this passage, is confirmed and developed in *laisse* 131.

But Roland's defect does not lead the author to "prefer" Oliver or to treat him as of comparable importance to Roland. It is clear that Roland is the central figure in the poem as a whole, and especially in the first half—until his death. He is the only man who declares that Marsilion does not intend to keep his promise of submission to Charles; now the poet has already told us (readers or listeners) the same thing. This weights our sympathy in advance on Roland's side. Then, while Oliver's deeds in the battle are heroic, like those of all the leaders of the French, Roland's are super-heroic (but never treated as incredible or ridiculous). After the death of all the rest—except Turpin, and again after *his* death— Roland and Roland alone holds the stage for many a *laisse*. (A good topic for oral discussion or an essay assignment might be found here.)

The fighting archbishop, Turpin, proves, at least, in the poet's view, that the crusading zeal of Charles and Roland is righteous. He promises Paradise to the French warriors; the penance he assigns for their confessed sins is to fight bravely! His prominence in the story is indicated by the fact that he dies last of all—except Roland. In this war church and state are indeed united.

Classroom Strategies

You will, of course, divide the poem for class assignments according to the time available, but here are a few convenient breaks in the narrative to the death of Roland:

1. [*Laisses* 1–27] Charles chooses Ganelon as envoy to Marsilion.

2. [*Laisses* 28–53] Ganelon and Marsilion plot treachery.

3. [*Laisses* 54–127, with some omissions in our selections]
   Destruction of the rear guard.

4. [*Laisses* 128–76, with some omissions in our selections]
   The last great deeds and death of Roland.

Topics for Discussion

1. The poet's attitude toward Roland.
   [Take account of the passages cited in *Topics for Writing* #3; then
   note that Roland dominates the action of the poem both before and
   after the disagreement with Oliver; overall as well as piece by
   piece Roland is paramount; note his well-nigh superhuman exer-
   tion after the rest of the French are all dead and the enemy either
   dead or fled, etc. He is a flawed hero but nonetheless the hero of
   the poem.]

2. Archbishop Turpin and the Crusaders' attitude.
   [Turpin's prominence as both fighting man and priest; his hearing
   the confessions of the French and assigning the penance of valor in
   battle; the final blessing of the slain leaders whose bodies Roland
   brings to Turpin; the repeated assertion that Christians are right
   and pagans are wrong (in the course of the poem).]

3. The supernatural and the superhuman elements in the poem.
   [Omens; dreams; the angel Gabriel; the exertions of Roland in the
   final scenes. Does all this amount to a miscellany of the incredible,
   tacitly ridiculed by the poet? Or is it so handled that the reader
   accepts it without demur, with no distress over its improbability in
   our prosaic, workaday world?]

4. Elements of oral poetry in *Roland*.
   [The frequent pattern of repetition of incidents or situations or
   items of dialogue—for example, Oliver's three requests that
   Roland blow the horn (1051–92) and Roland's three refusals,
   matched by Roland's later declaration that he will now blow it and

Oliver's dissent, both stated twice (1702–21). In climactic situations like these such repetition is still effective for the modern reader, though the partial repetition of identical phrasing shows that we have here a relic of oral practice.]

Topics for Writing

1. How does Ganelon persuade King Marsilion to plan an attack against Roland and the rear guard?

   [Begin with the talk between Ganelon and the Saracen envoy Blancandrin during their journey from Charles's headquarters to Marsilion's. Then Ganelon states Charles's message in the harshest, most offensive terms possible; and, acting as his surrogate, draws Marsilion's hot anger upon himself. But with Blancandrin's help this anger is diverted from Ganelon (and Charles) and directed at Roland. They now plan the destruction of Roland by means of the attack on the rear guard.]

2. The poet's parallel treatment of the courts and entourage of Charles and Marsilion.

   [Each is shown presiding over a group of leaders and advisers of the ruler; each has a select group of warriors (the twelve—*douze*—peers) distinguished above the mass; and heading these groups are Charles's nephew, Roland, and Marsilion's nephew, Aelroth. The peers do battle with peers on the opposing side; nearly all are spectacular fighters, though the French are (individually) superior (the Saracen victory is due to overwhelming numbers). Students' papers should quote or cite specific passages of the poem, usually moving from the first assemblies onward.]

3. Oliver's attitude toward Roland.

   [Begin with Oliver's protest when Roland offers to go as Charles's envoy to Marsilion (255–57). Go on to Oliver's urging Roland to blow the horn which will call Charles to the rescue (1049–92: Oliver asks three times and Roland refuses three times); then to Roland's wish to blow the horn when it is clear that the French will be destroyed, whereupon Oliver dissents—and breaks off the betrothal of his sister Aude to Roland (1702–21); then to Oliver's answer to Roland's question, "Why are you angry at me?" (1722–37), "'I will tell you what makes a vassal good: / it is judgment, it is never madness. . . .'" Finally there is an implicit reconciliation just before Oliver's death (2010–23).]

Further Reading

See the reading suggestions in the anthology, p. 1158.

MARIE DE FRANCE
Eliduc

Backgrounds

The author's interest is centered on the characters in the story, their emotions, thoughts, hopes, and fears. But a brief summary of the external action may be convenient. Eliduc, an excellent young knight in the service of the king of Brittany, is unjustly dismissed from the court. He decides to seek adventure abroad, comes with a small band of followers to the south coast of England; his wife, Guildelüec, remains at home in Brittany. Eliduc finds the king of that region of England in difficulty because of the oppression of an enemy, offers his help, and plans surprise tactics whereby the enemy forces are satisfactorily disposed of. The rescued king, delighted and grateful, engages Eliduc's service for a year. The king's young and beautiful daugther, Guilliadun, eventually learns of Eliduc's exploits and invites him to visit her. She falls in love with him at once but is afraid to say so—she can't guess how he feels about it. Her page, a young male servant, advises her as a confidant to send Eliduc a ring and a belt as tokens of friendship; he tries them on without comment but, as the page reports, he is apparently pleased. The author now tells us that Eliduc is "torn in two" between love of the princess and his promise of faithfulness to his wife in Brittany. Nevertheless, he says nothing of the true situation to Guilliadun but, with the king's cordial approval, becomes a friend of the princess. They now acknowledge their reciprocal affections; but Eliduc tells her that he will leave the country when his year of knightly service to the king expires. This does not distress Guilliadun unduly; she hopes to become his wife by that time.

Now the king in Brittany, beset by troubles, apologizes to Eliduc and asks him to return home and come to his assistance. When Eliduc tells Guilliadun what has happened, she begs him to take her with him; Eliduc says he will not thus abuse her father's trust, but he will return to England before whatever deadline she will set. Back in Brittany, Eliduc settles the king's affairs satisfactorily; but Guildelüec is disturbed by his apparent indifference to her. He tells her it's just that he must return to England to complete his unfinished task for the king there—that is what has been on his mind. He returns, meets the princess at a secret rendezvous, and they take ship for France. A storm arises, and a sailor blurts out the fact that Eliduc has a wife in Brittany; he suggests that the princess should be thrown overboard to save the rest from drowning. The sailor is quickly struck down and into the sea; but the shock of this discovery—besides seasickness—is too much for Guilliadun, and she falls down, apparently dead.

When the ship eventually comes into a harbor in Brittany, Eliduc takes the princess to a chapel where a holy hermit has recently been buried. This is quite near Eliduc's own home, where his wife receives him but with no knowledge about the princess. Eliduc delays the burial a few days; he is surprised at Guilliadun's seemingly healthful looks. Meanwhile with the help of a servant Guildelüec learns about the situation, in part; her grief for the princess's death and Eliduc's distress is wonderfully unselfish. (The restoration or revival of Guilliadun through the flower placed in her mouth—the weasel incident—cannot be usefully summarized; it must be read in the text.) Guildelüec now separates from Eliduc and becomes a nun, leaving him free to marry the princess—with the first wife's sincere good will. After many years of wedded bliss Eliduc and Guilliadun, in their turn, enter the cloister; and so ends the story.

Folklorists have found parallels to the weasel episode in many parts of the world; and in Cornwall (source of the Celtic people and language of medieval Brittany) weasels were called fairies because of their magic properties. (See Ewert, cited in *Further Reading* below.)

Most instructors will remember that Chaucer calls his *Franklin's Tale* a Breton lay and briefly describes the genre at the beginning of his story, which has its own magical element and is focused on a conflict involving love and duty, although the issues are quite different from those in *Eliduc*. Guilliadun's dialogues with her page and especially her soliloquies are the same methods of exposition found in early French romances such as the anonymous *Eneas* and the slightly later works of Chretien de Troyes. But Marie's adjustment and accommodation of the claims of the two ladies may be unique in medieval romance. Evidently she does not accept the doctrine of Andreas Capellanus (*The Art of Courtly Love*), which held that love and marriage are mutually exclusive; for she apparently approves of Guilliadun's plan to induce Eliduc into matrimony, and she certainly endorses their eventual marriage. But then what about the first wife, Guildelüec? It may be that her feeling for Eliduc is tacitly regarded as domestic affection; at any rate it is never described in terms of such rapture as possesses both Guilliadun and Eliduc. And although Eliduc clearly feels compunction about his treatment of each of the two women, the author never condemns him; instead she implies great sympathy with the dilemma which he faces—between the (equally valid?) "rights" of love and the obligations of matrimony. Whatever we may think of Marie's solution, it is a fact that many people, both men and women, resolved a middle-aged crisis in their lives by entering the cloister. Sometimes, doubtless, there was a vocation (to the monastic life) antedating marriage, which may have been more a matter of convenience than emotion.

Topics for Discussion

1. Do the terms in which the love of Guilliadun and Eliduc is described indicate that this emotion is something different from the affection between Eliduc and Guildelüec? If so, how might that influence the attitude of a medieval reader familiar with the "doctrine" of courtly love?

2. What would you think of a woman in our time who adopted the attitude of Guildelüec? Are we able to accept her "sacrifice"—or is it really a sacrifice?
   [Remember that her affection for Eliduc is genuine. On the other hand, consider the plausible consequences if she determined to "hold" her husband regardless of his feelings. (Your conclusions should be reached in the light of the author's portrayal of all three characters, Eliduc and the two women.)]

Topic for Writing

The author's characterization of Guilliadun.
[Her sincerity and ingenuousness, as indicated directly by the author and shown in her talk with her servant, the page; her growing confidence and assurance; the reader's sympathy with her can be complete because she does not know that Eliduc has a wife in Brittany; hence the shock of discovery and the sailor's accusation in the storm are enough to account for her apparent sudden death.]

Further Reading

See also the reading suggestions in the anthology, p. 1217.

Capellanus, Andreas. *The Art of Courtly Love* (ca. 1185). Translated by John Jay Parry. New York, 1941.
On the twelfth-century "doctrine" of love.

Ewert, A., ed. *Lais by Marie de France*. Oxford, 1963.
For Marie de France and *Eliduc* specifically, the Introduction and Notes are informative.

Aucassin and Nicolette

Backgrounds

The narrative is fluid and the only divisions are the unvarying alternations of passages in verse and prose, forty-one in all. It may be convenient, however, to divide the story into a few larger units for assignments and class discussion. The following plan provides a break where there is a substantial change of scene or situation.

1. From the beginning to the talk of the lovers, each in a separate building (I–XIV)
2. To the reunion of the lovers in the forest (XV–XXVI)
3. To their separation when the kingdom of Torelore is conquered by the Saracens (XV–XXVI)
4. Aucassin once more in Beaucaire; Nicolette once more in Carthage (XXXV–XXXVIII)
5. To the final reunion and marriage of the lovers in Beaucaire (XXXIX–XLI)

Suggested Topics for Discussion

In 1 (above) Aucassin's boldness, first in capturing Count Valence and then in setting him free when the Count de Beaucaire (Aucassin's father) breaks his promise to let him have a brief meeting with Nicolette is noteworthy. As with Aucassin's earlier capture by the enemy, this courage proves the supreme power of love in Aucassin's life. This total devotion represents a kind of counter-balance to the ingenuity and enterprise of Nicolette. Throughout the story she thinks of things to do— which Aucassin suffers frequent (though not total) desolation and inertia. Yet it is he who sings of Nicolette's healing the patient in the hospital by giving him an (inadvertent) glimpse of her leg. This may remind us of the incidents in the lives of saints; in variation, Nicolette's beauty replaces the saint's holiness as the power responsible for the cure. The absolute or total power claimed by parents and guardians and, of course, the efforts of the young hero and heroine to escape that control are noteworthy as background. But there is a difference between the two: the worst that can happen to Aucassin is imprisonment, whereas Nicolette is threatened with death, a threat which takes the form of human, animal and "natural" forces. And it is she who escapes from the tower by climbing down a rope of cloth which she makes for herself, then dives into the moat, and so comes close enough to Aucassin's underground cell to talk with him and toss a lock of hair to him through a small window. In this first sequence, extravagance, both of thought and action, and tempered with humor, sets an initial pattern for the narrative as a whole: the talk of Heaven and Hell, of the anatomical seat of love in the two sexes; and the spontaneity of Aucassin's capture and release of the enemy count.

In the next sequence (2, above), the lovers, acting separately, go into the forest where they find shepherds whom they try to pay for help in finding each other. The brashness of these rustics—who are casual indeed about their obligation—lends an additional element to the uncertainty and danger experienced by the pair: the shepherds will take the money but they won't exert themselves to earn it! The equal frustration of the lovers appears in their separate but identical exclamations—"It's up to God!" (The scenes with the shepherds are both dramatic and humorous; they may remind us, in some ways, of comic scenes with rustics in Shakespeare, for example: Autolycus and his companions in *The Winter's Tale*.) Also highly theatrical is the meeting of the pair in the hut that Nicolette makes and rests in while she awaits Aucassin.

In the following sequence (3, above), the reunited lovers engage passage on a ship—destination not given!—and a storm at sea drives the vessel to the kingdom of Torelore, where they find the king in bed with childbirth while his wife in with the army away in a war. (Somewhat similar practices, obviously without complete clinical features, have been reported by modern social anthropologists.) Aucassin, who (implicitly) regards this as arrant nonsense, rescues the king and leads him to the scene of the war. Here they find the two armies fighting with cheeses and vegetables. When Aucassin enters the battle and kills several of the enemy, however, the king checks him, explaining that deadly weapons are not used in that world. (Could this be a casual bit of anti-war propaganda?) In any event, the lovers sojourn in a castle in Torelore quite happily—for three years, as transpires at the very end of the sequence—until they are captured in an invasion of the Saracens. They are separated, and Aucassin is put on a ship that sails to Beaucaire—so he is back home!

The next sequence (4, above) shows Aucassin securely established as the successor to his deceased father; Nicolette arrives in Carthage, remembers her early years there as a daughter of the king and is duly recognized. But the present king wants to have her marry a "pagan" king, so Nicolette is once more thrown upon her own resources. Disguised as a *jongleur*, (an entertainer employing both music and words). she arranges passage on a ship to Provence (in the south of France) and goes through the country playing her viol (a stringed instrument played with a bow) until she reaches Beaucaire.

In the final sequence (5, above), Nicolette, still in disguise, describes the plight of Aucassin's beloved in a song which he hears. Not recognizing Nicolette in her disguise, he arranges with her to bring Nicolette to Beaucaire. After a week spent in getting rid of the disguise, Nicolette reveals herself to the still grieving Aucassin—and so they are married and live happily ever after. (Note that Nicolette has been careful to assure herself of her lover's steadfast devotion before she reveals her identity—she is a prudent as well as an ingenious young lady!)

Topics for Writing and Discussion

1. Do you think this anonymous story may have been written by a woman?
   [Consider the greater ingenuity shown by Nicolette and the comparatively passive role of Aucassin.]

2. Do you feel a slight contempt for Aucassin, who is shown weeping much of the time? Or is he active enough to escape your censure?

3. Do you find any clear differences between the sections in verse and those in prose—except for the comparative brevity of the verse section?
   [The Editor has no strong convictions about this.]

4. Can you give a reasonably full account of the humor in this narrative—including action, situation, and dialogue?

Suggested Reading

See the reading suggestions in the anthology, p. 1231.

DANTE ALIGHIERI
The Divine Comedy

Backgrounds

The headnote (pp. 1273–1284) provides a general view of the *Divine Comedy* as a whole as well as a more detailed account of the *Inferno* and the parts of the *Purgatorio* and the *Paradiso* included in our book. The headnotes and footnotes to the individual cantos offer ample guidance and abundant information about the persons, places, and thoughts encountered along the way.

Many people know—or know of—the *Inferno* but not the *Purgatorio* or *Paradiso* and hence infer that Dante was exclusively or at least unduly preoccupied with evil. We should point out that only one third of the *Divine Comedy* is focused on the bad; one third shows people in pursuit of the good (*Purgatorio*); and one third describes the enjoyment of the good (*Paradiso*).

Some people in our time are alienated by the doctrine of eternal punishment; why not redeem everybody, after suitable reformation? The first answer, of course, is that Dante was following orthodox Christian teaching. But there are other answers philosophically and aesthetically more satisfactory to our age. Do we want to see every villain in every serious film reformed? Could we believe in the repentance of Iago in Shakespeare's *Othello* or of Goneril and Regan in *King Lear*? The (psychological) truth about such men and women—and innumerable others who have actually lived in this world—is that they do not want to reform. They would be unhappy in heaven. What the *Inferno* reveals to us is the final state or consummation of the people who have chosen one of the various kinds of wrong conduct. The range is from the illicit lovers of the fifth canto to the figures enclosed in ice at the center of the earth in the final canto. Lawless passion was the lovers' choice—rather than reasonable restraint; now they are blown about by the winds; they have no hope of *peace*. The people in the ice endure the cold—the lack of feeling which enabled them to betray and kill their kindred on the earth.

It is worth noting that moral criteria may have changed since Dante wrote his poem. Homosexuality is apparently the only reason why Brunetto Latini is in hell; and the Florentine usurers also on the burning sands might now be regarded as respectable bankers. Dante was a conservative in economics.

The *Purgatorio* has been called the most *human* of the three parts of the poem—the part that comes closest to the experience and attitudes of most of us. For we are not hopelessly sunk in evil nor infallibly committed to good; but we should like to avoid the one and attain the other—if only we knew how to do it. The *Purgatorio* dramatizes and exemplifies the Christian teaching about the way. The front page of a newspaper or the daily telecast of news indicates that things are far from all right in our world today. The same was true in Dante's time. Conflict, violence, cruelty within and between families and nations are evidence that the human situation is not satisfactory. According to Christian teaching, the ultimate source (on earth) of these bad things is the uncontrolled passions and appetites of the individual human being. Long before Dante the Church had described these excesses as the Seven Cardinal (or Deadly) Sins: Illicit Love; Gluttony (any undue concern about food); Avarice and its opposite, reckless spending; Sloth (idleness as a way of life); selfish and unjustified Anger; Envy (the wish for another person's loss or failure); and Pride (not proper self-esteem but haughtiness and aggression). Each of these stems from a vice or fault, a flaw in the moral character of the man or woman. In Roman Catholic practice—modern as well as medieval—he or she should confess to a priest, ask God's forgiveness, repent sincerely, and promise to mend. The priest might also assign a penance which, especially in medieval times, might be painful or burdensome. It was assumed that most people would not have completed the process of purgation before death; hence the doctrine of Purgatory as an interval of purification (for a true Christian) between the end of earthly life and entry into heaven.

Dante's *Purgatorio* is based quite clearly and directly on Church doctrine and practice. But he is careful to assign self-discipline—or discipline gladly accepted—in a rationally appropriate manner. Thus his penitents exert themselves to the utmost in practicing the virtue opposite to the vice under correction at the time; so the proud behave humbly (symbolized by the heavy weights they carry on their backs—in a canto not included in our selections); and Pope Adrian, who had been too fond of material wealth, is literally brought down to bare earth. The suffering of the soul in Purgatory would be meaningless if it were permanent, if it served no purpose. It is important to remember that Purgatory is an interlude, a preparation for heaven. Moreover, Dante intended his readers to apply the example of his poem to the amendment of their lives while still in this world.

It is worth remarking that there are no terraces on the mountain of Purgatory for such specific crimes as murder or robbery. The reason is that these, and all crimes, are motivated by one or more of the seven cardinal vices; when the man or woman has got rid of the inclination to evil, there will be no temptation to kill or steal. On the other hand, murderers and robbers are classified as such in the *Inferno*—because a vice, or flaw of character, may have variable consequences. It may amount only to self-indulgence without direct harm to another person; or it may lead to the worst imaginable crimes.

The importance of Dante's personal participation in the purgatorial experience, delineated in the last cantos, has been fully discussed in the headnote (p. 1280). In our age of moral "permissiveness" patterns of discipline and self-reformation may not be popular or even familiar to many students. The contrary slogan, Do what you please (with due regard to the policeman around the corner), was a replacement not long ago. More recently, there has been a tendency to ignore or manhandle the policeman. That is, for many people, there is a rejection both of internal standards of conduct and of external enforcement. In the view of some, if things—or people—go wrong, the institutions of society are responsible. As teachers of Dante we should make it clear that, while ready to criticize institutions such as the Church and State, he places the final responsibility on the individual human being. It is human beings who create or corrupt institutions.

Classroom Strategies

The reader's immediate experience of the poem should come first; then that experience can be integrated in an increasingly wide range of events, ideas, and horizons. As to class assignments, obviously they must depend on the amount of time available for the segment (Dante) as a whole; two or three cantos might be average.

In our time it cannot be taken for granted that most students will be familiar with the basic doctrine and belief of organized Christianity, that is, the Church. But Dante, like Chaucer and every other medieval and Renaissance writer, could assume this knowledge and hence allude to it with confidence that he would be understood. Indeed, it was condensed in capsule form in the Creed regularly recited in many services of worship. The following is one version, known as the Apostles' Creed:

I believe in God, the Father almighty, creator of heaven and earth. I believe in Jesus Christ, his only Son, our Lord. He was conceived by the power of the Holy Spirit and born of the Virgin Mary. He suffered under Pontius Pilate, was crucified, died and was buried. He descended to the dead. On the third day he rose again. He ascended into heaven, and is seated at the right hand of the Father. He will come again to judge the living and the dead. I believe in the Holy Spirit, the holy catholic Church, the communion of saints, the forgiveness of sins, the resurrection of the body, and the life everlasting.

Of course, it is not suggested that the Creed be taught systematically; but an occasional reference to one or another of the statements in it may clear up many a passage in our authors.

The teacher should take full advantage of the episode of the grafters in Cantos XXI and XXII. Students who are turned on by nothing else will enjoy this crude, malicious, sly, malevolent cartoon comedy once it becomes clear to them. The milieu of low-level corrupt office-holders has not changed much since Dante's time; we still talk about "sticky" fingers and cartoonists often wield the tar brush or its equivalent. Furthermore, the poignance of Virgil's rescue of Dante at the end of this sequence provides a good opportunity to discuss the relationship between the two: how it changes and deepens in the course of the journey. The conclusion of the topic must await the *Purgatorio*: Virgil's farewell and Dante's sudden awareness that Virgil is no longer at his side.

Topics for Discussion

1. The suitability of the penalties to the sins in the *Inferno*.
   [This is relevant throughout, including the area outside the nine circles; thus those in the ante-Hell—those sometimes called the moral neutrals—are plagued by annoying *little* things, unpleasant insects, etc. The "virtuous pagans" in the first circle are not actively punished; they live without the good of participating in God, as Christians must do by definition. The poet does not usually explain why the various conditions in Hell are appropriate; hence we can profitably think about the matter. Fire, in sundry form, is familiar to us as a punishment; ice, which Dante makes the ultimate penalty, may seem strange to us at first. Reflection may well change our view.]

2. The differences between upper and lower Hell.
   [Basically, the people in the upper Hell were guilty of (excessive)

self-indulgence. They loved not wisely but too well—other persons, material goods (thus either as misers or spendthrifts), food and drink, or their own aggressive impulses (Anger). Primarily, they did not deliberately seek to injure other persons. Those in the lower regions (Violence and Fraud) did precisely that—in a great variety of ways.]

3. Possible differences between Dante's perspective and ours.
[It has been suggested that one category of the Angry in the *Inferno*—the incorrigibly morose—might now be treated as patients in a mental hospital. Similarly, modern views of homosexuality do not regard it as either a sin or a crime; and the same can be said of suicide. Dante's view depended on the idea that we belong to God as our Creator; He has prescribed the manner and set the limits of our lives in definite ways; we dare not interfere.]

4. Mini-tragedies in the *Inferno*.
[It has been said that Dante's portrayal of a number of the most notable figures in the *Inferno* amounts to a series of microscopic tragedies: Paolo and Francesca in the Canto V, Pier della Vigne in XIII, and Ulysses in XXVI are notable examples. These are people very attractive in personality, intellect, or even character; but they knowingly made the wrong decisions and so decided their own fate.]

Topics for Writing

1. For some of the major figures of the poem, personality and character are indicated by the speeches which Dante puts in their mouths.
[Thus, in Canto V of the *Inferno*, Francesca's good manners are indicated by her courteous greeting of Dante; her "romantic" temperament by the tercet in which she tells of her homeland; her adherence to the "doctrine" of courtly love by the three tercets each beginning with the word "Love"; her habit of blaming something besides herself shows through in the reference to the book about Lancelot; and perhaps her vindictiveness in the single verse in which she foretells the punishment of her slayer (ll. 103–04).
[In Canto XIII the lawyer-poet Pier delle Vigne may seem to play—seriously—with words as he contrasts and pairs "locking

and unlocking," "inflamed" (verb, then past participle, then verb again), all in a severely logical and antithetical account of his unfortunate experience (ll. 58–78).

[In Canto III of the *Paradiso*, Piccarda, a nun, talks volubly enough when explaining theological issues to the earthly pilgrim (Dante), but speaks with marked restraint, modesty, and reticence in answer to questions about her own life (ll. 103–8).]

2. The method of contrasting pairs of persons.

[In *Inferno* X the Florentine aristocrats Farinata and Cavalcante (the elder) rise to talk with Dante from their shared tomb among the unbelievers. Farinata is proud, haughty, disdainful of unknown characters like the present visitor (Dante)—[he] "stared almost contemptuously, / before he asked: 'Of what line do you come?'" (ll. 41–42) Their ensuing dialogue is interrupted by Cavalcante, who asks about his son, Dante's closest friend at one time. Distressed at Dante's uncertain answer, he is overcome by grief and sinks down into the tomb. Thereupon Farinata resumes his remarks just as if there had been no interruption.

[In the Circle of Evil Counselors (*Inferno* XXVI–XXVII), we come to the Greek Ulysses, deviser of the Trojan horse, and to an Italian politician of the thirteenth century. Virgil conjures the flame which is Ulysses to utterance remote, detached, impersonal (so far as its auditors are concerned), but in itself lofty and splendid. After a bit the flame which the soul of the politician has now become (Guido da Montefeltro) addresses Dante, asks for news of Italy, and, telling Dante he is sure the story won't get out, indulges his urge to tell how he was tricked into a final sin that accounted for his present situation. Thus this garrulous old gossip is juxtaposed to the sublime Homeric hero.]

3. The grafters and the demons of popular lore. (*Inferno* XXI, XXII, and XXIII.1–54)

[The more or less grotesque and comical names of the demons who have charge of the grafters in their ditches and pools of pitch; the tricks they play on sinners trying to escape momentarily; their readiness to deceive the travelers with bare-faced lies, solemnly spoken; the rough handling of the sinners, like bags of stuff, carried on a demon's shoulder. The crouching, fearful, utterly undignified figure of Dante the traveler in this episode; its biographical counterpart in the charge of misuse of funds while an office-holder in Florence.]

Further Reading

See also the reading suggestions in the anthology, p. 1283.

Auerbach, Erich. *Dante, Poet of the Secular World.* Translated by Ralph Manheim. 1961.

Clements, R. J., ed. *American Critical Essays on Dante.* 1969.

Fergusson, Francis. *Dante's Drama of the Mind: A Modern Reading of the* Purgatorio. 1953; reprinted 1968.

Freccero, J., ed. *Dante: A Collection of Critical Essays.* 1965.

Singleton, Charles. *Dante Studies 1, Commedia: Elements of Structure* (1956) and *Dante Studies 2, Journey to Beatrice* (1958).

Slade, Carole, ed. *Approaches to Teaching Dante's* Divine Comedy. In the MLA series Approaches to Teaching Masterpieces of World Literature. New York, 1982.

GIOVANNI BOCCACCIO
The Decameron

Backgrounds

The First Day

This introduction is the counterpart, with some differences, of Chaucer's *General Prologue*. Each provides the setting for a long sequence of tales. There is a measure of chance or coincidence in both groups of storytellers. Boccaccio's seven young ladies, happening to meet in a church (though they are already friends or acquaintances), decide to leave plague-ridden Florence and live with more safety on their country estates; they invite three young gentlemen, also well known to them, to share their plans. Chaucer's twenty-nine pilgrims—traveling alone or in twos or threes or even more—all happen to have come for a night's lodging to an inn or tavern in Southwark, across the Thames from London, on the route to Canterbury. Boccaccio's company decide to spend part of each day in telling stories, and agree that on the first day each of the ten is to tell a tale on a topic of his or her own choosing. In Chaucer's account the innkeeper takes charge of proceedings; he plans four tales to be told by each traveler; the order is to be determined by lot, and he says the Knight is due to tell the first tale.

Chaucer has no real equivalent of Boccaccio's extended and vivid account of the plague in Florence. Curiously, this account is apt to remind the English or American reader of the well known *Journal of the Plague Year* written by Daniel Defoe. But the latter, realistic as it sounds, was the work of an author who lived two generations after the London epidemic of 1665. On the other hand, Boccaccio knew the Italian plague of 1348 from his own experience. His description of the mode of life of the company of young folk in the country, though idealized, is perhaps not too far from actuality. The physical comforts, the apparent abundance of food and other necessities, the ease with which the people move from place to place, all these reflect what was possible or even usual among the wealthy class of Italians in the fourteenth century. They also have the pleasing manners of gentlefolk; they treat one another with courtesy and consideration—from which good-natured jest and humor are not excluded. It may seem idyllic to us, but it was probably none the less realistic.

The Second Tale of the Fourth Day

This is the story of Brother Alberto and Madonna Lisetta. The head-note (see pp. 1468–1469) mentions the major elements of the story; instead of a summary here, then, let me point out certain features.

To begin with, Alberto is not a genuine friar; he only pretends to be and gets away with it. And before the end he is very thoroughly punished for his outrageous masquerade as the angel Gabriel; thus the claims of morality are sustained (as they are not always in the *Decameron*). The traditional malice obtaining between one Italian city and another is evident in the pervasive disparagement of Venice and its citizens. In the first paragraph there is "Venice, that receptacle of all forms of wicked-ness (p. 1482); quite early on, Lisetta is described as "a Venetian (and, as such, a gossip like all of them)" (p. 1482); and the comment on the gross deception which is part of Alberto's punishment is, "And this is what they call good old Venetian honesty" (p. 1487). (One may be reminded, incidentally, of Iago's insistence on the notorious fickleness of Venetian women—aimed at Desdemona—in Shakespeare's *Othello*.) Although clearly a hypocrite, Alberto acquired a reputation for sanctity among the Venetians greater than that of Saint Francis in Assisi.

At various points Lisetta is designated as "Lady Lighthead, who was as smart as salt is sweet" (p. 1483), "Lady Silly," "Lady Dimwit," and "Lady Halfwit." This repetitious characterization makes it easier to believe that Lisetta—or someone equally stupid—could be deceived by the Angel Gabriel imposter. Here one may note a difference between the American tall tale and the European *fabliau*. In the tall tale the exaggera-tion, the humor, and the fantasy are the important qualities; incredibility is usually taken for granted. In a fabliau such as this one, on the other hand, it must be made plausible that the dupe or victim, at least—if no one else—finds the deceiver's story credible. And of course the more credulous the dupe the more credible the deception; Lisetta's rivalry with the Virgin Mary for the devotion of Gabriel fits here.

Some items are gratuitous good sport, like the remark about Lisetta's neighbor, the congenital gossip, to whom it seemed "as if a thousand years had passed before she was able to repeat what she had learned" (the advent of Gabriel as Lisetta's lover); or the bite under the left nipple which Lisetta gave Alberto-Gabriel.

Granted its premises in the characters of Alberto and Lisetta, the tale is well plotted and executed. It is appropriate if crude irony that Alberto should receive his punishment in another masquerade—as a bear, his body covered with real honey and feathers, and hunted in St. Mark's Square in Venice.

The Ninth Tale of the Fifth Day

The tale of Federigo and the falcon may remind us of one of the best known short stories of the American author O. Henry. In "The Gift of the Magi" a poverty-stricken young couple in early twentieth-century New York City want desperately to give each other a Christmas present. The wife sells her fine head of hair, her crowning glory, to buy a watch chain for her husband's gold watch; he, meanwhile, arranges to sell the watch in order to buy a set of combs for her hair. The depth of feeling and the cruel irony of the outcome are the essential elements of the story.

In the tale of Boccaccio there is the same cruel irony, but there is also delicacy as well as depth of feeling. We realize how painful it is for the lady to ask Federigo for his falcon—though she has no idea of the sacrifice which he will then make. He, in turn, pretends that he thought only the falcon worthy of her meal—he had plenty of more ordinary food. But the reader knows that there was really nothing else in the house to eat, that day, at least. Federigo conceals the depth of his poverty out of regard for her feelings, not his own.

Topics for Discussion

1. The wit and humor of the story of Alberto and Lisetta.
   [The satirical epithets allotted to Lisetta; the part played by her woman friend, along with *her* attitude; details of the double personality of Alberto-Gabriel; the "poetic justice" of the conclusion.]

2. Should we admire Federigo and the lady to whom he was devoted?
   [The "doctrine" of faithful though unrewarded devotion; its relation to the character of the man; the probability or plausibility of a modern parallel; why the O. Henry story is not really such (the odds are far less serious); is the happy ending convincing?]

Topics for Writing

1. Why is the story of Brother Alberto and Lisetta literature? Like many *fabliaux*, this may have existed in the form of an anecdote

before Boccaccio made it a part of the *Decameron*. Turn it back into an anecdote by condensing it into a single paragraph. Then point out the differences between your paragraph and Boccaccio's story.

2. A comparison of the story of Federigo and the falcon with O. Henry's "The Gift of the Magi" or with some other appropriate story of your own choosing.

[How carefully are the incidents related to the character and personality of the people in the story? Thus, how credible is the action? (This does not mean how statistically frequent are such incidents.) On the basis of each story, what would you predict as to the future happiness of the couple?]

Further Reading

See also the reading suggestions in the anthology, p. 1469.

Musa, Mark, and Peter E. Bondanella, ed. and trans. *The Decameron*. A Norton Critical Edition. New York, 1977.

In addition to twenty-one of the *novelle*, this edition contains a number of essays of contemporary reaction and modern criticism.

Sir Gawain and the Green Knight

Backgrounds

Part I [*Beheading of the Green Knight* (ll. 1–490)]

The poet quickly tells how, after the fall of Troy, various of the surviving Trojan warriors migrated to the west and founded new nations; among them Brutus came to Britain; later Arthur ruled as king in Camelot. This will be a wondrous tale of events during a Christmas-New Year's holiday there. Arthur, his queen Guenevere, and Gawain, his nephew, are at a high table or dais; many other knights sit at other tables; all await the feast; but Arthur has vowed not to begin until someone comes to tell him of a "wonder." Suddenly a huge horse and rider, both covered in green, dash into the hall and approach the dais; the visitor has neither spear nor shield but carries a branch of green holly in one hand and a large axe in the other. He asks who is in charge here; Arthur answers and invites him to dismount and be treated as a guest. He declines, saying he has heard of the prowess and courtesy of Arthur's knights; he comes in peace to propose a Christmas game. Arthur assents, and the Green Knight offers his head to be stricken off with the axe—on condition that a return blow be accepted a year and a day hence. When all the company remain silent, he taunts them harshly, whereupon Arthur in anger and shame steps forward to accept the challenge. But now Gawain intervenes, asking that he be allowed to take over in place of the king; Gawain modestly says he is the weakest of all in body and mind and of no consequence except for his kinship to the king. "This folly," he says, fits not a king. His request is granted, and now the Green Knight, repeating the conditions of the challenge, dismounts, lies down, uncovers his neck, and is neatly beheaded by Gawain's blow with the axe. But the Green Knight rises, catches his head up from the floor, mounts his horse, and tells Gawain to come next year and look for the Knight of the Green Chapel, who will be ready with the return blow. He then rides rapidly out of the hall; the company resume their feasting.

Part II [*Gawain's travels take him on Christmas Eve to a castle and host near the Green Chapel* (ll. 491–1125)]

The seasons pass in due course until All Hallows (November 1), when Gawain is ready to start on his journey in search of the Knight of the Green Chapel. He bids king and friends farewell; he is richly armed, as his horse, Gringolet, is handsomely caparisoned; the pentangle (five-pointed star figure) on Gawain's shield includes in its symbolism his devotion to Mary, Queen of heaven and all his moral virtues. As Gawain departs, some of the court regret that the affair was not better handled: it is a shame that he is likely to lose his life, "Beheaded by an elf-man, for empty pride" (681). In the course of Gawain's solitary journey, he is threatened by wild animals and wild men and hampered by winter cold and sleet; he prays to Mary for guidance. Presently he catches sight of a splendid castle and surrounding grounds; approaches, is greeted by the porter, who lets down the drawbridge. The lord of the castle welcomes Gawain and he is finely entertained, wined, and dined. There are two ladies in the host's family, one comely and beautiful, the other ugly and graceless. After the visit has lasted from Christmas Eve till St. John's day (December 27), Gawain says he must continue his search for the Green Chapel; his host assures him that it is close by, and so Gawain can stay on as a guest for three more days. The host then proposes a game: he will go hunting each day, while Gawain rests (after his tiring journey) in the castle; each evening the host will give Gawain whatever he has got on the hunt and Gawain will give him whatever he has received in the castle.

Part III [*The three hunts and the three temptations* (ll. 1126–1997)]

As noted in the headnote (see p. 1492), the same narrative sequence is maintained for all three days: first, the start of the hunt; then the visit of the lady, the host's wife, to Gawain's bedchamber; then the conclusion of the hunt, the evening meal, and the exchange of gifts. On the first day the host and his company hunt deer and bring home many carcasses, duly presented to Gawain; he duly gives the host a single kiss. The second day comes the boar hunt; and Gawain correctly gives the host two kisses. The third day the quarry is a fox; and Gawain correctly bestows three kisses on the host but silently withholds the silk belt which the lady had given him, with the promise that it would insure the wearer against death.

Part IV [*Gawain accepts the Green Knight's return stroke and afterward goes back to Arthur's court* (ll. 1998–2530)]

Early on New Year's morning Gawain sets out to keep his rendezvous; the young guide whom the host assigned to him warns him of the great danger facing him at the hands of the savage Knight of the Green Chapel and says he (the guide) will keep silent if Gawain avoids a meeting; Gawain says he must keep faith, and trusts to God. Proceeding, Gawain soon comes to a sort of mound; he hears nearby, but out of sight, someone sharpening a blade on a grindstone. Gawain calls out, giving his name, and the Green Knight comes over the crest of a hill carrying a huge Danish axe. Gawain duly prepares to receive the blow, but twice the Green Knight feints, bringing the axe down but not touching Gawain; the third time he lets the blade graze Gawain's neck, drawing a few drops of blood. Thereupon Gawain leaps up and offers to resist any further blows. But the Green Knight now explains that he was the host in the castle (of Bercilak); the two feints correspond to the two days on which Gawain carried out the exchange faithfully and in full; the slight scratch made by the third blow was Gawain's due because he kept back the silk belt—but only because it might save his life. Gawain quickly gives back the belt and reproaches himself bitterly for cowardice and covetousness. But the Green Knight declares Gawain, who has confessed the fault and suffered the penance (of the third stroke), as pure as the day he was born; and invites him to return to the castle, where his wife (the lady who had visited Gawain in his bedchamber) will be glad to see him. The host also gives the belt once more to Gawain, who must keep it as a reminder of the event; Gawain says he will keep it as a warning of his spiritual weakness and peril. In answer to Gawain's question, the Green Knight says that the old, ugly lady in the castle is Morgan le Faye, King Arthur's half-sister; she is an enchantress and an enemy of Guenevere, and hence was responsible for the visit of the Green Knight to Camelot. Gawain makes his way back to Arthur's court, where he tells the whole story; the belt is used as a model of a baldric to be worn by knights of the court.

The earliest extant literary treatment of the "Beheading Game" is in the Irish prose narrative *The Feast of Bricriu* (*Fled Bricrend*), dated approximately in the eighth century. Cuchulainn, the great warrior of the Ulster cycle of tales, is engaged in a contest with other fighters for the right to the "hero's portion" at a feast. A rough-looking figure of magical powers invites each of them in turn to an exchange of blows in the manner of Gawain and the Green Knight; but the time interval is one day instead of a year. The others fail to keep the appointment for the return blow; Cuchulain alone is faithful; he receives an entirely harmless blow and is declared the winner of the contest. (The Irish episode is translated in Kittredge, *A Study of Sir Gawain and the Green Knight*.) The Irish plot was taken over by French and perhaps other medieval storytellers; our (anonymous) author probably knew it in *The Book (Le Livre) de Caradoc*, which appears among the "continuations" of the Old French Perceval romance. (For discussion and summaries, see Larry D. Benson, *Art and Tradition in Sir Gawain and the Green Knight* [1965].) The temptation plot was also familiar from various romances (see Benson); of course it has an ancient history, e.g., the story of Joseph and Potiphar's wife in Genesis 39:7–20, as well as the deeply tragic Greek tale of Hippolytus and Phaedra. The author of the English romance may have been the first to combine the two plots.

In his descriptions and characterizations he also makes abundant use of tradition. Thus the knight in green costume, carrying a bough of holly, was a familiar figure representing the verdure of spring in the new year. And, not combined with this but rather juxtaposed is the green color of his skin; this, along with the enormous shock of hair covering his shoulders, may well have reminded medieval listeners or readers of the figure of the Wild Man, the uncouth stranger who often erupts in royal courts (in romances). Both traditions are doubtless related to prototypes of ultimate (pre-Christian) ritual significance; one thinks of spring festivals and sacrifices, the renewal of the Waste Land at the end of winter— though it is unlikely that the fourteenth century audience made conscious connections of this kind.

In the portrayal of Gawain our poet makes an independent use of tradition. In this poem Gawain is a brave, spotless Christian knight, imbued with the five chivalric virtues and devoted to the Virgin Mary, his heavenly patroness; he is, of course, keenly sensitive in any matter of truth or honor. But, while making him also peerless in courtesy (conduct as a cultivated gentleman), the poet definitely does not attach to Gawain the habits of a medieval Casanova. But that is just the reputation that Gawain had acquired in romance tradition by the late fourteenth century. What the poet does is to have the temptress—the wife of the Green Knight—pretend to believe that Gawain had well earned this latter reputation and ought to have no hesitation about living up to it. She is playing a game, of course; with the resources of a magic household and entourage and a shape-shifter for a husband, she incurs no risk, however Gawain may respond to her overtures. Thus she is free to deploy the whole gamut of invitation, including praise, entreaty, pretended unhappiness at his rejection, disbelief that he can really be Gawain—no holds need be barred and none are. This is a hilariously comic situation and the author takes full advantage of it.

Gawain, on the other hand, is deterred by his situation as a guest of the lord of the castle and the agreement to exchange winnings at the end of each day; by the fact that such an intrigue is a sin; and by his preoccupation with the approaching rendezvous with the Green Knight. Yet we can see that he feels deeply the obligation to behave always with courtesy (good manners and consideration of the lady's emotions). Nevertheless, the poet indicates that Gawain was genuinely moved, at least on the third day; we are told at the beginning of the visit that he delights in the lady's company—and there is a reminder that Mary had better look after her knight.

The parallel patterning of the hunts and the lady's visits has been noted. Probably it is significant that the third hunt, of the fox—regarded in that age as vermin—is paired with Gawain's breach of faith in not giving the belt to his host—a reprehensible act even if extenuated by the circumstances.

The humor of the situation after the Green Knight has delivered the final stroke must not be missed. Gawain instantly springs up ready to defend himself (against further attack, beyond the terms of the agreement); and the Green Knight quietly stands there, doubtless laughing to himself. Presently he explains the whole design. But the amused reader can sympathize with Gawain in his chagrin at the deception that has been practiced upon him; he has been under such pressure for so long! Even the most ardent feminist should forgive his outburst against the wiles of women. Indeed, the art and skill of the poet maintain the reader's sympathy with and esteem for Gawain through the many scenes in which he inevitably becomes a figure of comedy.

Classroom Strategies

You must see to it that students discover the many and various delights of the romance. Once they get into it, they will see how much fun it can be—as well as being a serious treatment of important issues. Early on, some of the vivid descriptive and "action" passages might well be read aloud in class. Later, some of the dialogue between Gawain and the lady should receive oral dramatization, with parts appropriately assigned to members of the class.

Topics for Discussion

1. Reasons for Gawain's chagrin and self-disgust.
   [When he throws the girdle at the Green Knight, he realizes that he has been made a fool of—but that it is his own fault; but it is also true that he has been obliged to play a game without knowing the rules; and he has shown a flaw by not returning the girdle earlier (as promised by the terms of the agreement)—a fault that he *need* not have committed—as he has just discovered. In his view—at the moment, at least—the flaw cancels out his persevering resistance of the other temptations which the lady had pressed upon him.]

2. What is the verdict of others (than Gawain) on his conduct?
   [Sir Bercilak (the Green Knight himself) lets the axe barely scratch the skin of Gawain's neck, and afterward declares him wholly absolved, invites him to return to the castle for more festivity. Arthur's court adopts the girdle as a badge of honor—rather than shame or disgrace. The reader is likely to see the narrative as a series of extreme tests imposed (without his full knowledge) on a superlative knight, courtier, and man of scrupulous honor. He passes them all with flying colors—with one slight exception, and there he believed his life was at stake. Since the author leads the reader to this conclusion, it must have been his also.]

3. Does the author indulge in too much descriptive detail?
   [There is certainly a rich abundance: the festivity at Arthur's court; the elaborate clothing and arming of Gawain for the journey; the details of the three hunts; etc. But is the description static? Or is something happening all the time within the descriptions? And could there be a difference between the spontaneous interest of the fourteenth-century listener and the twentieth-century reader?]

Topics for Writing

1. Characterization of the Green Knight.
   [To some extent a dual personality: the outlandish visitor at Arthur's feast and Sir Bercilak, Gawain's host at the castle. How are these necessarily somewhat different? Is there an underlying unity?]

2. The story as a Christmas "game"—in two parts.
[The initial setting at Arthur's court; the wait for a wonder; the Green Knight's challenge (which is noted as a "folly" but nevertheless must be taken seriously); the Christmas season a year later at Bercilak's castle; the triple exchange of gifts; the happy conclusion of both plots on New Year's morning.]

3. Gawain as a graceful nay-sayer.
[A close look at Gawain's part in the dialogue with the lady on the three mornings; how he maintains his (attributed) reputation for courtesy but still remains modest about himself; how he avoids involvement without giving offense; the details of his acceptance of the girdle.]

Further Reading

See the reading suggestions in the anthology, p. 1493.

GEOFFREY CHAUCER
The Canterbury Tales

Backgrounds

General Prologue

The Knight, his son the Squire, and their servant the Yeoman, make up a group of three traveling together. The account of the Knight is representative and typical, rather than based on any individual actual person. He is a professional soldier of notable experience and exemplary character. It has been shown that various English knights took part in most or all of the campaigns mentioned. Such a young soldier as the Squire might well have served with English armies in France in one or more campaigns of the Hundred Years' War.

Next comes another group of three: the Prioress, another nun who serves as her secretary, and an accompanying priest; neither the secretary nor the priest is described in the General Prologue. Chaucer's attitude toward the Prioress has been much discussed among scholars. It has been pointed out that she has many of the qualities to be expected in a fashionable lady of the period but not necessarily in a nun: meticulous table manners, graceful costume, the use of (insular!) French. The "love" emblematic on her brooch may be ambivalent—religious or ordinary earthly; her tenderness about the pet dogs—not monastic—seems to be an individual trait. Chaucer seems amused by the various items *not* generally approved for nuns, yet fully appreciative of an exquisite person.

Chaucer's treatment of the Monk is rather different. He does not merely tell us that he is an ardent hunter and that he is often away from his monastery, etc.; he repeatedly notes that these things were contrary to monastic "rule" and precedent. Consequently, when Chaucer declares his approval of the Monk's way of life, some kind of irony must be involved. One view is that, in the *Canterbury Tales*, there are two Chaucers: one is the sophisticated author, the other is the simple, suggestible pilgrim; and that sometimes we hear the voice of one, sometimes of the other. Thus Chaucer the author painted the portrait of the Monk, but Chaucer the pilgrim liked and approved his way of life. Without making so sharp a division as this, we can at least agree that Chaucer occasionally pretends to say what would contradict other clear positions or attitudes; he enjoys a moment of make-believe.

Unlike monks, friars were expected to leave their "house," to go out into the world and serve, especially, the poor and helpless—after the example of St. Francis and other founders. But Chaucer makes it evident that this Friar had all the traits of an expert salesman and used them assiduously for his own enrichment and enjoyment—leaving the poor to themselves.

The next several pilgrims require no comment here; then we come to the Parson, who, like the Knight, receives a full and entirely favorable treatment. Later still, there is the Summoner, a thoroughly unsavory and corrupt but also comic figure. He is not a member of the clergy; instead, he is a kind of policeman or constable attached to the church court presided over by an archdeacon. The Summoner is apparently an associate of the Pardoner, who comes next in Chaucer's list. The latter's occupation is discussed in the headnote (see p. 1555). Here it may be added that the Pardoner has often been regarded as a eunuch *ex nativitate* (by birth, congenitally); it has also been shown that Chaucer's description and language might apply to homosexual characters. There may thus be innuendo in the mention of the association between the Summoner and the Pardoner. And the present account should be kept in mind when the reader comes to the bitter altercation between the Pardoner and the Host at the end of the Pardoner's Tale.

The Miller's Tale

The Prologue: When the Knight has told his tale—a romance of chivalry and of courtly love (not included in our selections)—the Host invites the Monk (next in social rank to the Knight) to continue with the storytelling. But the Miller, partly drunk, insists on telling his tale at once. It is in some ways a parody of high romance, but primarily it is a very fully developed fabliau.

The Tale: John, a comparatively rich old carpenter of Oxford, has a pretty young wife, Alison; and there are two young servants, male and female. They have a boarder living in the house, Nicholas; he is a student at the university and a semi-professional astrologer. He and Alison plan an (uncourtly!) intrigue; but they will have to be cautious—the husband is jealous. Meanwhile the parish clerk, Absalom, is infatuated with

Alison (who has no interest in him) and likes to serenade her under the window at night.

Nicholas shuts himself up in his room for a time; John, who likes the young man, comes to his room to inquire. Nicholas explains that he knows from his astrology that a flood greater than Noah's is in the offing; but they can save themselves if they keep the news a secret. The carpenter must hang huge baskets from the ceiling or loft and he, Alison, and Nicholas will climb up and bed down, each in one of the baskets. (The servants have been sent out of town.) Then Nicholas and Alison—the weary John has gone to sleep—climb out, go downstairs and so to bed. Presently Absalom comes singing and pleading for at least a kiss from Alison. She sits on the windowsill, her rear projecting outward; Absalom's kiss chills all his amorous itch and inspires him with a plan for revenge.

Obtaining a colter or plowshare well heated at one end from a late-working blacksmith, Absalom returns and asks Alison for another kiss. This time Nicholas projects over the window; Absalom is ready with the hot iron. When Nicholas yells "Water! Water!" the carpenter wakes up and instantly cuts the rope holding his basket (expecting that form of navigation during the flood), falls to the floor, and breaks his arm. In the aftermath Nicholas and Alison insist that only the foolish John believed a flood was imminent.

The Pardoner's Tale

The Prologue: In this exuberant address to his fellow pilgrims the Pardoner boasts about his skill in getting money from the simple, rustic people who listen to his preaching. His text, "The root of evil is greed," serves to loosen their wallets and fill his own. His fake relics, he assures them, will cure ills of domestic animals, prevent suspicion of wives by husbands, increase the yield of crops—if a suitable offering is made. But note this: it won't work if the person making the offering is guilty of any really serious unconfessed sin. (Thus he intimidates anyone who did not come forward with an offering.)

The Tale: The Pardoner offers this tale as a specimen of his preaching. First, he briefly sets a scene: three young men are in a tavern; they eat and drink to excess, indulge in much profanity, and roll dice. Here the Pardoner inserts a long denunciation of gluttony, drunkenness, profanity, and gambling, with allusions to the Bible, examples from secular history, and a lively imitation of the snoring of a person who has taken too much alcohol—"Sampson, Sampson"—yet Samson never drank wine! Resuming the story, the revellers hear a bell outside the tavern. Learning from the waiter that it is rung for a man recently slain by this thief Death, they (are just intoxicated enough to) resolve to go immediately in search of this Death, intending to kill him.

Before long they meet a mysterious old man whom they question roughly. Without saying who he is, he describes himself as a hopeless wanderer who would welcome Death; but Death won't have him. The revellers then demand, with threats, that he tell them where Death can be found. He directs them to follow a crooked road to a grove nearby; they will find Death waiting under a tree. They do as he says; but what they find is almost eight bushels of fine gold coins.

After this they forget all about Death and set about ways of guarding the money for themselves. It is decided by lot that two will stay with the gold while the third goes into town to buy food for the (overnight?) wait which they must count on for safety. While one is away the other two plan to kill him as soon as he returns; and he buys poison to put in one of the jugs of wine which he carries back to the grove. Both designs succeed and soon all three are dead.

Apparently carried away by his own eloquence, the Pardoner, having quickly concluded his sermon, invites his fellow pilgrims to come forward and make offerings; that is, he tries to treat them like his rural congregations. When he suggests—playfully or not—that the Host should begin, being the most involved in sin, the latter answers him angrily and abusively; finally the Knight insists on a reconciliation and the incident passes.

The Nun's Priest's Tale

The headnote (see pp. 1555–56) outlines the sequence of events in this tale; no further summary need be given here. The narrator is of course the Priest who accompanies the Prioress and her secretary on the pilgrimage. He is not described in the General Prologue, but Chaucer, in the line immediately preceding the tale, calls him "this goodly man, Sir John." With only this hint, the reader must form his or her own impression of the man. There is little or nothing on which to build a physical image. On the other hand, much is indicated about personality, education, learning, temperament, and sense of humor—by the way in which he tells the story, including his acceptance of the Host's assignment.

Topics for Discussion

1. Of the Lawyer, the Franklin, and the Physician in the General Prologue, what remarks by Chaucer might indicate something less than total approval of each? Try to relate the qualifications to the portrait as a whole; bear in mind that these men are neither scoundrels nor saints.

2. In the Miller's Tale, how does the overall characterization of John, Alison, Nicholas, and Absalom make it plausible that each would act in the way the story tells it? Take into account such things as John's credulity and (qualified) respect for Nicholas's learning; Alison's youth and beauty; Absalom's naive taste in love songs.

3. Is the Miller's Tale pornography?
[This would involve an effort to define pornography, or at least to decide its essential feature(s). Is Chaucer's story ever suggestive or prurient? Or is it instead honest and forthright? The same questions might be asked in the discussion of Boccaccio's tale of Brother Alberto and Lisetta.]

4. The variety of aspects and settings in which death is referred to in the Pardoner's Tale.
[Consider: the bell heard by the three young men in the tavern (182); the waiter's talk about "a sly thief" (193); the resolution of the young men (210ff.); the talk of the mysterious old man (239ff.); his directing them to a grove (280); the pile of gold (288ff.); the apothecary's drug (362ff.); the (pretended) bit of friendly wrestling. When and where is there personification? (The use of a capital *D* is a clue.)]

Topics for Writing

1. Men and women of the Church.
[The Prioress, the Monk, the Friar, the Oxford Student, the Parson, and the Pardoner are described in the General Prologue. The Priest accompanying the nuns is characterized in the Prologue to his tale. The Oxford Student is a devoted cleric and serious scholar; the Parson is a diligent and faultless servant and moral guardian of his

parish. Chaucer's account of the Prioress is ambivalent: is it basically sympathetic? He admires the skill of the Friar and the Pardoner; but what is his judgment of them otherwise? After noting all these, come back to the Monk and try to assess Chaucer's estimate. Finally, dispose of the question, Was Chaucer in favor of the Church or opposed to it?]

2. Chaucer's pilgrims in Dante's *Inferno*.

[The headnote (see p. 1552) suggests that some of the rascals among them might have found a place in one or another of the subdivisions of the Eighth Circle, devoted to Fraud, or dishonesty. Choose several characters and discuss their fitness for such a category. Use both plain statements and indirect indications of both poets.]

3. The Nun's Priest's Tale as representative of Chaucer.

[Discuss such items as these: the quiet, friendly humor in the initial account of the widow's household; the husband-and-wife traits of the cock and hen; the irony of Chantecleer's refutation of Pertelote's counsel about dreams—and then following it; the narrator's evoking of topics like predestination or feminine advice—but not pursuing them; the final happy ending, and the moral.]

Further Reading

See also the reading suggestions in the anthology, p. 1558.

Gibaldi, Joseph, ed. *Approaches to Teaching Chaucer's* Canterbury Tales. In the MLA series Approaches to Teaching Masterpieces of World Literature. New York, 1980.

FRANÇOIS VILLON

Backgrounds

The first poem, a *ballade*, is often referred to in English as the "ballad of the Hanged." In Villon's time, and long after, the bodies of executed criminals were often left hanging indefinitely, exposed to the elements and to predatory birds. Without softening the macabre imagery associated with this situation, the poem combines with it the earnest prayer of repentance and the repeated lyrical refrain, " . . . pray God that He absolve us all."

The *Testament* is made up of a series of sections of uneven length, with loose transitions from one to another. Lines 1–48 express Villon's resentment of the harsh treatment he endured as a prisoner of Thibault d'Aussigny, bishop of Orleans—may God be as merciful to the bishop as Thibault was to Villon! It is said that we should pray for our enemies; hence, Villon will pray for Thibault in the manner of the Picards (who reputedly prayed not at all), or else in the language of Psalm 108, verse 7—which amounts to a satirical irony: "Let his days be few and let another take his office"! Lines 49–111 offer a serious prayer to Christ, express the poet's devotion to the Virgin Mary and his gratitude to King Louis, who released him from prison.

Lines 129–68: To be sure, Villon is a sinner; but, as the story of Alexander and Diomedes tells us, it is poverty and weakness that make criminals; prosperity would change many a sinner's way of life. Lines 201–328 combine regret for his heedless youth with a keen sense of the transience of life and the certainty of death, painful, solitary, desolate.

Lines 329–56: Here is the best known sequence of the entire poem, using the familiar motif, *Ubi sunt?* ("Where are they?"), which can be followed by a short or long series of names. Those Villon inserts here are still fairly well known: Heloise, Abelard, Bertha, mother of the emperor Charlemagne, and Joan of Arc. And here is the famous refrain, *Mais où sount les neiges d'antan?* ("But where are the snows of last winter?") After a passage omitted in our anthology comes a sequence parallel to the last named one, with a variation in the refrain, "So much blows away on the wind" (ll. 385–412).

The next sequence (ll. 413–560) begins with the universality of death and moves gradually to the soliloquy of the Helmet-seller, once a beautiful woman, now an unsightly crone—with her catalogue of physical decay. Lines 625–72 offer a disillusioned view of love between the sexes, with the refrain, "Lucky the man who has no part in it." Lines 833–909: Here are various bequests but especially the prayer which Villon composes for his mother's use, including the refrain, "In this faith I wan to live and die." Later sequences offer more bequests, including an inscription for the poet's grave, and a final series of stanzas with the refrain, "As he made his way out of the world."

The instructor may wish to talk with the class about the vivid, evocative imagery of the poem; about the medieval sense of sin expressed often in several contexts; and also about the not wholly muted human protest about the fate apparently imposed on mankind.

Topics for Discussion and Writing

1. What thought underlies the *Ubi sunt* ("Where are they") question found in Villon?
   [(That death ends everything, including, eventually, the fame achieved by great deeds—nothing remains but a bare name, if even that. But is the relation of this thought to the rest of the poem the same in Villon?)]

2. Compare and contrast the feelings about women and decay expressed in Villon's poem with those in the Baudelaire sequence below (pp. 2128–42).

Further Reading

See the suggestions in the anthology, p. 1622.

Everyman

Backgrounds

The longer form of the title is given early in the speech of the first character, the Messenger: "The Summoning of Everyman" to a final reckoning with God. The play is not divided into acts and scenes, but lines 1–183 serve as a framework and may be considered as the equivalent of a first act. After the Messenger's announcement, God in a speech of sixty-two lines declares his disappointment with mankind: His redemptive sacrifice on the cross is generally ignored, and the human situation seems to grow steadily worse. Hence He calls on Death to summon mankind to judgment. Everyman comes on stage and is given the summons by Death, who cannot be begged or bribed to delay Everyman's answer; instead, Everyman must prepare at once to go. Here Death leaves the stage and does not return.

Now Everyman asks a long series of his companions for their help; they begin with ready promises, only to renege when they learn where Everyman must go—so much for Fellowship, Kindred, and Goods (riches, wealth). Now (Everyman's) Good Deeds is willing to go with him but has been bound to the earth by Everyman's sins; she calls on Knowledge, who directs Everyman to Confession, who recommends Penance; after Everyman's earnest prayer of repentance and acceptance of penance, Good Deeds is released and now free to accompany Everyman. (That is, Everyman is now absolved of his sinful condition.) Strength, Discretion, Beauty, and the Five Wits will now assist Everyman (as long as he lives on earth)—that is, the natural endowments of human nature can now be directed rightly instead of sinfully. Five Wits lectures Everyman on the importance of the Priesthood; it is the priest who dispenses the seven holy sacraments of the Christian life. Everyman goes briefly offstage to receive holy communion and extreme unction. Soon Everyman grows weak; he learns that Strength, Discretion, Beauty, and the Five Wits (our familiar five senses, touch, sight, etc.) will not go with him into the cave of death; only Good Deeds will do so and thereby assure his acceptance in heaven—which is announced by an angel (probably a voice off stage).

Everyman is a supreme example of a literary work with allegorical characters, that is, not individual men and women but personified abstractions or generic groups such as Fellowship or Kindred or Goods or Good Deeds. As we have seen in other pieces, allegory was a favorite pattern of literature in the Middle Ages. Our headnote shows that the abstract characters of *Everyman* may speak on stage very brisk, crisp, sharp dialogue. The action also moves rapidly and purposefully. It is clear, on reflection, that the play dramatizes the central moral or spiritual situation of the Christian believer, or, at any rate, the medieval Christian. Absorbed by the business and pleasures of earthly life, he (or she) may not often remember the inevitability of death and the certainty of divine judgment. A sudden reminder may alarm and presently disillusion; there follows a genuine realization that "you can't take it"—or "them" (other persons with whom your own life seems inseparably involved)—with you. The desertion of Everyman by one after another of his cherished companions is a poignant experience shared by the reader or spectator.

Topics for Discussion and Writing

1. The role of Strength, Discretion, Beauty, and the Five Wits.
   [It is noted immediately after Everyman's reorientation that they will now direct and assist him on his journey. But when he approaches the cave of Death, they too, like his earlier companions, depart and leave him. What realities of human life do the two stages of their relationship represent? In what sense can it be said that Good Deeds, alone, goes with Everyman into the grave?]

2. Why are Fellowship, Kindred, and good effective figures in the play?
   [They at first cheerfully promise to go with Everyman on his projected journey—without bothering to ask where he must go. When they learn his destination (Death and the Judgment of God), they promptly renege, one after the other. This desertion is a poignant experience for Everyman—and for the reader or spectator as well.]

3. Compare *Everyman* with the twentieth-century play (or film) *You Can't Take It with You*.
   [In both there is a withdrawal from the usual pattern of life in the world. The cause or motivation is different, but the result is a readjustment in both cases, and the two are not entirely dissimilar.

The defense of the new perspective in the dialogue of the modern piece might correspond to the (religious) reordering in Everyman.]

Further Reading

See the reading suggestions in the anthology, p. 1639.

Masterpieces of the Renaissance

FRANCIS PETRARCH

Backgrounds

Petrarch's collection of lyric poetry is known as the *Canzoniere* ("Song Book") and sometimes also as the *Rime sparse* ("Scattered Rhymes"), a title taken from line 1 of the introductory sonnet. Neither of the two is Petrarch's title; his own had been, significantly, in Latin— *Rerum Vulgarium Fragmenta*, "fragments" written in the "vulgar" tongue, i.e., current poetic Italian as opposed to Latin.

The main image of Petrarch, as it has been through the centuries and justifiably remains, is that of the author of sonnets written in honor of his beloved Laura or somehow related to that central experience. Our selections belong wholly to that category. It should be noted, however, that the *Canzoniere* comprises in all 366 poems numbered by the poet himself; and though an overwhelming majority of these are sonnets (317), many are written in other forms, notably the much longer and metrically varied *canzone*, of which there are 29. Still other forms represented in the collection are the sestina (9), the ballad (7), and the madrigal (4). Excellence in the poetic art was closely identified in Petrarch's day with technical skill in handling a number of verse patterns and in achieving variety within strict metrical norms. It was also closely identified with music. "Lyric" poetry is named for "lyre," a musical instrument; *canzone* is the Italian for "song"; and the root of the word "sonnet" is in the Latin *sonus*, "sound." Musical accompaniment was regularly seen as part of the "performance" of a poem; in fact, sonnets by Petrarch have been set to music up to our own century.

The ordering of the *Canzoniere* was made by the poet himself; to see it exclusively as a poetic diary of his love for Laura from its inception through its countless modulations to her death and to the continuing celebration of her image is to forget that not all of the *Canzoniere* is devoted to Laura. Sonnets 136–138, to give a particularly extravagant example, are invectives against the papal court at Avignon; and the *canzone* numbered 78—one of the most famous poems in the Italian language—is a lament on politically divided Italy, with an exhortation to peace, in what we may call the mode of "cultural patriotism." (A significant quotation from this poem will be found in our Machiavelli selections, at the very close of *The Prince*.) These exceptions allowed for, however, it is fair to say that poems in praise of Laura alive make up the larger part of the collection, and poems commemorating her after death most of the rest.

During his life Petrarch was in contact, professionally and otherwise, with courts, the most memorable being that of the Pope at Avignon, in Provence. That region also provides the physical landscape against which Petrarch's love for Laura is imagined. His sonnets can be partly described as courtly love poetry in the sense that they originated in an aristocratic milieu.

Love poetry has, of course, a long tradition from remotest antiquity on. Petrarch's immediate and obvious antecedents are Dante and poets such as Guido Cavalcanti (cf. Dante, *Inferno* X. 52–72, and *Purgatorio* XXIV. 19 ff. [not included in the anthology]) and the Provençal "troubadours." Apart from quotations in Latin, the only non-Italian lines in the *Divine Comedy* are spoken by the poet Arnaut Daniel in his native Provençal tongue (*Purgatorio* XXVI. 140–147, [not included in the anthology]). Petrarch was also steeped, of course, in the culture of antiquity; and the major Latin love poets—Ovid, Tibullus—figure prominently among his sources.

Equally evident in his work are manifestations of the Christian tradition. One is the insistent connection that he makes between his love and the Passion of Christ, as shown in Sonnets 3 and 62. Another is his sense of love as guilt, in the expression of which he initiates the now-familiar Romantic image of the poet as lamenting sufferer. Closely related to both of these is his framework of repentance and confession as if after a sinful life. This, as found in the *Canzoniere*, has its chief source in the *Confessions* of St. Augustine, probably the most important influence in Petrarch's intellectual life. It would not be amiss, in fact, to think of the *Canzoniere* as Petrarch's own Confessions.

Our prose selection, the letter to Dionisio on the ascent of Mount Ventoux, is an allegory of the sinner's repentance and contrition under the decisive Augustinian influence.

Classroom Strategies

Undoubtedly the least useful strategy is to take the selections from the *Canzoniere* as parts of a poetic diary and follow the many failed attempts to reconstruct the work as an autobiographical love story. Petrarch had practical experience in matters of love—had, in fact, some illegitimate children by a mistress. But it is equally clear that his poems are not only a purification of love in its usual terrestrial senses, but are also conscious models of literary convention. The persons of the speaker and his beloved have almost as little historical identity as those of the author and the object of any popular love song. A practical way to cope with this problem, if the Dante selections in the anthology have been previously studied, is to attempt a comparison and contrast between the strictly unearthly view of Beatrice and whatever is earthly in the image of Laura. Also, as already mentioned, a complete "execution" of a Petrarchan sonnet is probably best imagined with musical accompaniment. At the very least, emphasis should be placed on the musicality of Petrarch's language; and it would be a good idea to have some of the poems read out loud in the original, vowel-rich Italian. (Italian pronunciation is easy to learn; and a colleague conversant with Italian may be available on campus.)

Topics for Discussion and Writing

1. The figure of the speaker of the poem and his varied attitudes between elation and despair.

2. The Petrarchan sonnet and its structure in comparison with the Shakespearean pattern. In particular, compare the endings of the sonnets and the relative effectiveness of Petrarch's closing lines, in Sonnet 90 for example, and that of the closing couplet in the Shakespearean form of the sonnet.

3. Choosing an appropriate passage from the *Paradiso* selections and one of the sonnets on Laura in death, indicate specific differences in the handling of the two feminine images.

4. Petrarch was a public man, a diplomat, and an extremely influential

poet. So was, for example, Sir Thomas Wyatt, who introduced the Petrarchan sonnet to England. (Of Wyatt's thirty sonnets, published in *Tottel's Miscellany*—the anthology of English poems published by Richard Tottel in 1557—ten are translations from Petrarch.) Would such a multidimensional individual be conceivable today?

5. Although we read Petrarch in translation, there is no reason why a topic for discussion shouldn't be (with possible comparisons to the situation in other national literatures) the part that a literary language may have in establishing or indeed creating the identity of a country.

Further Reading

See also the reading suggestions in the anthology, p. 1669.

Bergin, Thomas G. *Petrarch*. 1970.
A useful study by the Yale Italian scholar and translator of Dante, Petrarch, and other authors.

Bergin, Thomas G., ed. *Selected Sonnets, Odes and Letters*. 1966.
With introduction, principal dates in the life of Petrarch, and selected bibliography. A good source for further readings from Petrarch's works.

Harrison, Robert Pogue. *The Body of Beatrice*. 1988.
Chapter 5 is "The Death of Dante's Beatrice and the Petrarchan Alternative."

Donadoni, Eugenio. *A History of Italian Literature*. 1969.
See the chapters on Petrarch's life and on his Italian works. A standard, reliable account of the history of Italian literature, widely used as a textbook in Italian schools.

Trinkaus, Charles Edward. *The Poet as Philosopher: Petrarch and the Formation of Renaissance Consciousness*. 1979.
Examines how Petrarch's "poetic mentality penetrated and shaped his thought."

Wilkins, Ernest Hatch. *History of Italian Literature*. Revised by Thomas G. Bergin. 1974.

Chapter 10 is dedicated to Petrarch. One of the best among the few histories of Italian literature written in English. Professor Wilkins is also a renowned Petrarch scholar.

DESIDERIUS ERASMUS
The Praise of Folly

Backgrounds

The Praise of Folly is divided into four sections; our selections are from the first, second, and fourth parts. The work, originally written in Latin, is a satire for which the author has adopted, with tongue in cheek, the structure and manner of a public oration. The "goddess" Folly, after giving her own jocose genealogy as the illegitimate daughter of the god of wealth and plenty (Part I), describes the manner of her birth and identifies the symbolic persons who attend her as she appears before a varied assembly of listeners. She proceeds to declare herself (Part II) the true life-giving goddess on the ground that every man in the act of procreation inevitably makes a fool of himself—hence the very conception of life is Folly's doing. From this premise follows the conclusion that all truly human activity must necessarily contain the life-giving element of folly/foolishness. Folly conducts this argument colorfully, relying on such classic devices of oratory as rhetorical questions, apt quotations, and, above all, vivid anecdotes. Prominent among the targets of her satire are the Stoic philosophers, whose attempt to "purge the wise man of all strong emotions" (p. 1686) she naturally scorns. What could such a regimen result in but a "marble imitation of a man" unfit for any responsible position ("What army would want such a general? What woman such a husband?").

Not unaware of life's pains and disappointments, Folly prescribes as remedy a good measure of "foolish" self-love and self-deception. Here again, in a sequence of quick satirical strokes she celebrates the foolish and happy victims of deceit along with their deceivers. A doctor, for instance, "is honored . . . to the degree that he is impudent. Medicine . . . is a branch of the art of flattery as much as rhetoric is." As deceivers, lawyers rank next to doctors:

> Perhaps they should be placed first, but I hesitate to join the philosophers, who unanimously laugh at lawyers as being so many asses. Nevertheless, all affairs, both great and small, are arbitrated by these asses. Their lands increase; while the theologian, who has mastered a trunkful of manuscripts, lives on beans, and wages a gallant war against lice and fleas . . . . (p. 1548)

Asses, in other words, wait upon other asses, and "the happiest man is the one who is most thoroughly deluded" (p. 1692). Other categories of foolish but happy maniacs are listed and illustrated in as many brilliant little sketches—hunters, gamblers, nobility buffs, the superstitious.

At this point the speaker—quite transparently a mouthpiece for Erasmus the Christian humanist—shifts to religious "superstitions," to "things . . . that are so foolish that I am almost ashamed of them myself . . . ," such as the belief in the specific powers of particular saints: "One gives relief from toothache, another aids women in labor, a third recovers stolen goods. . . . Some are helpful in a number of difficulties, especially the Virgin Mother, whom the common people honor more than they do the Son" (p. 1694). Further on, in the same vein: "You will also see more devotion being paid to such fabulous and poetic saints as George, Christopher, or Barbara than to Peter or Paul or even to Christ Himself" (p. 1696).

The culminating association between religious piety and Folly occurs in the final section, where the character of the "Christian Fool" is depicted. Showing in familiar scriptural quotations Christ's preference for the meek and simple-minded, Folly claims among her followers the Savior himself, who, "although He possessed the wisdom of the Father, became something of a fool in order to cure the folly of mankind" (p. 1699). Along this line, in the grand finale of her oration, Folly vividly describes the experience of the mystic and defines it as "that portion of folly" that will not be taken away by death and as "something very like madness," a "madness" that is only "the slightest taste of the happiness hereafter." She realizes at this point, however, that she has forgotten who she is and has "run out of bounds," and comes to the gracefully ironical and self-deprecating conclusion of her "hodgepodge of words" (p. 1702).

The Praise of Folly, though it is far and away Erasmus's most popular work, occupies a very small place within the wide range of his activity as a writer, scholar, translator, editor, theologian, and polemicist. He is said to have completed it in a week (citing the quotations from memory) while he was the guest of Thomas More at Bucklersbury in the autumn of 1509 and possibly for this reason is also said to have ascribed little value to it. Whatever the truth may be in this regard, the piece is as impressive in its learning and as sober in its implications as anything he ever wrote. There is no doubt either about its literary merits, the elegance and liveliness of its language, the gusto of its author's droll inventions. Behind the humorous facade, Erasmus familiarity with the great texts of the ancient and the medieval worlds—with the Greco-Roman as well as with the Judeo-Christian tradition—is fully visible. More particular models may also be cited. From the ancient world, the Greek satirist Lucian, some of whose work Erasmus had translated into Latin, and, from Erasmus's own time, Sebastian *Brant's Ship of Fools* (*Narrenschiff*, 1497), of which there was a Latin translation in 1500, an English one in 1509.

Classroom Strategies

Our selection can be managed in one assignment. As with Petrarch and most other authors in this section, it may be advisable to explore first the degree to which the class is acquainted with the main elements of the Greco-Roman and the Judeo-Christian traditions. Questions on mythological concepts and themes, such as "Zeus/Jove, father of the gods," or on the historical conflicts between Roman Catholic and Protestant churches in the period of the Reformation will yield information on how to proceed. A basic point to be stressed is that at the time Christianity was also politics, religious divisions and doctrinal controversy being everywhere rampant. Discussions of the meaning of the Reformation and Counter-reformation may need to be elicited together with class views of the function of satire—both in that era and in our own. Ensuing discussion should bring out the point that Erasmus favored direct contact with Scripture and a return to a simpler purified ritual. In examining the passages about "superstitious" Christian practices, it will be clear that he had particularly the Roman Catholic Church in mind. Unlike the extreme reformers, however, he wished to preserve the unity of the Church and to improve it from within so he was also well received in papal circles. Under the polemical, flippant surface, it is important to detect the wise and conciliatory nature of Erasmus piety. At the same time, beneath that surface, it is important to note the home thrusts at absurdities still very much with us today.

Topics for Discussion and Writing

1. Take what seem to be the most memorable objects of Folly's mockery (the Stoics, the Roman Catholic Church, various categories of fools and maniacs, etc.) and ask the class to explain by what means the satirical effects are obtained.

2. Satire may work in two opposite directions at the same time—that is to say, both criticize and undercut the criticism; both praise and undercut the praise. Work on specific passages to see how this happens. Give special attention to the handling of wisdom versus foolishness.

3. The presence of the author is sometimes more, sometimes less detectable under the mask of Folly. With particular emphasis on the selection from Part IV, identify passages where the author's presence shows clearly.

4. Satire has been described as presupposing, in the object satirized, some sort of deviation from an accepted or even ideal norm. Discuss what norms can be inferred from a reading of *The Praise of Folly*—what kinds of acts and attitudes, in other words, does the author value?

Further Reading

See also the reading suggestions in the anthology, pp. 1681–82.

Bainton, Roland H. *Erasmus of Christendom*. 1969.
An illustrated biography, with emphasis on Erasmus as a Christian philosopher. With notes and bibliography.

De Molen, Richard L., ed. *Erasmus of Rotterdam: A Quincentennial Symposium*. 1971.
Of particular relevance to the problems of Erasmus's religiosity are the essays "Erasmus the Reformer" and the annotated translation of "A Devout Treatise on the Pater Noster." With notes and selected bibliography, plus a brief chronology of the major events in Erasmus's life.

Huizinga, Johan. *Erasmus and the Age of Reformation*. Translated by F. Hopman. 1957.
A thorough, illustrated study, originally published in 1924, of Erasmus's life and career by the famous author of *The Waning of the Middle Ages*. Chapter IX deals with *The Praise of Folly*.

Olin, John C. *Six Essays on Erasmus.* 1979.
Essay 4 is on *The Praise of Folly.*

Thompson, Geraldine. *Under Pretext of Praise: Satiric Mode in Erasmus' Fiction.* 1973.
A study of Erasmus's fiction with emphasis on Erasmus as an educator and on his use of irony. Chapter II deals with the *Praise of Folly* as a parody as well as a moral indictment of European society in Erasmus' time.

Tracy, James D. *The Politics of Erasmus: A Pacifist Intellectual and His Political Milieu.* 1978.
Erasmus's place in European intellectual history as a political philosopher, with emphasis on the "national matrix" of his political opinions.

Zweig, Stefan. *Erasmus of Rotterdam.* 1934.
By an eminent novelist and biographer.

NICCOLO MACHIAVELLI
The Prince

Backgrounds

The Prince in a very general sense belongs to the same category as *The Book of the Courtier*, presenting sets of instructions and ultimately the description of an ideal type (the "employer" of the courtier, as it were). Yet from the very first brief chapter a briskly didactic tone differentiates it unmistakably from Castiglione's work:

All the states and governments that ever had or now have power over men were and are of two sorts: either republics or princely states. And princely states also are of two sorts: either hereditary . . . or else new. And the new ones are either brand-new . . . or they are like grafts freshly joined to the hereditary states of a prince. . . . New acquisitions of this sort are either accustomed to living under a prince, or used to being free; they may be acquired either by force of other people's arms or with one's own, either by fortune or by strength [*virtù*].

To each of the twenty-six chapters of *The Prince*, Machiavelli gave a strictly undecorative explanatory title, originally in Latin, then the standard language of scholarly communication. The style of the work makes it one of the supreme examples of vigor and originality in the history of Italian prose. The general distribution of the material is announced in Chapter 1. Chapter 2 takes up hereditary princedoms. Chapters 2 and 3 deal with the conquest and maintenance of new provinces by a state already possessing its own structure and form of government. Chapters 6 through 9 handle newly formed princedoms acquired by the force of arms (6–7), by crime (8), or by the choice of fellow citizens (9). Chapter 10, as a kind of corollary, discusses the military defense of such newly formed states. Chapter 11 moves to "ecclesiastical states," i.e. the dominions of the pope, their unusual nature, and the vast current power of the papacy. Chapters 12 through 14 examine what to Machiavelliand to most modern statesmen—is the major problem in the government of a state—the organization of its armed forces. According to Machiavelli, the prince must not enlist mercenaries but rather have his own armies, the art of war being the only one that pertains to a sovereign. Chapters 15 through 23, in turn, concentrate on the qualities and codes of behavior that should characterize an efficient ruler and inspire his conduct. The uses of praise and blame, of liberality and stinginess, of cruelty and clemency, and finally of keeping or not keeping promises are expressed in a form so definitive and lucid that they can hardly be summarized. For a specimen, see the second paragraph of Chapter 18, which is possibly the most famous and controversial passage in the history of political writing.

Criteria of efficiency and political expediency pervade the advice given to the prince in Chapters 19 through 24. These treat such diverse matters as how to avoid contempt and hatred (19); the utility of protecting the city-state with fortresses (20); the means to acquire a prestigious reputation, the dangers of neutrality, and the recognition to be granted artists and men of talent (21); the way to select and judge private counselors (22), with a corollary on avoiding flatterers (23). Chapter 24 concentrates on the present situation of Italian princedoms and prepares for the last two chapters, where, as indicated more elaborately in our headnote (see p. 1704), the "realistic" and the "poetic" methods are mingled.

The origin of *The Prince* is best described in Machiavelli's letter to Francesco Vettori (pp. 1580–81). Vettori, a prominent public figure under the Medici, was a friend and frequent correspondent of Machiavelli's, in spite of political divergencies; he had been instrumental in obtaining from Pope Leo X (Giovanni de' Medici) Machiavelli's release from imprisonment (cf. our headnote), followed by his confinement to the small estate he owned near Florence, where he wrote *The Prince.* From early in 1513, Machiavelli had begun the writings that were eventually to become his *Discourses on the First Ten Chapters of Livy,* the culminating result of his meditations on Roman history and of his passionate interest in its teachings. In Machiavelli's case, as we know, the strict meaning of Renaissance as the "rebirth" of ancient culture has a particularly concrete validity; for him, the Romans offered supreme models in all areas of human endeavor, most particularly as examples of that political and military competence that in the princes of contemporary Italy he found wanting.

The reasons generally given for Machiavelli's interruption of the *Discourses* to write *The Prince* between July and December of 1513 are highly speculative. Possibly once launched on the task of political analysis, he felt an understandable urge to draw on his own experiences as a political man and observer of political events in his own time and place. Possibly, too, he hoped that his political sagacity as shown in *The Prince* would capture the attention of the dominant Medici family and bring him a new employment with them.

Machiavelli's sources are mainly his readings in ancient history and his own political experience. Though *The Prince* has resemblances, as noticed earlier, to the established genre of the manual of instruction, its matter, manner, and impact put it beyond easy classification. In Castiglione, our previous instance of this kind of literature, apparent similarities of content and conception only put the differences in sharper focus. Castiglione was not unaware of the uses of power, and his courtier's highest manifestation of loyalty is the service of his prince on the battlefield. But his accent falls on the esthetic aspect of human actions, on "style" in performance, and on government of the inner man rather than government of other men. In Machiavelli, on the other hand, even the final "Roman dream" has its roots in his practical notion of Roman political competence, efficiency, and military preparedness.

Classroom Strategies

The Prince offers no special textual difficulties. Its statements, however startling, are as cuttingly clear as anything in political writing. The examples drawn from history may be puzzling inasmuch as they refer to particular and often obscure episodes; yet the contexts in which they are presented, plus our footnotes, should suffice to suggest the type of situation and the theme they illustrate. Maps may be helpful, not to teach geography or history, but to create in the student's mind some concrete idea of the location and respective sizes of such political entities of the day as the Kingdom of France, the Papal States, and the larger Italian city-states. As for the "moral" aspects of Machiavelli's teachings, a look forward to the "devilish" Machiavelli image through the centuries and particularly to the Elizabethan stage "Machiavel" may be in order. Finally, here as always, reading significant passages out loud will help bring out the dramatic aspect of Machiavelli's prose.

Topics for Discussion and Writing

1. Granted that Machiavelli's own historical context is remote, how far does his pattern of contrasts between political ideals and con-

crete realities apply today? What do modern rulers of states mean by *realpolitik*?

2. Attempt to define in specific passages the borderline between "realism" (practical advice, emphasis on military preparedness, etc.) and "myth" (the ideally equipped leader, the mirage of a unified Italian state). A close analysis of the last chapter, or even only of its last two paragraphs, may be one of many ways to see how the terms of that contrast can coexist, as it were, in the same breath.

3. Taking specific passages from *The Prince*, identify the characteristics that make Machiavelli's style effective.

4. Discuss the extent of Machiavelli's "amorality," and his basic alibi that "if man were good . . . ."

5. Compare and contrast Machiavelli's idea of Fortune with the religious idea of man's free will and, on the other hand, with the meaning of "luck" when we refer to a contemporary political leader as being lucky.

Further Reading

See also the reading suggestions in the anthology, p. 1705.

Anglo, Sydney. *Machiavelli: A Dissection*. 1969.
A study of Machiavelli's works and political thought through analysis and quotations from his works; with bibliography. Hale calls this book "refreshingly iconoclastic but somewhat too tart."

Bondanella, Peter E., and Mark Musa, eds. *The Portable Machiavelli*. 1979.
A good general introduction to Machiavelli's life and works. The introduction is brief and cogent, and includes sections on the historical context of *The Prince*, politics and history in Machiavelli, and on Machiavelli today. A good anthology with ample possibilities for further readings.

Hulliung, Mark. *Citizen Machiavelli*. 1983.
Separates Machiavelli from the tradition of "civic humanism" and describes him as "the first and one of the greatest subversives of the humanist tradition."

Mazzeo, Joseph Anthony. *Renaissance and Revolution: The Remaking of European Thought*. 1965.
See the chapter on Machiavelli.

Pitkin, Anna F. *Fortune Is a Woman: Gender and Politics in the Thought of Machiavelli*. 1984.
A study of Machiavelli "in terms of ambivalence about manhood."

Pocock, J. G. A. *The Machiavellian Moment*. 1975.
See particularly Chapter VI, B, "Machiavelli's *Il Principe*." An attempt to "selectively and thematically define . . . the moment, and the manner, in which Machiavelli's thought made its appearance within the specific historical context of the Florentine republic"

Wilkins, Ernest Hatch. *A History of Italian Literature*. Revised by Thomas G. Bergin. 1974.
Chapter 23 deals with Machiavelli and Guicciardini.

BALDESAR CASTIGLIONE
The Book of the Courtier

Backgrounds

The Book of the Courtier is a book of etiquette meant to be useful to
gentlemen (and ladies) who lived and worked at court in the service of
aristocratic rulers of states. Its form, traditional in Renaissance literature,
is that of a dialogue, or more precisely of a conversation. Even more
specifically, it is a transcription, formalized but nonetheless brilliant and
sometimes witty, of after-dinner talk among people well versed in the
customs and requirements of court life. Its style in the original has long
been regarded as a model of proper Renaissance Italian, classically
formal and yet supple and graceful. Its larger setting is one of the states
that composed the mosaic of the then-divided Italy, the duchy of Urbino.
Its narrower setting may be imagined to be one of the halls in Urbino's
splendid ducal palace. The conversationalists, or dramatis personae, are
assembled from different parts of Italy and represent some of the most
illustrious families in their respective city-states: a Gonzaga from Man-
tua, a Bembo from Venice, a Medici from Florence. The local ruler, the
duke of Urbino, Guidobaldo da Montefeltro, is irremediably ill and has
the habit of retiring early. Hence the evenings at court, with their conversations and games, are ruled over by the authoritative but gentle duchess
Elisabetta, who often delegates her authority to the countess Emilia, née
Gonzaga, one of her ladies-in-waiting. One such evening is imagined by
Castiglione to have been the origin of his famous work. Various forms of
entertainment are suggested by different members of the party; the one
chosen, somewhat unexpectedly, is a purely intellectual "game" proposed by a count Federico Fregoso from Genoa. The "game" will consist
in composing, through well-regulated debate, a description of the qualities and functions of a worthy courtier, or indeed of "forming with words
a perfect Courtier."

The work is divided into four parts corresponding to the four evenings
of the debate. Part I, after the exordium and the choice of the "game,"
describes the qualities and capacities required of the model courtier, from
the indispensable nobility of his birth to his dexterity in his major pro-
fessionthe handling of arms in war, in dueling, and in peaceful tourna-
ments. There follow rules and recommendations concerning physical and

moral virtues, speech, manners, generosity, the ornaments of culture and the arts. Book II partially elaborates on and perfects some of the themes of Book I, adding details on music, dance, gracefulness, benevolence, humaneness, and the art of conversation, including counsel on how to handle, in the proper measure, word play, jokes, irony, witty repartee, and *burle* (practical jokes). Book III discusses the *Donna di Corte* or *Donna di Palazzo*, i.e. the lady-in-waiting or other female member of the court. The qualities, education, and norms of behavior appropriate to her are elaborated on in their similarities to and their differences from those of the male courtier. Examples of feminine excellence are taken from all ages and praised; immodesty and ostentatiousness are blamed.

The first part of Book IV deals with the ways in which the courtier, who is not only a loyal subordinate but also a wise counselor to his prince, may conquer the latter's good graces by advising him wisely on such varied matters as war and peace, the active and contemplative life, justice, magnanimity, religion without superstition, and the respective merits of different forms of government. The latter part of the book centers on the sentiment and practice of love by the courtier, in youth and in old age, and finds its culmination in Pietro Bembo's discourse on earthly love transforming to divine love, just as the work itself moves from matters of civilized behavior to concerns of the soul. Our selections, both from Book I, contain the most classic and influential passages on the nature and accomplishments of the courtier. Of the "Words" that, according to the announced purpose, shall "form" the ideal picture of the courtier, some are key terms, particularly "grace" and *sprezzatura*, a Castiglione coinage usually translated as "nonchalance." (For further definition, see below.)

The "courtesy book" as a genre was common in Renaissance culture. The form goes back to Plato's dialogues, and "Platonism" in a generic sense is to be found also in Castiglione's aiming at an ideal form (the *perfect* courtier). But the major source of Castiglione's treatise is, of course, his own experience as a courtier. Though much of that experience in its practical results was negative and disappointing (see the biographical data in the anthology, p. 1718), Castiglione continued to pursue his established aim through his long years of labor on the book with an ever-increasing tendency to idealize what was rarely ideal.

Classroom Strategies

A major difficulty in teaching Castiglione is the remoteness of the society and customs he depicts. On the other hand, *The Book of the Courtier* offers a splendid opening for discussions of the practical usefulness of utopias in establishing an ideal, however unattainable, and of the other kinds of "how-to" books in which our own age abound. The *Book*'s own description of its courtly milieu may be enhanced by obtaining from your art department illustrations of the place (the ducal palace at Urbino) and some of the participating characters (e.g.; the portrait of Castiglione himself by Raphael or Piero della Francesca's portrait of the duke of Montefeltro). One may also bring the participants closer by reminding the class that they are, in their way, simply government officials in an age when aristocrats had the responsibilities of public office.

The other possible stumbling block—the artificiality of Castiglione's dialogue—should not be exaggerated. The custom of orchestrated conversation survives even in modern times, not only in the society represented, say, in the first chapter of *War and Peace*, but also in such contemporary institutions as the panel or round-table discussion or the television talk show. Moreover, since a large part of our selections concerns the courtier's achieving such expertise in the arts of dueling and dance that he can exercise them without apparent effort—i.e. with *sprezzatura*, Olympic sports activities offer a wide range of comparisons.

Topics for Discussion and Writing

1. On the assumption that the students have read the Boccaccio selections in the anthology, a clarifying discussion can center on the characters in the *Courtier* as compared and contrasted with those who take turns telling each other tales in the *Decameron*.

2. A parallel topic can center on the function of the "frame" story as an organizing element in both works.

3. Discuss the individual qualities given to the main characters in the *Book of the Courtier*, considering also such matters as differences in age and personal history.

4. Attempt a definition of *sprezzatura* more detailed and inclusive than the simple, approximate translation as "nonchalance."

5. Define the likenesses and differences in the ideal of Renaissance man as presented by Castiglione and Machiavelli.

Further Reading

See also the reading suggestions in the anthology, p. 1719.

Hanning, Robert W., and David Rosand, eds. *Castiglione: The Ideal and the Real in Renaissance Culture.* 1983.
Among the ten excellent essays in this collection, the following are perhaps of greatest relevance to our discussion: Chapter 1 (Thomas M. Greene, "*Il Cortegiano* and the Choice of a Game"), Chapter 4 (Eduardo Saccone, "*Grazia, Sprezzature, Affettazione* in *the Courtier*"), Chapter 7 (Robert W. Hanning, "Castiglione's Verbal Portrait: Structures and Strategies"), and Chapter 10 (Louise George Clubb, "Castiglione's Humanistic Art and Renaissance Drama").

Wilkins, Ernest Hatch. *History of Italian Literature.* Revised by Thomas G. Bergin. 1974.
See chapter 24, "Castiglione and Other Prose Writers."

Woodhouse, J. R. *Baldesar Castiglione.* 1978.
A "reassessment of *The Courtier*," the book opens with chapters on life at court and the courtly educational ideal. There follow individual analyses of the four books of the *Courtier* and the subjects with which they deal.

MARGUERITE DE NAVARRE
The Heptameron

Backgrounds

For an account of the "frame story" as given in the prologue of the *Heptameron*, see the latter part of the headnote, pp. 1733–44. A definitive text of Marguerite de Navarre's collection has not been established and probably never will be, owing to the situation of manuscripts (seventeen of them exist, not at all identical in the numbering and ordering of the stories included) and of early printed editions. The first printed edition appeared in 1558, nine years after Marguerite's death, edited by a prominent scholar, Pierre Boaistuau, under the title *Histories of Fortunate Lovers*. The present title appeared a year later in *Héptaméron des Nouvelles*, a printed edition done by Pierre Gruget, who divided the stories into "Days" with ten stories each and gave more space to prologues and dialogues, although he censored some names and passages, as well as three entire stories that had to do with the corruption of Franciscan monks. Among the manuscript texts, the one produced by the scholar Adrien de Thou in 1553 is of particular interest; oddly enough, it "calls itself *Le Décaméron* of Marguerite, and seems to leave empty pages for missing tales to complete the hundred implied in the title" (P. A. Chilton).

Even from these sketchy notes it is clear that a definitive canon of the stories does not exist. Details are available in Chilton's introduction to his translation (see the anthology, p. 1734), which is based on the best available scholarship and contains seventy-two stories, ten for each of seven days and two for a barely started eighth day. Each "Day," in addition to its prologue, has a long title that summarily indicates the type of stories it contains. The First Day, from which our first selection is taken, announces "A Collection of Low Tricks Played by Women on Men and by Men on Women." Our second selection is from the Third Day, entitled "Of Ladies Who Have Goodness and Purity in Love and of the Hypocrisy and Wickedness of Monks." The general title for the Fourth Day, from which our third selection is taken, is "Principally of the Virtue and Long-Suffering of Ladies in the Winning Over of Their Husbands, and of the Prudence of Men with Respect to Their Wives for

---

the Preservation of the Honour of Their House and Lineage."

Marguerite de Navarre presents a peculiar type of storytelling, as each story is followed by a discussion of its moral and social implications among the storytellers themselves; thus we have something of a mixture of two genres, the short story and the treatise in the form of a dialogue or conversation. A major example of the latter is Castiglione's *Book of the Courtier* (see p. 1719 in the anthology). For the short story as Marguerite handles it, three precedents can be indicated: the medieval *fabliau*—a short tale in verse form, typically with a humorous and bawdy subject; the *lai*, a longer narrative in verse form, an example of which is Marie de France's Eliduc (see p. 1216 in the anthology); and most importantly the *novella*, of which the major medieval exponent was Boccaccio (see p. 1467). Boccaccio's *Decameron* had first been translated into French by Laurent Premierfait in 1414; a new translation, mentioned in the prologue to the *Heptameron*, was commissioned by Marguerite herself and done by a member of the court of Francis I, Antoine Le Maçon; it came out in 1545.

Classroom Strategies

Marguerite's stories present no difficulties in terms of plot development and narrative sequence. As for their content, particularly with regard to the codes implied in the characters' behavior, it may be in order always to keep in mind some basic facts. This is a group of people who belong to the higher echelons of aristocratic society, indeed to the inner circle of royalty, at a time of kings "by divine right" and of extremely classified societies; whether they tell stories about their peers (which sometimes verge on the "juicy piece of gossip") or about characters of inferior social status, they act as people who do not feel bound by common standards of judgment but who have established standards that are valid for persons of their own rank.

Hence the literary qualities of the stories, the naturalness with which they handle such otherwise potentially shocking situations as overt matrimonial infidelity, incest, assassination, the cuckolding of a king, or the bawdiness of a monk. This general attitude is reflected in the relative simplicity and directness of Marguerite's narrative manner. Discussion of it may present good opportunities to familiarize students with such notions as objectivity in fiction, point of view, and authorial comment. Actually, Marguerite's manner and technique may prove to be more subtle than they appear at first, especially in the relationship between the stories themselves and the commentary that follows each of them. It could be pointed out that the conversations among the characters, all of them narrators in turn, ultimately create a variety of "voices" or "points of view" for the same fictional material; hence Marguerite's narrative, however deceptively simple, may turn out to be quite sophisticated and "modern."

Topics for Discussion and Writing

1. Compare the handling of "bawdy" materials in our first two selections and in Boccaccio's Second Tale of the Fourth Day (see p. 1482 in the anthology). Compare, especially from the point of view of style in narrative and in dialogue, the handling of love and matrimonial situations in our third selection and in Boccaccio's Ninth Tale of the Fifth Day (p. 1488).

2. The characters of Parlamente and Hircan are generally identified with Marguerite herself and with her second husband, Henri de Navarre. Take these two characters' words as they appear in some of our quotes from the prologue (see the headnote in the anthology, p. 1732) and in the conversation following our third selection, and attempt to describe the implied notions of what constitutes a rational, successful matrimonial relationship in the world of the *Heptameron*. Also use contributions from other characters surrounding this central couple.

Further Reading

See also the reading suggestions in the anthology, p. 1734.

Gelernt, Jules. *World of Many Loves: The Heptameron of Marguerite de Navarre*. 1966.
    Views the work as a "Renaissance treatise on love" and traces in its background the "idealistic" line from courtly love to Renaissance neoplatonism and the "realist" tradition of the *novella*.

Kinney, Arthur F. *Continental Humanist Poetics*. 1989.
    See Chapter 4 on the *Héptaméron*.

Meijer, Marianne. "The *Héptaméron*: Feminism with a Smile." In *Regionalism and the Female Imagination*. 1977–78.
A short article from a contemporary point of view.

Norton, Glyn P. "Narrative Function in the *Héptaméron Frame-Story*." In *La Nouvelle Française à la Renaissance*, ed. by Lionello Sozzi and V. L. Saulnier. 1981.

FRANÇOIS RABELAIS
Gargantua and Pantagruel

Backgrounds

Gargantua and Pantagruel, as we know it now—whatever the history of its composition, the dates of its parts, and the authenticity of its final part—is an immense and seemingly chaotic work of fiction, divided into five books. It is possible, however, to extract an intelligible "story line" from the seemingly haphazard movements of its narrative course. The necessary premise to any successful encounter with it is that it operates on two levels—fantasy and realism—which are variously balanced and merged. The locale at the opening of Book I is a kingdom, for which Rabelais borrowed from Sir Thomas More the name of Utopia, but it is at the same time a large French country estate. The gigantic king-squire is Grangousier. He and his queen, Gargamelle, beget a giant-son, Gargantua, who enters the world from her left ear while she is lying in a meadow and who calls immediately for wine. After this comes the story of Gargantua's education in Paris. It is a story told in semi-fantastic, often comic terms, but tracing what was then a highly controversial transition from medieval scholasticism (a term whose meaning students should be asked to look up) to the subjects and methods of the "new" learning: see our selections from chapters 14–24 (pp. 1753–66).

Later on in Book I Gargantua will leave Paris, answering his father the king's summons to war. The so-called Picrochole War is a mock-heroic version of a country brawl between people of two neighboring estates, with, however, many of the characteristics of wars between nations. The cake-peddlers of nearby Linne ("King" Picrochole's domain) have refused to sell their wares to Grangousier's shepherds, one of whom knocks down a Picrochole baker. The "incident" is used by Picrochole as an excuse to invade Grangousier's territories, but his overblown "imperialistic" designs are thwarted by Gargantua's gigantic physical stature and power. (There are such vaguely pre-Swiftian details as his combing cannon balls out of his hair, or inadvertently eating several pilgrims in his salad.) Another valiant and picturesque war hero is the monk Friar John of the Funnels; after the enemy is conquered and pardoned, he is allowed as a reward to build the monastery of his dreams, the Abbey of Thélème (see chapters 52–57, pp. 1766–75).

Book II is Pantagruel's book. Like his father, Gargantua, Pantagruel is sent to Paris to study. The new learning now happily dominates, and Gargantua's letter to Pantagruel (pp. 1777–80) is a kind of manifesto of the proud intellectual achievements of the period. Shortly thereafter, a major new character makes his entrance—Panurge, the still-familiar type of student who grows in age without ever getting his degree: poor but generous; astute and malicious; an erudite and practical joker; and as much a proverbial figure in French literature as Pantagruel himself. The two young men become inseparable; their most significant adventure in Book II is the war against the Dipsodes (the root, the same as in "dipsomania," is Greek for "thirst"), who are conquered, Pantagruel becoming their king.

Book III introduces a question that pervades the rest of the work: should Panurge marry? To find out, Panurge and Pantagruel make several fantastic journeys to consult a sibyl, a poet, a magician, a doctor, and a philosopher. Finally a madman, Triboulet, advises them to seek the Oracle of the Holy Bottle. For that purpose, they go on further fantastic voyages, which take them, among other destinations, again in a pre-Swiftian manner—to the island of the Papefigues (Protestants or "Pope-snubbers") and the island of the Papimanes (Catholics or "Pope-enthusiasts"). Finally in Book V, taking a shortcut through the frozen ocean north of Canada, Panurge and Pantagruel reach Northern India and the subterranean location, under a vineyard planted by Bacchus, of the Holy Bottle. Its oracular response is the single word TRINCH ("DRINK!"). The assuaging of thirst, actual and also symbolical, physical and intellectual, proves to be the cultural metaphor of the entire work.

Before Rabelais made them heroes, raising them to a high place in the literary culture of France, Gargantua and Pantagruel existed as characters in French folklore. In other words, they already had the kind of house-hold popularity now enjoyed by some of our comic-strip heroes endowed with exceptional muscle and superhuman powers. In French folk-tradition, Gargantua was a gigantic figure famous for his exceptional voracity, while Pantagruel was a pleasant little devil whose favorite work was making men thirsty. It was Rabelais who, among many other innovations, made them father and son. The composition of *Gargantua and Pantagruel* was as leisurely as the work itself. The first of its parts to see the light was what is now Book II. This was published in 1532 under the pseudonym Alcofribas Nasier, an anagram of Rabelais' own name, with a long title, as was then the fashion: *The Horrible and Fearful Facts and*

Brave Deeds of the Renowned Pantagruel, King of the Dipsodes, Son of the Great Gargantua. It was intended as the continuation of a preceding anonymous book, *The Great and Inestimable Chronicles of the Great Giant Gargantua.* Rabelais' own and quite different *Gargantua*, the present Book I, was published two years later. Books III, IV, and the spurious Book V were published with considerable intervals between them (1547, 1552, 1564).

Rabelais' characters, apart from their folksy lineage, may be related to such previous literary giants as Morgante and Baldus, respective heroes of mock-heroic poems by Luigi Pulci (1432–1484) and Teofilo Folengo (1491–1544). Their attribute of longevity is, of course, traceable as far back as the heroes of Genesis. More generally, the disparate elements assembled in Rabelais's work are a reflection of his unique life experience (see p. 1750), his multiple occupations, and his extraordinary learning. Even a summary biography of the man throws light on the sources of the work: for the Abbey of Thélème, his experience with monastic life; for the education of the giants, his knowledge as a scholarly humanist and practicing physician; and so on.

Classroom Strategies

Like *The Praise of Folly*, Rabelais's work can help your classes learn how to detect serious ideas in comic and, in this case, particularly extravagant garb. The new reader may have some difficulty with the twists and turns that the author gives to such august texts as the Holy Scriptures—typically, for instance, in his handling of the biblical pattern of "begats" in tracing the genealogy of his heroes. The idea to be suggested and elaborated upon in such cases is that a humanist must be well at ease in a tradition (in this case the Judeo-Christian tradition: Rabelais, in however unorthodox a fashion, was a monk) before he can take the liberty of twisting and parodying that tradition. Laughter does not necessarily indicate disrespect, but often an affectionate familiarity. With Rabelais' mixture of realism and fantasy there should be no problem. Young audiences have long been trained in that area by science fiction and films. Our selections are intended to emphasize both the fundamental seriousness of Rabelais' purpose and the sheer fun to be derived from his method.

Topics for Discussion and Writing

1. It has been observed that in the course of the story Rabelais often seems to forget the gigantic size and superhuman nature of his characters. Find specific examples of this "oversight" and attempt to explain its significance (for instance, in Gargantua's letter to Pantagruel, we hardly think of father and son as supernatural giants).

2. Describe the implications of the fact that Pantagruel's kingdom is named Utopia. Discuss the idea that utopias are useful in showing the way to an unattainable perfection.

3. Discuss possible comparisons between Rabelais's and Erasmus's views of religious practices, comparing passages in which both seem to oppose pompous, exhibitionistic piety.

4. Compare Rabelais and Castiglione on the mental and physical education of a gentleman. Keep in mind that Pantagruel is also a prince, and receives the traditional education for his rank.

5. Discuss the idea that the Abbey of Thélème's orderly, pleasant life depends on an aristocratic sense of honor.

6. Although Rabelais wouldn't have known the phrase, *Gargantua and Pantagruel* can be called in part a "generational novel." What are possible similarities and contrasts with the generation gap as we experience it in our own time? Discuss the role of one single humanistic or scientific change in altering the outlook of our own period.

Further Reading

See also the reading suggestions in the anthology, p. 1752.

Bowen, Barbara C. *The Age of Bluff: Paradox and Ambiguity in Rabelais and Montaigne.* 1972.

Coleman, Dorothy G. *Rabelais: A Critical Study in Prose Fiction.*
1971.
An in-depth study of "the richness of Rabelais's vocabulary and
the galvanizing dynamics of his style," as well as of "some of the
general orientations of his work," his characters, choice of form,
and so on.

Cruickshank, John, ed. *French Literature and Its Background.* Vol.1,
The Sixteenth Century. 1968.
Chapter 2, by G. D. Josipovici, is dedicated to Rabelais.

Febvre, Lucien Paul Victor. *The Problem of Unbelief in the Sixteenth
Century: The Religion of Rabelais.* Translated by Beatrice Gott-
lieb. 1982.
A thorough treatment of the question of Rabelais's religious ideas
in relation to the time in which he lived, by an important French
scholar.

Losse, Deborah N. *Rhetoric at Play: Rabelais and Satirical Eulogy.*
1980.
Quite specialized, with quotations in the original French.

Screech, M. A. *Looking at Rabelais.* 1988.
An Oxford lecture by an eminent Rabelais scholar.

MICHEL DE MONTAIGNE
Essays

Backgrounds

Montaigne's *Essays* are divided into three books, each containing a different number of essays of widely varying lengths and, of course, subjects (fifty-seven in Book I, thirty-seven in Book II, thirteen in Book III). The essays are designated as "chapters," a term that can be misleading, not only because a collection of essays is not a work of fiction but also of the ostensibly haphazard way in which the "chapters" follow one another. Each essay, therefore, would lend itself to individual mention and description. Yet some sense of progression and development can be detected.

Montaigne began to work on what was to become his famous collection of essays when he was thirty-eight years old and had already had considerable experience of the world. Retired now to the library of his castle, he had a private purpose in his writing—not, however, that of keeping a chronological diary but rather that of assembling a scrapbook in which to record passing thoughts and memorabilia. Thus the work began as a collection of rambling observations and meditations on Montaigne's readings, on events past and present, on general human attitudes, foibles, qualities, oddities. Many of his chapter or essay titles start with "Of" followed by the name of a human virtue, vice, custom, etc. "Of" sorrow (I, 2), idleness (I, 8), liars (I, 9), fear (I, 17), pedantry (I, 24), friendship (I, 27), sleep (I, 44), smells (I, 55), drunkenness (II, 2), conscience (II, 5), the affection of fathers for their children (II, 8), riding post (II, 22), anger (II, 31). Such titles, as well as those featuring maxims or proverbs—"That the Study of Philosophy Is to Learn to Die" (I, 19), "That We Laugh or Cry for the Same Thing" (I, 37), "That Our Desires Are Augmented by Difficulties" (II, 15), "Cowardice, the Mother of Cruelty" (II, 27), "All Things Have Their Season" (II, 28)—introduce essays showing the same qualities of casual progression as the work as a whole and coming to the justification of their titles in comfortable, roundabout ways. Our selection from Book I, for instance, the famous essay "On Cannibals," opens with a little episode from Roman history, then mentions the unnamed friend who had spent a long time in a section of Brazil and relates to the author some observations made there; gradu-

---

ally, but only gradually, the focus shifts to the main subject, cannibals, and to the personal acquaintance of the author with one of them. The author seems able to maintain a detached, often ironical attitude throughout, however bizarre or horrible his material.

That such an attitude may be ascribed to the influence of a particular philosophical system is doubtful; many not entirely successful attempts have been made to formalize Montaigne's thought, usually in terms of a progression from the Stoicism of his much-admired Seneca and an initial confidence in the authority of human reason, to a more balanced, temperate "natural philosophy" and a deep albeit undramatic contemplation of the limits of human judgment. The thirteen long chapters of Book III, written at a more advanced age and after new private and public experiences (such as Montaigne's four years as mayor of Bordeaux), would then be the ultimate statement of that wise "natural philosophy," not without touches of "Epicureanism." Though there is some truth in this, Montaigne remains a striking example of his own idea of the changeable nature of man; he has "slipped through the fingers of even the most daring critics," as he himself says of the Emperor Augustus. Hence the safer, simpler, and most obvious way to trace a line of development in the three books of the essays is to see it in terms of increased focusing on the individual Self. Our selections, however sketchily, exemplify such a progress, from Montaigne's early eclecticism to a consideration of mankind's "presumption and littleness," to the overtly central purpose of analyzing the exemplar at hand, himself.

The originator of the "essay" as a literary genre, Montaigne can hardly be said to have had predecessors in that form. His mode of writing can be related, however, to a kind of book very fashionable at the time: collections of informative bits of knowledge and wise sayings in all areas from grammar to geography, from mathematics to history, of which Erasmus's *Adagia* is perhaps the best surviving example. One of the major purposes of such collections, besides moral teaching, was to enable one to display one's familiarity with antiquity. They also exemplify a view of history, and particularly of Roman history, as a source of teachings and models of behavior—a view that in his own different way Montaigne entertained as enthusiastically as Machiavelli. Ancient Roman archetypes of the genre were found in such works as *Memorable Deeds and Sayings* by Valerius Maximus, a writer of the first century A.D., or in Aulus Gellius's *Attic Nights* (second century A.D.). In the shaping of Montaigne's thinking in the earlier parts of the *Essays*, a similar role may be attributed to the philosophical writings of the Stoic philosopher Seneca (ca. 50 B.C.–A.D. 40), while the way Montaigne handles historical characters testifies to his knowledge of and professed admiration for Plutarch (A.D. 45–ca. 125). Montaigne's deep familiarity with an enormous number of other possible "sources" is shown in the very abundance of his quotations from, and his opinions on, a wide range of writers. Naturally his most obvious source remains the observation of life and of himself.

Classroom Strategies

Readers new to Montaigne may be disturbed by the large number of quotations from texts with which they are unacquainted. The best way to cope with this reaction is to demonstrate the fitness of the quotation to its context. It should also be remembered that the passages Montaigne quotes were as familiar and commonplace to him as proverbs; memorizing well-turned sentiments from the classics was a normal school exercise at the time, and keeping a notebook of striking aphorisms was the habit of every educated adult male. The quotations supply a further coloring of universality to Montaigne's themes, most of which belong to all times and are demonstrably still very much with us—the relativity of the ideas of civilized and uncivilized behavior; the position of man in an ever more widely explored and yet mysterious universe; the complex, self-contradictory nature of human intelligence; and so on.

Analysis of Montaigne's texts also offers good ground for the discussion of literary style. Montaigne's great influence is due not only to his subject matter but also to his "tone of voice," the gait of his prose, and his tempered, ironical manner, which is both detached and yet very personal. It is an influence that extends even to such writings of our own day as the newspaper feature article and syndicated column, as well as to the "Talk of the Town" section in *The New Yorker*.

Topics for Discussion and Writing

1. Granted that it is impossible to extract from Montaigne's view of the world a well-organized philosophical "system," examine closely the meanings he attaches to any one of the following: nature, reason, justice, courage.

2. Montaigne writes of the "disorders of our poor country" (p. 1804)

and states that "there is no small pleasure in feeling oneself preserved from the contagion of so corrupt an age" (p. 1818). Our present world can hardly be seen as free from tumultuousness and corruption. Discuss whether, and to what degree, Montaigne's position as we deduce it from our readings and from the main elements of his life, would be conceivable and morally justifiable in our own age.

3. Discuss the quotation as a rhetorical device to support an argument and give it authority. Examine five to ten particular quotations in Montaigne and discuss their effect. What examples can you think of in electoral oratory of our own day in which references to respected national figures of the past and quotations from their utterances are used for similar objectives? Discuss, of course, differences as well.

4. Examine Montaigne's attitude toward scientific discoveries and the idea of progress. Make possible comparisons with Rabelais's notions of the betterment of humankind through education.

Further Reading

See also the reading suggestions in the anthology, pp. 1792–93.

Bencivenga, Ermanno. *The Discipline of Subjectivity: an Essay on Montaigne.* 1990.
By a philosopher specializing in language analysis.

Cruickshank, John, ed. *French Literature and Its Background.* Vol. I. 1968.
One chapter, by C. R. Baxter, is dedicated to Montaigne.

Gide, André. *Montaigne: An Essay in Two Parts.* 1929.
By one of the important French writers of the century.

McGowan, Margaret M. *Montaigne's Deceits: The Art of Persuasion in the Essays.* 1974.
By a student of French Renaissance aesthetics and rhetoric.

Sayce, R. A. *The Essays of Montaigne: A Critical Exploration.* 1972.
A thorough, detailed analysis, with quotations in French.

MIGUEL DE CERVANTES
Don Quixote

Backgrounds

Don Quixote is divided into two parts (the first of fifty-two chapters, the second of seventy-four), published separately with an interval of ten years between. Like *Gargantua and Pantagruel, Don Quixote* mixes realism and fantasy, but with the obvious difference that the fantasy is not here external but located in the mind of the hero. He is an impoverished gentleman who owns a small country estate in the Spanish province of La Mancha. As the whole world today knows from the innumerable films, plays, paintings, and sculptures inspired by his story, he is so infatuated with the reading of romances of chivalry and particularly with the image of the knight-errant and his code—heroic adventurousness, helpful generosity toward the weak and the needy, the service of justice, acts of valor for valor's sake and as an offering to a beloved lady—that he decides to equip himself in the proper manner and single-handedly revive the profession of knight-errantry. Quixote's spear and shield are old relics, his horse is the lean nag Rozinante; he leaves home at dawn, unnoticed, through a secret door. To complete his credentials as a knight-errant he chooses for the object of his devotion a peasant girl, whom his imagination transforms into the Lady Dulcinea del Toboso. Stopping at an inn, which he sees as a castle, he compels the crooked innkeeper in a scene accompanied by much jesting and slapstick comedy to dub him knight.

After leaving the inn Don Quixote's first actions are his pathetically futile defense of a farm boy being lashed by his master, and his unsuccessful attempt to force a group of merchants from Toledo to perform an act of faith, i.e., to swear to the incomparable beauty of Dulcinea without having seen her. In the ensuing brawl Quixote is unhorsed and badly mangled. A fellow villager finds him in this condition and takes him back home on a donkey (Chapters 1–5, pp. 1823–44). Since Quixote's troubles are attributed to his mad infatuation with the chivalry books in his library, the local curate and barber proceed to burn them; but this proves to be a futile action, for he resumes his wanderings (Chapter 7, p. 1845) now with his newly appointed squire, Sancho Panza. Their first adventure probably the most famous of them all—is a fight against windmills, which Quixote declares to be giants; their second, an encounter with two Benedictine monks on their mules, whom Quixote sees as enchanters abducting a lady. The consequent scuffles culminate in Quixote's battle with a choleric attendant in the lady's retinue (Chapter 9, p. 1852).

After the significant exchanges between Quixote and his squire in Chapter 10 (p. 1856), chapters 11–14 (pp. 1860–84) take us to a pastoral world. The salient points in this beautiful section are: Quixote's eloquent evocation of the Golden Age; the shepherds' story of young Grisostomo, who dies by his own hand for love of Marcella; and Marcella's defense of her feminine code. When master and squire resume their wanderings, they stumble into trouble with the "wicked Yanguesians," whose mares are coveted by Rozinante, and become the victims of tumultuous events at an inn which in Quixote's vision again becomes a castle. This is the place where Sancho is tossed on a blanket (one of the most famous Sancho episodes) as a reprisal for not having paid their bill. There follow some of the more legendary Quixotic exploits: the attack on a flock of sheep, which the Don sees as an enemy army, and the disastrous effort to liberate a chain of galley slaves (Chapters 18, p. 1884, and 22, p. 1888).

Chapters 23 through 32 (not included in our selections) are the Sierra Morena chapters. In that region of woods and forests Quixote decides to spend a period of retirement and penance, in imitation of his knightly models; from there he dispatches Sancho to his lady Dulcinea with a letter for her. The squire never delivers the letter but returns to the Sierra Morena with the curate and the barber, their aim of course being to bring the Knight of the Mournful Countenance back to his senses and his home. In the interval between departure from Sierra Morena and return to the village, they spend a period, long and full of incidents (chapters 32–46), at the place they had left in Chapter 17, the inn/castle of which Sancho has dire memories.

Both the Sierra Morena and the inn sequences are enriched by exemplary cases of romantically difficult loves, presented through the technique of the story-within-the-story, of which Cervantes originated the fashion. In the intimate setting of the inn, the intricate vicissitudes of the two major couples—Cardenio and Lucinda, Fernando and Dorotea—have their happy endings. Their connection with the main *Quixote* plot is made through the character of the beautiful Dorotea, who on the urging of the curate and the barber has persuaded Quixote to leave Sierra Morena and return to the inn—to him an enchanted castle—by playing the part of Princess Micomicona, a "damsel in distress." To the outside world (when Quixote and Sancho are in danger of arrest for their attempt to liberate the slaves) Quixote's rescuers use as a plea his insanity, but in dealing with him they use his own visionary notions and convince him that he is himself the victim of enchantments as they carry him back to his village (Chapter 52, the last of Part I, p. 1761). Of the curate's and the barber's two aims—to bring Quixote home and to "cure" him—the first has been achieved, but not the second.

The most important thing that happens to Quixote and Sancho at the beginning of Part II is the realization that their adventures have been narrated in a book. Quixote, of course, is not cured (in the first chapter of Part II he has declared to the curate and the barber: "A knight-errant I shall live and die"), nor is Sancho less desirous of becoming "governor of an island," as his master has promised him. It is Sancho who tells Quixote that they have been put into a book, the source of that information being the young Sansòn Carrasco just back from the University of Salamanca where he has received his bachelor's degree. Chapter 3 (p. 1902) is the point at which Cervantes, through Quixote conversing with Carrasco, amiably glorifies the popularity of his book (i.e., Part I) in other countries as well as Spain and debates the objections of the critics as reported by Carrasco.

From Chapter 8 on, the two adventurers are on their way again. In the country around El Toboso, Sancho saves himself from trouble by assuring Quixote that his failure to recognize the beautiful Dulcinea in the country wench confronting him comes from devilish spells and enchantments (chapters 8–10). As they move on toward Saragossa, there is a troublesome encounter with a company of players in their costumes—strange apparitions including "the Devil"—on their way to a performance of *The Parliament of Death*. The two most memorable encounters follow (chapters 12–17, pp. 1908–1943).

The first is with Sansòn Carrasco. Carrasco, having joined the ranks of the would-be rescuers of Quixote from his folly, tries to do something decisive about it by meeting Quixote on his own terms: as a knight (first called the "Fearless Knight of the Mirrors," then the "Knight of the Wood"), Carrasco plans to challenge and defeat Quixote in a duel. The plan fails as the Knight of the Wood is himself unhorsed and vanquished by the fury of the mad Don. Quixote's other significant encounter is with a kind, wise gentleman, Don Diego de Miranda, who witnesses Quixote's courage as he provokes a lion to come out of its cage and fight. Appropriately placed after Quixote's victorious interlude, this episode—a pivotal instance of Quixote's idea of gratuitous valor—has a semi-comic ending which is fully balanced by Quixote's speech on "the meaning of valor," one of his most movingly eloquent speeches. Aroused to a puzzled admiration, Don Diego invites Quixote to be his guest. Chapters 19 through 21 consist once more of a "story-within-the-story." It tells of the planned marriage between the fair Quiteria, loved by the poor shepherd Basilio, and the rich Camacho; on the day of the wedding Quiteria is abducted by Basilio, her true love, much to her delight and with Quixote's wholehearted support.

From this point on, the four main narratives of *Don Quixote*, Part II, treat the hero's descent to the cave of Montesinos (Chapters 22–23); Quixote's and Sancho's long stay at a castle as the guests of a duke and duchess (Chapters 30–67); their stay in Barcelona, the scene of Quixote's last duel and lamentalbe defeat (Chapters 64–65); and the hero's return to his village and his death (Chapters 73–74). The peculiar character of the Montesinos sequence is that it is narrated by the hero himself to his incredulous listeners after he has been lifted from the cave; to all appearances it is a dream in which Quixote has been granted visions of ancient kingdoms and of his enchanted Dulcinea. A dreamlike atmosphere also pervades the long scenes at the castle, but now it is a manipulated illusion, the result of theatrical pranks played by the duke and duchess and their retinue of idle jesters on the knight and his squire, who are now famous everywhere for their drolleries. One of the castle scenes concerns Dulcinea: a prankster, dressed as Death and pretending to be the magician Merlin, reveals as the harsh condition of her disenchantment that Sancho must submit to 3,300 lashes, a sentence that of course will never be carried out. Another scene involves Sancho. Conducted, blindfolded, to a nearby village which he supposes to be the island of Barataria, he is given the promised governorship. Sancho's victory consists in the fact that he will prove to be a good "governor," beloved by the villagers. The crucial Barcelona episode (Chapters 64–65, pp. 1943–47) is staged by Sansòn Carrasco, who turns up in a new disguise as the Knight of the Moon and this time defeats Quixote. The Don, after flirting with the idea of a new life enacting a pastoral play instead of a romance of chivalry, returns to his village to sicken and die (Chapters 73–74, pp. 1947–55).

Three literary traditions make their presence felt in *Don Quixote*: the epic or romance of chivalry, the adventure story of the *picaro* or vagabond, and the pastoral narrative of shepherds and their loves. The qualities of the chivalric epic may be sampled by the student in our selections from *The Song of Roland* (p. 1155) and those of the chivalric romance in the tales of King Arthur and his knights of the Round Table, especially such episodes of courtly love as that of Tristan and Isolde or that of

Lancelot and Guinevere. The latter, it will be recalled, is so moving to Dante's Paolo and Francesca (*Inferno*, Canto V, p. 1302) that it inspires their sinful love and leads to their destruction. The two collections of stories—that centering on Roland and his uncle, the great king Charlemagne, and that centering on Arthur—are combined and subjected to new twists in the major Italian Renaissance poems, *Orlando Innamorato* ("Roland in Love") by Matteo Maria Boiardo (ca. 1441–1494) and *Orlando Furioso* ("Roland Insane") by Ludovico Ariosto (1474–1533). Both of these poems were well known to Cervantes and the latter is possibly the immediate source of the Sierra Morena episode and other passages in Don Quixote.

The "picaresque" tradition is named from the *picaro*, the stock rogue-hero of many popular tales dealing with life in the undergrounds of society, where robbers, tramps, and various eccentrics meet. This tradition contributes to the "realistic" or "Sancho" aspects of Cervantes's story. Its major literary formulation is the anonymous novel *Lazarillo de Tormes* (first published in 1554), the influence of which was enormous at the time and indeed may be traced through eighteenth-century English fiction and down to our own time.

As for the pastoral romance, this tradition has its roots in Greek and Roman antiquity from Theocritus to Virgil and flourished during the Renaissance in such works—known to Cervantes and cited by him—as the *Arcadia* of Jacopo Sannazzaro (1457–1530) and most particularly the *Diana* of Jorge de Montemayor (ca. 1520–61).

What matters for us, of course, is what Cervantes made of these backgrounds: a work so new and absorbing that it is impossible to lay it down, and peopled by two creations, Quixote and Sancho, who have become part of our everyday mental furniture.

Classroom Strategies

Our selections from *Don Quixote* are best handled in three assignments. A first can center effectively on the figure of Don Quixote as a blind hero, fool, and ultimately wise fool, with the contributions of successive attitudes to our complex of feelings about him. A second can focus in similar ways on Sancho and his functions in the story. And a third can deal with the nature and development of the relationship between the two.

Analysis and discussion of *Don Quixote* call for some use of the terms "parody" and "satire." Parody is ordinarily a magnification of the characteristics of a particular style to the point at which its absurdity becomes unmistakable—in the case of *Don Quixote*, the inflated highfalutin style of the chivalric romances. Yet apart from the early quotations from Quixote's readings, obviously inserted to parody that style, his own speeches in the course of the story, and the general nature of his eloquence, move increasingly away from parody toward a speech that registers both his delusion and the idealism that feeds it. The term "satire" is equally inadequate for describing Cervantes's tone. Satire, in its usual sense, aims to expose an object or a person to ridicule and censure with implicit reference to a higher standard of conduct. In Cervantes the case is more complex. The argument can be made, in fact, that Quixote, far from being an object of satire, unconsciously becomes the satirist—of, say, crooked innkeepers or aristocratic pranksters—by exposing their cruelty, childishness, and vulgarity. In addition, and more generally, Cervantes's complex attitude toward the world of medieval chivalry can hardly be considered unmitigated satire. The serious interest and the underlying importance of Quixote's actions and speech can be demonstrated by observing their effect on other characters, particularly Sancho, whose warm response to Quixote's genuine chivalry of heart should correct any tendency to identify the two men with a superficial polarity between idealism and realism.

Topics for Discussion and Writing

Don Quixote is perhaps unparalleled as a starting point for broad discussions of the art of fiction in general and its place in a literate society. Our first three suggestions are along those lines.

1. We may grow attached to a fictional character in such a way that it becomes a solid point of reference, something "truer than life." Granted that Quixote and other characters in the novel have acquired that kind of "reality," take any number of examples, major and minor, and analyze by what verbal devices that author produces our perception of them. Discussion may be interestingly extended to the differences between our perception of a character in fiction and one on stage or in a film.

2. *Don Quixote* has been and still is held to be "great" literature. Yet one of Cervantes's most respected contemporaries, Lope de Vega, considered it trash. There is evidence of a similar duality of

attitude toward the romances of chivalry in Cervantes's time, some readers regarding them with a mixture of overt contempt and secret fascination. Can you think of forms of writing in our own time that are similarly both admired and condemned?

3. What constitutes the hero of a piece of fiction? One way to put it is that he is the one who determines and qualifies the actions and attitudes of the other characters. Show with specific evidence that Quixote is a hero in this sense, examining the characters of Sancho, the curate and the barber, Don Diego de Miranda, Sansòn Carrasco.

4. Don Quixote has become a world figure not only as the hero of a celebrated novel, but also as one of the main emblems of Spain. Discuss ways in which he can be compared, in his popularity and representativeness, to heroes of ancient epics on the one hand and to modern heroes of fiction, film, and comic strip on the other.

5. Take the passage in Part I, Chapter 4, where Don Quixote confronts the merchants from Toledo (p. 1836); the general effect of the episode may be comic or pathetic, yet the underlying pattern of Quixote's speech is nothing less than the theological virtue of Faith. Choose and analyze other passages of Quixote's eloquence where serious concepts raise an apparently comic situation to importance and significance (e.g., the concept of valor in II, 17, p. 1936).

6. Quixote had been described as the most "autonomous" character in literature—a supreme example of the phenomenon by which a fictional character acquires a life of its own, independent of its inventor. See how this paradoxical situation is consciously dealt with by Cervantes, not only in our first selection from Part II, but more generally in the way in which the narrator "reports" on his hero to the reader.

Further Reading

See also the reading suggestions in the anthology, p. 1679.

Bjornson, Richard, ed. *Approaches to Teaching Don Quixote.* 1984.
Contains background, critical appraisals, etc., by various expert hands.

Brenan, Gerald. *The Literature of the Spanish People.* 1951.
Chapter VIII is devoted to Cervantes's life and works. Brenan, who is not only a renowned scholar but also a brilliant writer, has a vast knowledge of Spanish culture.

Mann, Thomas. *Cervantes, Goethe, Freud.* 1943.
Individual appraisals by one of the major fiction writers and essayists of the century.

Nelson, Lowry, Jr., ed. *Cervantes: A Collection of Critical Essays.* 1969.
Besides Nelson's enlightening introduction, the importance of two of these essays is due to the literary stature of their authors: Thomas Mann ("Voyage with Don Quixote") and W. H. Auden ("The Ironic Hero: Some Reflections on *Don Quixote*"). Also includes essays by some of the most outstanding literary critics: Harry Levin ("The Example of Cervantes"), Leo Spitzer ("On the Significance of Don Quixote"), and Erich Auerbach ("The Enchanted Dulcinea").

Predmore, Richard L. *The World of Don Quixote.* 1967.

Riley, E. D. *Cervantes' Theory of the Novel.* 1962.

Two famous views of *Don Quixote* by outstanding Spanish writers are:

Madariaga, Salvador de. *Don Quixote: An Introductory Essay in Psychology.* 1961.

Unamuno, Miguel de. *The Life of Don Quixote and Sancho According to Miguel de Cervantes Saavedra.* Translated by Homer P. Earle. 1927. (Originally published 1905.)

CHRISTOPHER MARLOWE
The Tragical History of the Life and Death of Doctor Faustus

Backgrounds

Marlowe's *Doctor Faustus* has similarities with Greek drama and with medieval religious plays in the sense that the general line of its story was known to its audiences and the destiny of its hero a foregone conclusion. Even on the first night every spectator knew that Faust would be damned, just as a citizen of Athens in the fifth century B.C. knew that Oedipus in the end would discover the truth about his tragic past and blind himself. A presentation of *Doctor Faustus* would therefore be like the public performance of an exemplary story belonging to a common cultural heritage.

Marlowe treats the story in the manner of an Elizabethan playwright, conscious of the varied tastes of his mixed audiences. After the chorus-prologue that announces the play's theme, Faust is seen in his study, traditionally monologuing on his dissatisfaction with the learning accumulated in his life as a philosopher, physician, and theologian, all activities in which he has excelled. Thirsting after extremes of knowledge, power, and sensual gratification, Faust urges—or rather commands—his friends Valdes and Cornelius to introduce him to the techniques of the occult and the black arts, which he seems promptly to master. With them he evokes Mephistophilis, the messenger who becomes the intermediary for his pact with Lucifer, sealed in blood. Mephistophilis will be at his service for twenty-four years during which he will enjoy magical power, invulnerability, and the capacity to turn into an invisible spirit.

The two principal backgrounds for Faust's exploits are Rome and Germany. Faust, a theologian and now a magician coming from Luther's Wittenberg, goes to Rome and makes fools of the pope and his cardinals and supports a German anti-pope. When he goes to Germany, he gains entrance to the emperor's court, becomes the object of admiring respect, and puts horns on the head of the only courtier who mocks him. Faust's mode of action at both courts—the Pope's and the Emperor's—makes him seem a trickster and prankster, yet significantly the dramatist has had him show the superiority of his power to that of the two major centers of power of the time, the empire and the papacy. For all his involvement in power politics, however, the apex of Faust's experience will be the traditionally supreme symbol of classic beauty, the vision of Helen, "the face that launched a thousand ships." By that time he is already torn apart by fear and remorse, and indeed he will end by physically being torn to pieces by devils.

There are three kinds of interruptions of the main plot, in addition to those of the narrating Chorus: from the Good Angel and the Bad Angel of medieval tradition (cf. Dante, *Inferno* XXVII. 110–24), who struggle for the possession of Faust's soul; from Faust's servant Wagner and the traditional Clowns of low comedy, whose intrusions provide rustically comic intervals; and from Faust's former peers, the Scholars who will "give his mangled limbs due burial."

The historical existence of a Dr. Faust seems certain; even more certain, and surely more relevant, is the fact that his legend continued to spread after his death until Faust as a character became the focus of one of the four major literary myths originating in the Renaissance period, along with Don Juan, Don Quixote, and Hamlet. The legendary doctor had early acquired notoriety as a man endowed with dangerous occult powers, and hence to be feared and flattered. From its earliest formulations the Faust image presented faces that have stayed with it through the centuries: that of the prankster; that of the man tormented by a religious conscience divided between orthodoxy and free-thinking; and that of the man aspiring not only to boundless knowledge but also to practical activity in the society of his time. This third aspect is, of course, essential to Goethe's conception of the character in *Faust*, Part II.

The accumulating body of legend and anecdote about Faust was gathered and published for the first time in 1587 by a certain Johannes Spiess in Frankfurt. This is the volume usually referred to as the *Faust Book*, which typically bears a much longer title, *History of Dr. Johann Fausten, the Well-known Magician and Necromancer*, etc., and presents the doctor's story as a frightful warning to the presumptuous, the unduly curious, and the godless. An English version of the work, the *History of the Damnable Life and Deserved Death of Dr. John Faustus*, was printed in 1592. Marlowe is the first artist to have realized the potential of the material that Spiess had collected; his influence therefore extends to Goethe, who first knew Faust in puppet-show adaptations of the story which English players had brought to the stages of his native Germany (see Goethe's *Faust*, Part I in Volume Two of the anthology), and beyond Goethe, to all of the Fausts that in the most varied shapes have since appeared in words to be read, spoken on stage, or sung to the music of such composers as Gounod, Schumann, Berlioz, Liszt, and Boito.

Classroom Strategies

By its very structure, and the variety of its episodes and their qualities and tones, *Doctor Faustus* may very plausibly seem difficult and confusing even to relatively experienced readers. One way to arm the student with patience and understanding is to give some notion of its textual history through the early printed editions of 1604, 1609, and 1616. The first one came several years after the first performances of the play and presumably contains interpolations by various hands, including those of producers and actors. The second and particularly the third editions include considerable insertions generally not attributed to Marlowe, among them the comic intervals.

This will also be a suitable moment to give the uninformed student some understanding (valid also for the reader of Shakespeare) of Elizabethan theatrical life. Particular reference might be made to the furnishing of texts by various writers who often collaborated on the same text and, because nothing was protected by copyright, could take a "good story" wherever they saw one and adapt it to their own purposes. Apart from the present maniacal feelings about protecting "original ideas," obviously contrary to Elizabethan habits, it may still be useful to mention the similar situation nowadays with respect to film scripts. These often go through many different stages and are rewritten by various hands unrecognizable in the final product, even though one of them may be that of William Faulkner (as in the potboiler *Land of the Pharaohs*, 1955).

To help them understand Faust's moving between orthodoxy and the black arts, students should probably be reminded that the borderline between necromantic dabbling with the occult and what we now call scientific research was not at all clearly established in Marlowe's day.

Topics for Discussion and Writing

1. One view of Faust's story is that he presents some of the intellectual aspirations and impulses to power of a "Renaissance man." On the other hand, Spiess's *Faust Book* sees him as an example of just punishment inflicted upon a godless sinner. From the evidence of the play, what do you take to be Marlowe's view?

2. According to Mephistophilis, Hell is not necessarily to be conceived as a definite place. Find and comment on those passages in the play from which we can draw a definition of the nature of eternal punishment.

3. Define the respective contributions of the Chorus, the Good and the Bad Angel, Wagner, and the Scholars to our estimate of the play's hero.

4. Marlowe called his play *The Tragical History of the Life and Death of Doctor Faustus*. "Tragedy" in Marlowe's time could refer simply to the disaster of a fall from prosperity and power to suffering and death, or it could refer to what we now more generally think of as tragic—i.e., the destruction or defeat of a person who is in some respects great or heroic or at least admirable by forces within him as well as without. How far does the play answer to the first definition? How far to the second?

Further Reading

See also the reading suggestions in the anthology, pp. 1957–58.

Birringer, Johannes H. *Marlowe's* Doctor Faustus *and* Tamerlaine: *Theological and Theatrical Perspectives*. 1984.
Examines "the specifics of Marlowe's dramatic style" and "the verbal and visual rhetoric of his plays," taking into account the apparent inconsistencies and contradictions in his work.

Friedenreich, Kenneth; Gill, Roma; Kuriyama, Constance B. *A Poet and a Filthy Playmaker: New Essays on Christopher Marlowe*. 1988.
Recent and valuable.

Gatti, Hilary. *The Renaissance Drama of Knowledge*. 1989.
Chapter 4 is on *Doctor Faustus*, especially seen in relation with Giordano Bruno's writings.

Jump, John D., ed. *Doctor Faustus*. 1965.
With a lengthy introduction on Marlowe; the history, dating, editions, authorship, literary sources, and stage history of the play.

Leech, Clifford, ed. *Marlowe: A Collection of Critical Essays*. 1964.
With chronology of important dates and selected bibliography. Essays include "Christopher Marlowe" by T. S. Eliot, "The Damnation of Faust" by W. W. Greg, "The Damnation of Faust" by J. P. Broadbank, and "The Equilibrium of Tragedy" by Una Ellis-Fermor.

Meehan, Virginia M. *Christopher Marlowe: Poet and Playwright*. 1974.
A study of Marlowe's style, figures of speech, imagery, etc. Chapter 5 is dedicated to *Doctor Faustus*.

O'Neill, Judith, ed. *Critics on Marlowe*. 1970.
This collection of essays is divided into two sections: Critics on Marlowe 1592–1930 and Modern Critics on Marlowe, which includes essays by Leo Kirshbaum ("*Doctor Faustus*: A Reconsideration), Nicholas Brooke ("The Moral Tragedy of *Doctor Faustus*"), and Arthur Mizener ("The Dualism in *Doctor Faustus*").

Weil, Judith. *Christopher Marlowe: Merlin's Prophet*. 1977.
The title of this study refers to a quotation from the end of Rabelais' *Gargantua*, and sees Marlowe as a "rhetorical provocateur" who uses a mixture of "sense with nonsense, allegory with the violent energies of farce and tragedy" in his plays.

WILLIAM SHAKESPEARE
Hamlet, Prince of Denmark

Backgrounds

Hamlet, Prince of Denmark—even in the title the play's hero is presented within the framework of a country and a royal court. He is, in fact, the most eminent member of that court; and the court as a setting and organizing structure is as typical of Renaissance drama as of the drama of antiquity. In *Hamlet* we soon realize that this setting is not a Denmark remote and medieval, but a modern state, of the kind described and studied by such political writers as Machiavelli; and that this kingdom is undergoing a crisis caused by inner corruption and foreign threats.

The previous king of Denmark—Hamlet was his name, too—has been assassinated by his brother Claudius, who has inherited the throne (through a partly elective procedure) and married his brother's widow, i.e. his sister-in-law, Gertrude. In certain social codes, one of which Prince Hamlet obviously accepts, this is marriage within the forbidden degrees—is, in short, incest. But there is also trouble from without. On the ramparts of the castle at Elsinore, sentinels stand guard against a foreign threat of invasion, embodied in Fortinbras, prince of Norway. The ghost of the murdered king appears there, seeking to be avenged. Hamlet promises to obey, and while seeking evidence that the apparition was in fact his father's ghost and spoke truth, puts on an appearance of insanity to avoid suspicion that he may be planning to kill the king. For the time being the court interpretation of his insanity is that its cause is love for Ophelia, daughter of the lord chamberlain Polonius. Hamlet "loved" Ophelia "once" but now treats her with cruel sarcasm.

When a group of travelling players visits Elsinore, Hamlet devises a plan, his "mousetrap": he has the actors perform a play, *The Murder of Gonzago*, about a royal fratricide similar to the one committed by Claudius, and Claudius's visible reaction when he sees it performed confirms the ghost's truthfulness. In an immediately following scene with his mother, whom he accuses of complicity in the murder, Hamlet suddenly suspects that the king may be listening behind a curtain. Actually it is Polonius; and when Hamlet thrusts his sword through the curtain Polonius is killed. The king, now aware of danger, sends Hamlet on a mission to England accompanied by two courtiers, Rosencrantz and Guildenstern with the instruction that he be executed there. By a ruse, Hamlet turns the king's trick back on to Rosencrantz and Guildenstern, and returns to Denmark to complete his mission as avenger of his father's death. There, soon after, he encounters the funeral cortege of Ophelia, who has gone mad and drowned herself. Her death and Polonius's bring Laertes (her brother and Polonius's son) back to Denmark on a similar avenging errand. An elaborate show is planned—a sort of counterpart to Hamlet's "mousetrap," but more complex and devastating—by the king and Laertes, allied in their desire to liquidate Hamlet. Laertes will challenge Hamlet to a duel in which they will fight as if in sport, but secretly the point of Laertes's foil will be poisoned. A cup of poison to be administered when Hamlet is thirsty will also be ready as a possible last resort. During their encounter Hamlet is hit and thus mortally wounded, but by an exchange of weapons manages to give Laertes a mortal wound also. The queen in ignorance of the plot drinks from the poisoned cup. Laertes, dying, confesses his and the king's plot to Hamlet, and Hamlet kills the king. In his own dying speech he urges his friend Horatio to live on to report truthfully on the past tragic events and gives his vote to Fortinbras for the succession to the throne.

Hamlet constitutes all by itself an important area of Elizabethan scholarship. But the main lines of what we know about its sources and composition are relatively clear. The plot of *Hamlet* originates in the account given of Prince "Amleth" in books III and IV of the *Danish History* (*Historia Danica*) written by the Danish chronicler Saxo in the late twelfth century and first printed in 1514. The story reappears in Book V of *Tragic Histories* (*Histoires Tragiques*) by the French historian François de Belleforest (1530–1583), first printed in 1576. In all probability Shakespeare knew neither of these two sources—the *Hystorie of Hamblet*, an English adaptation of Belleforest, was published only in 1608, and indeed seems to have been influenced by Shakespeare's play rather than vice-versa. What Shakespeare did know was an earlier play on the same subject, now lost, but mentioned in several places, including the *Diary* of Philip Henslowe, the most important theatrical manager of the time. That play was being performed during the late 1580s and early 1590s. The likelihood is strong that its author was Thomas Kyd, whose *Spanish Tragedy* (first printed in 1594) is the best-known example of what was then a very popular genre, the "revenge play." Of course, the starting point of any class study of *Hamlet* should be to consider how far it surpasses the simple idea of a "revenge play."

Classroom Strategies

One profitable strategy is to trace the aspect of mystery that Shakespeare seems to have built into the play—its riddling language, its continual questions, the obscure motivations of the characters (why *does* Hamlet chide himself for delaying? how much does the queen know? on what account does Ophelia go mad and drown?)—from its first words ("who's there?") to its last. Does this stress on mystery affect your response to the play? If so, how?

Useful too is consideration of the range of idioms in the play: those of the soldiers on guard; of the ghost; of Claudius; of the Player King and Queen; of Ophelia in madness; of the queen in describing Ophelia's death; of Osric; of the grave-diggers; of Hamlet. What suggestion do we find that Hamlet speaks all these idioms, and how does this affect our estimate of him? Hamlet praises Horatio for being steadier than he—but would one choose to be Horatio rather than Hamlet? Why and why not?

A third and most important strategy is to avoid putting all the emphasis in class discussion on the motivation of the prince. The play bristles with an exciting variety of incident, mood, imagery, and (as noted above) personalities depicted through their speech. The surest way to bring out these qualities is to ask successive teams of students to read aloud, or even try to act out a few of the multitude of encounters and confrontations that the play provides.

Topics for Discussion and Writing

1. Both *Doctor Faustus* and *Hamlet* present central characters who have become literary "myths." It is obvious that Hamlet is a more mature, complex, and tightly structured work, but it is still very much worthwhile to discuss what makes it so. An excellent place to begin is with the death scenes of the two heroes.

2. Compare the character of Polonius—his behavior and speech—to that of the ideal courtier, and of the dialoguing courtiers "forming him with words" in Castiglione's book. Do likewise for Osric.

3. Consider Hamlet's "antic disposition" in the light of the themes of folly and madness in Erasmus and Cervantes.

4. Hamlet has been described (by Rebecca West) as a "bad man," and it has been argued that he is even more of a politician than the king his uncle. Drawing specific evidence from the play, do your best to support this proposition. Then, again using specific evidence, do your best to refute it.

5. Imagine yourself a director and then describe as accurately as you can your ideal handling of the play's opening scene. Or of the closet scene between Hamlet and his mother (III.iv, p. 2070). Consider especially what you wish the scene to contribute to the tone and effect of the play as a whole.

Further Reading

See also the reading suggestions in the anthology, p. 2014.

Aldus, P. J. *Mousetrap: Structure and Meaning in* Hamlet. 1977.
With bibliographical note. An analysis of Shakespeare's tragedy as literary myth, focusing on "Aristotelian criticism of dramatic structure" and Platonic concepts of metaphoric form in literary myth.

Bloom, Edward A., ed. *Shakespeare 1564–1964: A Collection of Essays by Various Hands.* 1964.
Seventeen essays, including two on *Hamlet* and one on Shakespeare criticism from 1900 to 1964.

Cohen, Michel. Hamlet *in My Mind's Eye.* 1989.
This deals also with a production of the play.

Gatti, Hilary. *The Renaissance Drama of Knowledge.* 1989.
Chapter 4 is on *Hamlet.*

Harbage, Alfred. *William Shakespeare: A Reader's Guide.* 1971.
A guide to Shakespeare's language, verse, and style. Works are described chronologically, scene by scene, followed by a brief analysis of each.

Hoy, Cyrus, ed. *Hamlet.* A Norton Critical Edition. 1992.

Contains sections on the text of *Hamlet*, intellectual backgrounds, sources, and essays in criticism. With notes and bibliography.

Knight, G. Wilson. *The Wheel of Fire*. Revised 1948.
The section on *Hamlet* ("The Embassy of Death") is well-known for its "positive interpretation" of the character of the king.

Wilson, John Dover. *What Happens in* Hamlet. 1959.

JOHN DONNE

Backgrounds

The bulk of Donne's poetry first appeared in print in 1633, two years after the poet's death. Until then Donne's poems, with very few isolated exceptions, had circulated only in manuscript form, as was more often than not the custom of those days. Problems of dating and chronological sequence are thus very difficult in Donne's case, but fortunately this scarcely matters. His most characteristic qualities are present throughout his career.

Certainly Donne knew the classics, such as the Latin love poets; and he was aware of the Petrarchan tradition. (He used a line from a Petrarch *canzone* as his *ex libris*.) That tradition continued to be felt in England to Donne's day as well as on the European continent where it originated. (Scholars have calculated that in Italy and France alone, during the sixteenth century, no fewer than 300,000 sonnets in the Petrarchan manner were printed, the large majority of them being love sonnets.) There are "certain Petrarchan features in some of Donne's lyrics," as Theodore Redpath has pointed out (see below in *Further Reading*), yet the majority of his poetry "is quite divergent from Petrarch in spirit." In fact, there seems to be agreement on the general idea that Donne's manner implies a reaction to the mannerisms and clichés of "Petrarchism."

As in the case of other poets of his generation, Donne's poetry is nourished by the extraordinary diverse experiences and activities that his time, country, and historical circumstances offered to a man of his education, gifts, and social position. Hence the variety and the up-to-dateness of his materials and his imagery. His poetry presupposes an equally varied audience of scholars, courtiers, wits, and also of voyagers, merchants, soldiers, judges, lawyers. Finally, in the framework of literary history as exemplified in our anthology, Donne's treatment of the man-woman relationship can be placed at the opposite end from the canons and formalities of "courtly love."

Classroom Strategies

Possibly the best way to introduce students to the reading of Donne's poems is to attempt with them a definition of the "speaking voice"—its tone, its character, its function. Reading out loud will be helpful. So will be some reference to Petrarch sonnets as the simplest way to bring about a feeling of Donne's difference and novelty. From the Petrarch sonnets we draw the image of a lover in isolation. His voice, as he addresses the beloved, distant lady (or speaks of her in the third person) may present a considerable variety of tones, from joyful celebration to lament and nostalgia; yet it persistently maintains the quality of a lover's confession, or of a meditation on his present state and on the evoked past. On the other hand, the speaking voice in the typical Donne poem resounds in the present; it is a voice in action. Its function is to set up a dramatic situation. While the Petrarchan kind of poem, even when addressing the lady, suggests isolation, the Donne poem, instead, sounds like the speaker's side of an animated, voluble exchange on an imaginary stage.

Even the newest reader will easily see the significance of the basic differences in poetic forms between the two poets. The Petrarchan sonnet, with its established structure, is the proper vehicle for events and emotions recollected from memory, or in any case ordered into regular shape, metrics, rhyme. The characteristic unit of Donne's love poems is a stanza, either single (as in "The Apparition") or repeated (five times in "The Canonization," three in our other selections). There is, however, variety among stanza patterns, so that each seems created to fit the tone of the particular poem.

We may hold on to the theatrical metaphor when we approach individual love poems by Donne. The speaking voice is that of the principal actor who all by himself is staging a variety of situations where the main business is the rapport between man and woman, clearly in a society where the game of sensual love is played with both passion and intellectual sophistication. Although the speaker's voice is fairly consistent in its quality and originality, situations and moods change, so that the central character can be compared to a frequently type-cast actor performing in a variety of plays.

Using our selections as models, there is for example a particularly obvious kinship between the central characters in two such poems as "Song" ("... And swear / No where / Lives a woman true and fair") and "The Indifferent" ("I can love both fair and brown ..."), where the speaker enacts the young blade, the rake and show-off cynic, unperturbed by moral codes and by thought in general. The simplest observation of verse patterns will indicate great differences between the two poems, yet an equally high degree of musical potential, i.e., fitness to be sung in a social context where faithlessness in love is *de rigueur*. In a similar way, we can couple two poems such as "The Good-Morrow" and "The Canonization," where the speaker enacts the philosophical wooer, fashionably demonstrating (cf. Bembo in Castiglione's *Courtier*) the power of love to transcend mortality.

It is particularly obvious in such cases, of course, that imagery, metrical patterns, unusual and circuitous ways of conveying the main idea of the poem—all the ways of "staging" the situation—make all the difference, and that true experience of the poems can only be conducted through explication and exchange in the classroom.

Obvious as it may be that "dramatization is all," the student should not be allowed to forget that the main "idea" of a poem may be a cliché, consecrated by centuries of love poetry, Petrarchan and otherwise. There is no need to go into detail on the endless conventions and formalities of that tradition to realize that "Donne's originality is bound up with his use of common positions" (A. J. Smith [see *Further Reading*], p. 23), a fact that is particularly evident in the more complex poems such as "The Apparition" and "The Funeral." In the former, the "lover's death of his mistress' disdain, the midnight visitation, and the revenge or curse" are all stock motifs, to which are added, in the latter, such motifs as "the lover's interpretation of the token she has sent him, the lover's complete dependence on his mistress for life and being, the lover as love's martyr" (ibid.).

An even greater power of renovation is apparent in the two Holy Sonnets in our selections, where the traditional ideas are no less than the highest verities of the Christian faith. (For an interesting and provocative discussion of the quality and religiosity of these poems, see Sanders, cited below.)

Topics for Discussion and Writing

1. Discuss and define the differences between a Petrarchan and a Donne love poem, considering such elements as imagery, the implied character of the speaker, and the greater or lesser awareness of the "presence" of the person whom the speaker is addressing and of other possible "presences" and "voices," as the case may be.

2. Compare and contrast the religious element in Petrarch and Donne (see Petrarch's sonnets 3 and 62, and Donne's "The Canonization" and, of course, Holy Sonnets 7 and 10).

3. Compare and contrast the stanza pattern of "Song" to that of "The Apparition" and their respective appropriateness to the matter of the two poems.

Further Reading

See also the reading suggestions in the anthology, p. 2111.

Gardner, Helen, ed. *The Divine Poems*, by John Donne. 1978.
A basic edition, with critical and textual introduction and notes.

Gardner, Helen, ed. *The Elegies and the Songs and Sonnets*, by John Donne. 1965.
A standard edition, with commentary and critical and textual introduction.

Grierson, H. J. C., ed. *The Poems of John Donne*. 1912.
The classic modern edition, with critical and textual introductions and commentary.

Redpath, Theodore, ed. *The Songs and Sonnets of John Donne*. 1983.
Contains a lengthy introduction on the status of the Songs and Sonnets in English poetry and on the "psychological" and "literary" features of the poems, and on their relation to the Petrarchan tradition (the latter is discussed at length on pages 47–88). Each of the poems is followed by explanatory and critical notes.

Sanders, Wilbur. *John Donne's Poetry*. 1971.
The discussion of the Holy Sonnets comprises pages 111–39.

Smith, A. J. *Donne, Songs and Sonnets*. 1964; reprinted 1975.
A short and very useful study from the series Studies in English Literature.

PEDRO CALDERON DE LA BARCA
Life Is a Dream

Backgrounds

The weaving of two main threads in *Life Is a Dream* (the Segismund plot and the Rosaura plot) starts with the very first scene of the play. So does the mingling of literary genres—serious drama, comedy, fairy tale. The relationships among the characters, as they develop, seem to be ruled by both supernatural fatality and by the laws of comedy and novels of adventure—coincidences, recognitions, revelations.

Against a craggy, desolate background in a purely imaginary "Poland" we see a prison, its door wide open. Rosaura, disguised as a man and accompanied by the servant-clown Clarion, has arrived there as if by magic. In due time (I. 6753ff.) we will learn that the reason for her being in Poland is to search for the man who has seduced her, Astolfo. The two strangers hear coming from inside the prison the lamentations of Segismund and soon listen to his long speeches as he emerges from the "rude tower" where his father, King Basil, a believer in astrology, has had him locked up since infancy, having read evil portents in the stars at the moment of Segismund's birth (as we shall learn in detail in I. 431ff.). There is an aura of magic in the first encounter between Segismund and Rosaura: he is at once "bewitched" by her and she in turn states that heaven must have led her to that spot "to be comforted, if it is comfort / To see another sadder than oneself." Their passionate exchange is soon interrupted by the appearance of Clotaldo, Segismund's aged jailer and mentor. Clotaldo is ready to punish Rosaura and Clarion with death for having trespassed into the confines of the prison. The revelation (to Clotaldo) that Rosaura—dressed as a man—is his "son" is obtained through the theatrical device of the sword which the lady is carrying (I. 285ff.). Clotaldo, caught in a dilemma between a father's love and loyalty to the throne, decides to spare the trespassers' lives and take them to the royal palace and let the king decide their fate.

The scene moves to the royal palace, where Astolfo, Duke of Muscovy, and Princess Stella—the nephew and niece of King Basil—are discussing an arrangement between themselves for the succession to the kingdom; in a long speech (I. 378ff.), Astolfo proposes a political marriage but Stella has reason to doubt his faithfulness, the revealing "prop" this time being the portrait that Astolfo carries in a locket around his neck—a portrait of Rosaura. There follows King Basil's long speech to his assembled people (I. 431–607), in which he very elaborately describes the reasons why, in his determination "to cage up this newborn tiger," he has had Segismund confined. He then proceeds to discuss the problem of succession, "vacillating discursively" between the notion of the influence of the stars upon men and the Christian doctrine of man's free will (I. 560ff). He finally comes up with the rather hypocritical idea of having his son—who until this time, by his father's decree, has been trained as "a courtier to the mountains and neighbor to the beasts"— brought suddenly to the palace and placed on the throne in order to put his royal capacities to a test; should he prove unworthy, the father's "obligation of mercy" will have been "fulfilled," and Astolfo and Stella will be designated as Basil's successors.

The courtiers are dismissed as Clotaldo appears with Rosaura and Clarion. Clotaldo's attempt to reveal to King Basil that Rosaura is his "son" is brusquely interrupted (I. 625ff.) by the king, who curtails any further discussion by pardoning the two strangers. Exit the king, so that Act I ends with the conversation between Clotaldo and Rosaura which brings the double, bewildering revelation to Clotaldo—that the young stranger is in reality a woman, and that the man who has stained her honor is the Duke of Muscovy, Astolfo. Clotaldo is in a moral "labyrinth" ("My family honour's injured . . . / I'm a vassal [to Astolfo] and she's a woman . . . / The whole world is a prodigy.")

Act II opens with Clotaldo's report to the king: Segismund has been given a sleeping drug and transported to the palace. King Basil's plan is not to reveal to Segismund that he is his son and heir, and to make him believe that his royal experience is a dream, so that if he should "wake up in prison on the morrow / He might understand he had been dreaming"; also, in that notion "he will not be wrong, for in this world . . . all who live are only dreaming." Thus, poorly protected against the temptations of power, Segismund behaves like a capricious, beastly tyrant. Ignoring all norms concerning rank, points of honor, and courtship, he mistreats Astolfo and improperly courts Stella; when a servant reproaches him for doing so, he commits his wildest absurdity by throwing him out of a window into the sea. As he threatens to have Astolfo beheaded, King Basil appears. In the ensuing scene of recognition and exchange between father and son (II. 302–68) the basic issue of life versus dream is debated, the king warning Segismund to be kind and humble since he may only be dreaming; Segismund nevertheless claims that he has been cheated of his hereditary crown. Enter Rosaura, now in woman's clothing. Segismund's attitude toward her runs the whole gamut from instinctive adoration to beastly assault. Clotaldo's attempts to restrain Segismund are received with death threats. Astolfo appears in time to save Clotaldo's life; as Astolfo and Segismund are crossing swords the king appears with Stella and attendants (II. 498ff.). Segismund admits to having wanted to kill Clotaldo and exits in a threatening mood. Before he leaves, the king somewhat ambiguously predicts that Segismund will have to return to his prison.

Astolfo and Stella, now alone, rather obscurely debate on the value of astrology (II. 513ff.); the practical result of their exchange is Stella's warning that Astolfo should address his flatteries not to her but to the woman whose portrait he has been carrying in a locket. He protests his love and leaves to fetch the portrait in order to replace it with Stella's. At this point Rosaura appears; she has been serving in Stella's retinue under the name of Astrea, and is now asked by Stella to wait for Astolfo and receive the portrait from him. Naturally Astolfo recognizes Rosaura, who insists she is Astrea, and, through a rather farcical routine (672ff.), manages to get her portrait from him. Astolfo is left in a desperately awkward situation; Stella dismisses him with such epithets as "crude, coarse villain . . . ruffian of a wooer."

The scene moves to the prison tower where Segismund is again condemned to lie in chains in the company of Clarion, watched by Clotaldo and attendants. King Basil appears; he and Clotaldo listen as Segismund in a dream babbles about power and vengeance. As he awakes, Basil retires. The subsequent exchange between Segismund and Clotaldo, as well as Segismund's monologue, which concludes Act II, contain some of the essential themes of the play: that a man, whatever his station from king to pauper, in whatever condition from joy to suffering, should live his life as if it were a dream (Segismund, 788–814); and that "even in dreams . . . / Nothing is lost by trying to do good" (Clotaldo, 786–87). The final lines of Segismund's beautiful speech (811–14), answering the question "What is life?", are among the most proverbially famous in world drama:

> ...Una ilusión,
> una sombra, una ficción,
> y el mayor bien es pequeño,
> que toda la vida es sueño,
> y los sueños sueño son.

...an illusion,
A shadow, a delirium, a fiction.
The greatest good's but little, and this life
Is but a dream, and dreams are only dreams.

The first scene of Act III is in the prison tower and opens with the pathetic, humorous lament of the clown Clarion, who paradoxically claims that he has been imprisoned for keeping his mouth shut, thus contradicting the cliché of the loquacious servant. Drums and trumpets announce the arrival of soldiers. There is a comic scene when the soldiers mistake Clarion for the prince; then as Segismund himself appears, the First Soldier, as spokesman for the rebels, acclaims him their lord ("Hosts of plebeians, bandits, and freebooters, / Acclaim you king"). Now armed with the knowledge that all is illusion, Segismund, after forgiving Clotaldo, shows that he has also learned his jailer-mentor's lesson (II. 786–87, quoted above, and III. 137–39: "I know I'm in a dream, / But I would like to act well, since good actions, / Even in a dream, are not entirely lost"). Thus when Clotaldo announces that out of loyalty to the king he cannot join Segismund and the rebels, Segismund subdues his initial wrath and lets Clotaldo go, "for every man / Has his own honour."

The following scene takes place in the royal palace, where an atmosphere of imminent danger prevails. Astolfo, who along with Stella is the designated heir of King Basil, proclaims his bellicose intentions while the king's attitude seems to be one of resignation to fate. Stella, in some beautiful lines (III. 209–18) describes the predictable disasters of war. But as Clotaldo enters to announce that Segismund, now free, is valiantly fighting for his right to the throne, both the king and Stella are roused, and they exit to go to battle against him. Rosaura appears, holding back Clotaldo. The long ensuing exchange between the two (III. 234–332) artfully derives some of its dramatic tension from the fact that Clotaldo knows that Rosaura is his daughter and she does not. Clotaldo is torn between the moral duty to restore her honor (he has saved her life, but life without honor is worthless) by killing her seducer Astolfo, and his debt to Astolfo, who has saved *his* life. Rosaura remains firm in the belief that her only alternatives are regaining her honor of seeking a lonely death. She makes a dramatic exit and Clotaldo follows her, concluding their passionate dialogue: "If you are lost, / My daughter, let us both be lost together!"

The scene shifts to Segismund's camp; he maintains a wisely sober attitude in victory, knowing that "plaudits . . . when I wake, will turn to bitterness." Announced by Clarion's flowery rhetorics, Rosaura appears, attired as a woman warrior, once more dazzling Segismund ("Her light blinds me"). In her long, beautifully eloquent speech (III. 358–498), Rosaura gives a summary of her past life. Her mother's story and her own have followed a similar pattern—both women have been abandoned and betrayed by their lovers, Clotaldo in the first case (he will declare himself Rosaura's father only at the very end, III. 721–24) and Astolfo in the second. Now that Astolfo is claiming the throne for himself and Stella, Rosaura has come to offer her services to Segismund, to ensure both his claim to the throne and her own honor by vanquishing Astolfo. Segismund, the newly wise prince, subdues his masculine instincts and concludes his speech with a pledge: "Having to see your honour is requited, / I must not see your beauty."

Before the predictable happy ending, an original touch is provided by the paradoxical death of the clown Clarion, the only war casualty, killed on the very spot where he thought he would be safe from the raging battle. There follows the climactic moment of the main plot (Basil-Segismund), when father and son finally meet face to face and work out their reconciliation (III. 638–711), forgiving errors, each one kneeling at the other's feet. There are some seemingly odd but characteristic touches in the happy ending. It will be proper for Astolfo to restore Rosaura's honor by marrying her, but not without having made sure—as Clotaldo publicly declares that he is Rosaura's father—that her stock is as noble as his own. Similarly, when Segismund offers his hand to Stella as a consolation for having lost a prince of Astolfo's rank, he stresses the propriety of this act by observing that Stella is "no less in birth and rank." Finally, Segismund's decision to have the leader of the rebels (the "First Soldier") imprisoned for life in the dungeon from which those very rebels had liberated him ("No traitor is of use after his treason") implies an extremely rigid notion of what constitutes honor and kingly behavior.

Some stock situations in the plot and characters of *Life Is a Dream* had appeared very early in the history of fictional literature. The theme of the man who undergoes an important experience of some sort while in a drugged state and is afterwards made to believe that the whole thing was a dream, can be traced back to collections of Oriental tales including the one that became most famous in Western culture, the *Arabian Nights* (the story of Abou Assan and the Caliph Haroun al Raschid). The situation of the man who is taught a lesson through a fictitious "dream" has been much used in the Oriental and Western traditions; the major storyteller of the Middle Ages, Boccaccio, provided a bawdy variation on this theme in his story of the jealous Ferondo (*Decameron*, Third Day, Eighth Tale). The theme of a king who has his son imprisoned as a consequence of what the stars have foretold can be traced back to the frame story of a prominent Oriental collection of tales, *Barlaam and Josaphat*. The characters of Barlaam and Josaphat have a long history in the Greek, Roman, and Christian traditions and were used by Lope de Vega, Calderón's predecessor as the leading Spanish dramatist, in his play *Barlán y Josafá*. Another play by Lope, *El hijo de Reduán*, in which the hero raised by shepherds in primitive ignorance is brought to court and acts like a wild man, was also a partial inspiration for Calderón.

As for Rosaura, the heroine of the second plot, her appearing disguised as a man and the damsel-in-distress aspect of her story and personality are recognizable situations in the tradition of comedy and of the sentimental novel. Similarly, her woman-warrior aspect has eminent precedents in the epic from, for example, Virgil's Camilla to Tasso's Clorinda. As we have seen, Calderón's play is also full of situations dealing with questions of honor, etiquette, and rank. This of course reflects aristocratic customs and usages as Calderón could have observed them (he himself had been a "young blade," and as a dramatist he wrote mainly for the court), but much of it may also be ascribed to exaggerated theatrical convention.

Classroom Strategies

First of all—difficult as this may seem—the new reader should be given a clear, cogent notion of "what happens in the play"; the summary given above should be of help in this sense. A study of *Life Is a Dream* can also offer a good occasion to familiarize students with such basic terms as "plot" (the hero's story) and "subplot" (Rosaura's story) and to observe the way the two combine to form a dramatically rich, varied whole. As in other cases, after a notion of the action and general structure of the play is obtained, it may be a good idea to read selected passages aloud, possibly also in the original Spanish; it shouldn't be difficult to find a colleague or student on campus who is fluent in Spanish. The purpose of such a reading is to acquaint students with the peculiarities of Calderón's versification and rhythms, which are difficult to render in an English translation (which may unavoidably tend to acquire Shakespearean connotation). As for the passages to be selected, there is an embarrassment of riches. Some examples that are crucially representative of individual characters and almost constitute poems in themselves include the end of Segismund's lament (I. 112–34); the close of his speech at the end of Act II (795–814); Stella's speech on the horrors of war (III. 206–18); and the peroration in Rosaura's address to Segismund (III. 486–98).

After having established as clearly as possible the structure and the development of action in the play, some literary analysis would be in order, particularly to observe and define the qualities in Calderón's style that may at first be somewhat disconcerting to the new reader. Here is language that mingles a lofty tone, rich imagery, and overabundant eloquence with well-reasoned argumentation and sententiousness. Careful reading should prove that Calderón's style aptly reflects a view of the world that is composed both of reality and imagination, intellectual subtlety and high passion. Good examples are provided by passages that have to do with conflicts between human nature and binding codes of behavior (e.g., Clotaldo in I. 289–344; Rosaura in II. 570–618).

Finally, since the action is indeed often related to aristocratic codes of behavior and "points of honor," it should be remembered that such mechanisms may certainly have become dramatic conventions but that they did have their original source in social reality and custom. A brief, clear account of the concept of honor in Calderón's drama is Gerald Brenan's *Literature of the Spanish People* (see the anthology, p. 2119), Chapter XII, pp. 180–82. A longer treatment is in Northrup's introduction to his *Three Plays by Calderón* (see below), pp. xvi–xxiv.

Topics for Discussion and Writing

1. Calderón in later years wrote another play titled *Life Is a Dream* as one of his seventy *autos sacramentales* or edifying religious plays to be performed on certain Church occasions. Can we already detect the presence of, and preoccupation with, Christian doctrine in the drama that we are studying? If so, where and in what measure?
[Work, for instance, on Basil's speech in I. 432ff., and/or on Act II from the death of Clarion (592) to the end of the play.]

2. In more than one case the typical conflict in this play is between individual feeling and codes of honor. Take for example the scenes between Clotaldo and Rosaura (III. 234–332) and between Rosaura and Segismund (III. 355–560) and discuss them in terms of dramatic situation and the devices employed to obtain tension

and suspense; also discuss these scenes in terms of language and imagery.

3. The high drama of *Life Is a Dream* is played among characters connected with royalty and court life. Are "ordinary people" represented, and if so, how?
[See and discuss, for example, the mention of "the crowd" in III. 221–25; the handling of the character of the First Soldier, particularly at the end of the play; the character of the Second Servant in Act II; and most importantly the character of the clown Clarion throughout the play. Of the last two, consider particularly the way in which they die as examples of the handling of the theme of death against an aristocratic background (drama and absurd comedy; levity along with seriousness; touches of irony and macabre humor; it may not be inappropriate here to recall the death of Polonius in *Hamlet*).]

Further Reading

See also the reading suggestions in the anthology, p. 2119.

Bryans, John B. *Calderón de la Barca: Imagery, Rhetoric, and Drama.* 1977.
For the more advanced student; the quotes from Calderón's work are in Spanish.

Cascardi, Anthony J. *The Limits of Illusion: A Critical Study of Calderón.* 1984.
A study of formal and thematic aspects of Calderón's plays; the first chapter is "La Vida Es Sueño: Calderón's Idea of a Theatre."

Honig, Edwin. *Calderón and the Seizures of Honor.*
Chapter 8, "The Magnanimous Prince and the Price of Honor," is on *Life Is a Dream.*

Northrup, George Tyler, ed. *Three Plays by Calderón.* 1926.
The long introduction provides information on historical and social backgrounds, the sources of *Life Is a Dream*, and the metrical forms employed.

Wardropper, Bruce W., ed. *Critical Essays on the Theatre of Calderón*. 1965.
   Contains several essays on *Life Is a Dream* dealing with structure, Rosaura's role, Calderón's concept of the perfect prince, etc.

JOHN MILTON
Paradise Lost

Backgrounds

Milton's epic, *Paradise Lost*, is divided like Virgil's epic, the *Aeneid*, into twelve books. Its great theme is announced in the proemium (p. 2179) as that of man's transgression and fall, and the promise of redemption. Actually, the scope of the poem is vaster. Using a device common to both the Greek and the Roman epic—the *Odyssey* and the *Aeneid* in particular, i.e., a flashback in the form of a tale told by one of the characters in the poem (in this case the Archangel Michael in his speech to Adam and Eve in books V–VIII), *Paradise Lost* encompasses the story of the rebellious angels and *their* fall, the creation of Hell as their eternal abode, and of man and his earthly habitation surrounded by its celestial universe. Thus Milton, through Michael, has also undertaken the Dantean task of "delineating" events occurring in the Empyrean heaven, and in created Hell, "by likening spiritual to corporeal forms" (V. 573, not included in the anthology).

Immediately after the proemium and the invocation to the Muse, the curtain rises on the vision of Hell where the former Lucifer, now Satan, tells his legions of "a new kind of Creature to be created" and summons them to a council in his palace, "Pandemonium," which has suddenly risen from the depths of surrounding Chaos. In Book II, the infernal parliament debates whether it should engage in a new battle against God, or whether it should first verify the news of His having created a new world and a new being, man, possibly susceptible to Satanic influence. The latter plan is accepted and Satan leaves on his exploratory mission. Book III shifts to the vision of Heaven, where God sits on His throne, the Son on His right side. Here Milton takes up the task of presenting in poetic language the doctrinal problems of God's foreknowledge, man's free will, and his redemption. The omniscient God knows that man will fall, but clears Himself of "all imputation," having endowed man with free will; He declares His "purpose of grace," provided that someone is found who will "answer for" man's offense and undergo his punishment. The Son offers Himself and is exalted as the Redeemer.

The last part of Book III shifts back to Satan, who in the following

Book IV—after being torn by the passions of fear, envy, and despair—"confirms himself in evil." His first attempt on Eve, in the form of a dream, is frustrated by the intervention of the Archangel Gabriel, and he is chased from the Garden. In Book V, after Eve's account of her dream to Adam, Raphael as God's messenger descends upon Eden; he warns Adam of the imminent danger of temptation by the fallen angel, thus beginning his long flashback, which will end in Book VIII with Raphael answering Adam's questions on the celestial bodies and their movements. Adam in turn confides to Raphael what he remembers of his own creation and tells of God's warning about the Tree of Knowledge. At the end the two discourse on appropriate relationships between man and woman, and the archangel departs.

Book IX and the second part of Book X are our main selections (pp. 2180–217). Raphael has gone (cf. fn. 6, p. 2180) and the poet announces a change in tone from "venial discourse" to the tragedy of the transgression and fall. This is the section that deals with the poet's theme and purpose as announced in lines 1 and 26 of Book I: "Man's first disobedience," and the justification of "God's ways to man." It ends, at the close of Book X, with the prospect of life on earth—life as we know it—and with the first sinners recommending themselves as suppliants to the Son of God, who in Book XI intercedes for them with the Father. God decrees their expulsion from Paradise and sends Michael with a band of Cherubim to announce the sentence. Before executing it, the archangel from a hilltop sets before Adam a vision of the future life of man up to the Flood; his revelation continues in Book XII up to the coming of the Messiah and His incarnation, death, resurrection, and ascension. They descend the hill, and Adam awakens Eve from gentle dreams (p. 2218); the two are led by Michael out of Paradise.

Scores of plays and poems on sacred subjects, in English and in Italian (during his visit to Italy Milton had known local poets and even wrote poems in Italian) have been mentioned as having possibly contributed to inspire Milton's conception; such relationships in general belong to the area of specialized curiosities. Milton was extraordinarily well read in several languages; and there may be, for example, generic echoes from Dante (whom Milton greatly admired) in such early lines of *Paradise Lost* as "…sights of woe, / Regions of sorrow, where peace / And rest can never dwell, hope never comes / That comes to all, but torture without end…" (I, 64–69, not included in the anthology), or of Tasso's *Jerusalem Delivered* in Milton's conception of the infernal council in Book II. Or

Milton may practically translate a line from Ariosto's *Orlando Furioso* ("Things unattempted yet in prose or rhyme," I. 16) and effectively use it in a totally different context, much as Dante does when on his first meeting Beatrice he uses a line (*Purgatorio* XXX. 46) that in Virgil's *Aeneid* is spoken by Dido as she is falling in love with Aeneas. This is one of the minor ways in which the "great tradition" works.

More important, quite early in life Milton had conceived of a great work (at first, apparently, imagined as a drama) on the central story of the Judeo-Christian tradition. This was to constitute the crowning achievement of his variedly active life—an indication of the supreme place that he reserved for his activity as a poet. Thus Milton's main inspiration for *Paradise Lost* was the very awareness of the magnitude and height of his task. The significant lines 20–47 of Book IX also express his notion of the superiority of his poetic material (to him, accustomed to religious meditation and doctrinal debate, "chivalry" materials were not only inferior, they were "tedious") and implicitly of his own poetic power. And perhaps also those lines signal the feeling that he is the last in a tradition of poetry on a grand scale which had begun with the Homeric epics and continued through Virgil and through Virgil's Christian "pupil" Dante.

Classroom Strategies

Experience would indicate that in Milton's case as in others (cf. our notes on teaching Erasmus) a useful first measure is to test students' knowledge of the biblical events that constitute his material. There may be surprises in either direction. Specifically for our selections, a supplementary reading and explication of the relevant passages in Genesis may be in order. Young people possessing superficial knowledge and mental images of the story of the fall and its meaning as a *felix culpa* may find in that notion as dramatized by Milton a source of considerable intellectual stimulation and enlightenment. Attention should be drawn to Milton's poetic handling of the story of the temptation, fall, and promise of redemption, in a poetic style alternating between solemn discourse and lively drama. The ideal student should be able to discover that there is fascination in the Adam-Eve dialogue, conducted as it is by the poet both as doctrinal argumentation and as human drama. Also, as in other previous cases, it should be observed in detail how the poet incorporates Greco-Roman material and uses it in handling his biblical story. Our footnotes attempt to be helpful on all these levels.

Topics for Discussion and Writing

1. Analyze, in specific passages from our selections, the ways in which the concept of the fall as a *felix culpa*, a "happy fault," is dramatized by Milton.

2. If the last selections from the *Purgatorio* (p. 1435) have been read, compare the scene and function of the Earthly Paradise in Dante and in Milton.

3. Choose and analyze passages in which pagan and Christian imagery are fused in Milton.

4. In his description of "chivalry materials" in Book IX. 27–41, Milton seems to ignore the fact that this material also had a Christian world as its background and that the "battles feigned" were also between Christians and infidels. Contrast with the revitalization of that same material in Cervantes. Discuss whether the differences may be due to the diversity in cultural and religious backgrounds of the two writers.

Further Reading

See also the reading suggestions in the anthology, p. 2178.

Broadbent, J. B. *Some Graver Subject: An Essay on* Paradise Lost. 1967.
With illustrations and index. A thorough, detailed analysis of *Paradise Lost*, perhaps somewhat extravagant.

Demaray, John G. *Milton's Theatrical Epic: The Invention and Design of* Paradise Lost. 1980.
A critical interpretation of *Paradise Lost* with a view to its origins and development, Milton's theories and techniques, influences, and its relation to Renaissance dramatic forms.

Emma, Ronald David, and John T. Shawcross, eds. *Language and Style in Milton: A Symposium in Honor of the Tercentenary of* Paradise Lost. 1967.

Eleven essays on the linguistic background, theological language, spelling and pronunciation, Aristotelian notion of ethos and dianoia, grammar, imagery, and style of *Paradise Lost*. With selected bibliography.

Le Comte, Edward S. *A Milton Dictionary*. 1969.
A dictionary including "hard" words from Milton's works, entries on the individual works, and biographical data.

Leonard, John. *Naming in Paradise: Milton and the Language of Adam and Eve*. 1990.
Particularly appropriate to our selections.

Lieb, Michael. *Poetics of the Holy: A Reading of* Paradise Lost. 1981.
A religious interpretation, with illustrations and up-to-date bibliography. Deals with the basic religious context of *Paradise Lost*, the esthetic dimensions of that context, and the aspects of sacral phenomena in the work.

Summers, Joseph H. *The Muse's Method: An Introduction to* Paradise Lost. 1962.
Broadbent says that this is the most complete study of its kind.

Wittreich, Joseph Antony. *Feminist Milton*. 1987.